GROUNDED IN THE LIVING WORD

GROUNDED IN THE LIVING WORD

The Old Testament and Pastoral Care Practices

Denise Dombkowski Hopkins and Michael S. Koppel

William B. Eerdmans Publishing Company
Grand Rapids, Michigan / Cambridge, U.K.

Published 2010 by
Wm. B. Eerdmans Publishing Co.
2140 Oak Industrial Drive N.E., Grand Rapids, Michigan 49505 /
P.O. Box 163, Cambridge CB3 9PU U.K.
www.eerdmans.com

Printed in the United States of America

15 14 13 12 11 10   7 6 5 4 3 2 1

Library of Congress Cataloging-in-Publication Data

Hopkins, Denise Dombkowski.
Grounded in the living Word: the Old Testament and pastoral care practices /
Denise Dombkowski Hopkins and Michael S. Koppel.
p.   cm.
Includes bibliographical references.
ISBN 978-0-8028-6368-3 (pbk.: alk. paper)
1. Pastoral care. 2. Pastoral theology — Biblical teaching.
3. Bible. O.T. — Criticism, interpretation, etc.
I. Koppel, Michael Sherwood. II. Title.

BV4011.3.H66 2010
253 — dc22

2010013277

Unless otherwise noted, the Scripture quotations in this publication are from the
New Revised Standard Version of the Bible, copyright © 1989 by the Division of
Christian Education of the National Council of Churches of Christ in the U.S.A.,
and used by permission.

We dedicate this book to the next generations:
Dylan and Ryan Kirk, and Brian and Ariel Hopkins.
"May the Lord keep your going out and your coming in,
from this time on and forevermore" (Psalm 121:8).

Contents

Foreword

One of the challenges and opportunities in our current social crisis is the breaking down of old divisions and patterns of life and thought. This breaking down is no less evident in academic matters than in political and economic aspects of our common life. The older academic path, reflective of Enlightenment commitments to reasonable certitude, was to isolate knowledge into its several disciplines that were kept hermetically sealed off from each other. Interpreters were responsible only for being competent in their particular domain.

Now it is clear that the mystery of life and the explosion of knowledge make it impossible to contain thought or life in such rigid categories. Thus it is imperative that our study, when taken seriously, should be interdisciplinary, with an openness to be challenged, summoned, impacted, and eventually transformed by disciplines other than our own.

Hopkins and Koppel have written quite a remarkable book that is genuinely interdisciplinary. By "genuinely" I mean that each author is thoroughly grounded in and defined by a particular discipline and does not compromise the learning or perspective of that discipline. But these authors "genuinely" interact with each other and take into account the perspective of the alternative discipline. The outcome is a happy, generative offer of a new way into both disciplines.

There is no doubt that pastoral theology, insofar as it is a "church practice," has been ripe for serious engagement with biblical-theological work. Indeed, the so-called Pastoral Care Movement was formed in something of a rebellion against theology that was excessively rigid. As a consequence, the movement had to distance itself to some extent from the regnant theological categories of the time. It has been a long, slow road back to theological dimensions for pastoral theology, which has been preoccupied principally with psychological matters. In this volume it is clear that theological imagination and specifically the defining character of God enacted in the narrative matter decisively for Koppel's notion of pastoral theology.

Conversely, there is significant blowback for Scripture study. For a very long time that study has been in the grip of a more or less arid historical criticism that was preoccupied with historical questions; or, alternatively, there was commitment to doctrinal formulation in which the interactive nature of the text was largely lost. Indeed, arid historicism and doctrinal reductionism concerning the biblical text have tended to reinforce and evoke each other, as historical criticism served to "fend off" doctrinal reductionism. In this study, by breaking away from both arid historicism and doctrinal reductionism, Hopkins shows the way in which biblical study is, from the ground up, relational and interactive.

The grounding of pastoral theology in the holiness of God and the re-reading of Scripture in an interactive way have together resulted in a book that will have wide pastoral appeal. The authors move back and forth between personal narratives (including their own) to the deep claims of Scripture. They offer practical guidance for participation in such dynamic interpretation, though their offer is much richer than any how-to manual.

I suspect that this book will be taken up with eagerness in much church practice and in theological education. The book invites a fresh perspective on "faith and life" that has enormous implications for church practice. Beyond that, the book will be an important offer to the "cultural despisers" of such faith, who are here given a glimpse into truthful humanness which cuts way beneath conventional clichés that are bound to be misunderstood. The book is a welcome and mighty protest against our reductionisms (in both disciplines) that collude in the domestication of human energy and human hope. I am glad to commend this book and offer my thanks to these authors who have read widely, thought deeply, and risked honestly in exploring the wondrous mystery of human connectedness with its hurts and hopes.

WALTER BRUEGGEMANN
Columbia Theological Seminary
April 1, 2009

Foreword

Pastoral theology and pastoral care first rediscovered their theological imagination in 1970, when they realized that their practicing of their own unique heritage and faith resources led to the growth and development of persons. They began to realize that these resources are legitimate reservoirs for the holistic growth and development of persons. The initial coming to maturity of pastoral theology and pastoral care helped the pastor return to those faith resources, especially the ones that worked well with the psychological and counseling disciplines.

The second coming of age, however, took place in the late 1990s and in the early 2000s when pastoral theology and pastoral care began to recover the pre-Enlightenment understanding of the pastoral function of doctrine and Scripture. Doctrine and Scripture functioned pastorally when they became vehicles for encountering a trustworthy God. The Enlightenment undermined our trust and faith in God and in the church in favor of science. Postmodernity, however, enabled pastoral theology and pastoral care to rediscover how significantly Scripture and the church's faith resources could nurture people's growth. Thus, pastoral theology and care were ready when the study of Scripture began to change as well.

Postcolonial studies, as an offshoot of postmodern thought, emphasize multicultural approaches to biblical interpretation and pastoral care. Postcolonialism challenges outdated missionary practices which privileged a U.S. and Western orientation to and understanding of human beings and religious practices. Colonialism neglected an intercultural and international understanding that immigrants to the

United States brought with them to Bible study and pastoral conversations. An intercultural understanding recognizes that pastoral conversations and Bible study groups increasingly are impacted by immigrant persons who bring with them far different understandings of the Bible which reflect their cultural location. Thus, this groundbreaking book seeks to have pastoral theologians and pastoral care specialists be more open to multiple interpretations of the Bible that come from different social locations and cultures.

In addition, the authors address the need to view the Hebrew Bible in light of grace and law within the frame of covenantal care. For them the Hebrew Bible's view of covenant care fits well with the premodern pastoral use of the Bible. They point out that the image of covenant care in the Hebrew Bible forms the theological basis for understanding community in both the Hebrew Bible and the New Testament. Their point is that God's grace preceded the giving of the law, and that law and grace function together to center persons and communities around common values, principles, and virtues that reflect the God of the Bible. Thus, grace and law form the boundaries and parameters for the relational growth of all persons in community.

EDWARD P. WIMBERLY
Interdenominational Theological Center
April 2, 2009

Acknowledgments

Many have heeded the wisdom of this Chinese proverb: "A journey of a thousand miles begins with a single step." A revised translation reveals a significant nuance: "A journey of a thousand miles begins with the ground beneath your feet." Beginning from the ground beneath our feet means beginning wherever we are, rather than at the place we wish we were or that we construct ideally in our minds. We begin not knowing the journey's terrain, or when, or even if, we will arrive at our destination. Yet we gain energy with each successive step.

So it was with the two of us. We began our journey more than five years ago when we said to one another, "Let's teach a class together sometime." From that first step, we set in motion plans that eventuated in our co-taught course at Wesley Theological Seminary in the fall of 2006.

Beginnings marked by anticipation and enthusiasm generate momentum. The destination itself marks just another place in time where we are, just another piece of ground beneath our feet for taking another journey. Reaching significant markers and destinations calls us to celebration. We have walked side by side on our collegial, interdisciplinary journey and delight in sharing the fruits we have gathered along the way. Our co-taught course concluded late one mid-December afternoon. A striking sunset illumined the sky in transition to evening. The class stood together with us, beholding and marking the end of our time together. We thought, "We will remember this day." We did and we will. Now we arrive at the "destination" of this book's completion, aware of beginning new journeys with readers, students, family, friends, and colleagues in conversation. We hope that readers will find ground and light here for their own fruitful encounters in faith.

We speak as two authors with one voice in this volume, since we have jointly written and edited each chapter. Our harmonized voice, with both of us speaking together and sometimes individually, represents an intentional rather than an accidental approach. Aware of marginalizing tendencies within and between academic disciplines, we vowed to draw upon wisdom from our respective fields to serve a vision of collegial exploration of rich interpretive intersections between biblical and human texts. We invite clergy, laity, and seekers across the age spectrum to join us in our conversation. The questions for reflection and group exercises embedded in each chapter are meant to facilitate your participation.

We want to express our appreciation to people and organizations who have endorsed our collaborative teaching, research, and writing. Notably, for our jointly developed syllabus on the Hebrew Bible and Pastoral Care, we acknowledge the receipt of a Faith as a Way of Life Theological Renewal Award from the Yale Center for Faith and Culture. Each of us also received a Lilly Research Grant from the Association of Theological Schools, which funded our travel to two separate international conferences.

Many colleagues have journeyed with us along the way, especially former Dean Bruce Birch of Wesley Theological Seminary, who suggested our class and book title long ago; members of the Society of Pastoral Theology and the Society of Biblical Literature, who received our joint presentations and papers with helpful comments; the team at Eerdmans, particularly Sam Eerdmans, whose enthusiastic support of the book energized us, and Mary Hietbrink, whose fine editorial eye has sharpened our work; Amy Serridge, Wesley faculty support, who assembled our bibliography; Mary Bates-Washington, Executive Assistant to the President, whose indefatigable grace enabled the project's completion; treasured friends Dr. Eva Lew, Reverend Linda Hodson, Dr. Gwen Garrison, Edwin Peterman, and lifeline Eva Kaplan; and most of all, our students. The church is in their good hands.

DENISE DOMBKOWSKI HOPKINS *and*
MICHAEL S. KOPPEL
Lent 2010

Chapter 1

Intersections

Ivy's Story

Standing before the congregation, Ivy, a founding member and elder of her Presbyterian church in California, shared her story publicly for the first time. As part of a sermon series entitled "Easter Reflection," Ivy spoke of the agonizing soul struggle she had experienced after receiving a phone call one morning seventeen years ago that would forever change her life. Her eldest daughter, traveling to a meeting early that same morning, had swerved in the road to avoid hitting a child's toy and had wrapped her car around a telephone pole. She died instantly.

With tears and a wavering voice, Ivy shared her experience of emotional and spiritual devastation, recalling the bewilderment and intense questioning of her faith that followed. She also expressed her profound gratitude for her belief in God, however tattered this belief had become in light of her experience, and for the unwavering support of good friends, family, and church members who had wrestled with her in small-group Bible studies.

This Easter, Ivy remembered a poem she had written years ago about losing her daughter. The pastor had saved this poem and shared it with her in a later Bible study on Jonah. It was in this study that Ivy began to recognize and name her condition of being in the pit of despair, and to acknowledge her similarity to Jonah. Her ability to put words to the experience marked the beginning of what she now calls her "resurrection moment."

•   •

As this story indicates, ongoing participation in small-group Bible studies provided Ivy a ground for viewing and making sense of her experience. Ivy's pastor honored her struggles by saving her poem. Through study and shared reflection in a caring community, Ivy came to name her own experience, to know the power of biblical language in her own life, and to embrace on an intimate level of knowing the tensions and struggles at the heart of faith. Her journey from the pit of despair and grief to inklings of peace was not a short one. It was a gradual process that unfolded over years. Fortunately, the connection between the Bible and pastoral care is like ever-resilient elastic: we cannot wear out the possibilities or time limits for ways of meeting and stretching. Just as Ivy discovered, we too can come to know the Bible as a deeply trusted friend of the soul. As we listen to its living stories, to ourselves, and to one another over and over again, as we share, struggle, and celebrate, we may come to find ourselves in the Presence of the One who cares for all.

Ivy's story lifts up the value of communal caring, safe enough space for the sorting through of life's experiences, gracious accompaniment and patience, and the transforming power of connecting to biblical stories. Her story challenges the fast-paced, distraction-filled, multi-scripted culture which we inhabit. How do we as pastoral care givers function amid the materialism, consumption, unhealthy sexual images, and hype of our society? Noting the connection between "hype" and "hypodermic," we suggest that, whether we are aware of it or not, we are injected every day with sensationalism, excess, and deception. In this Botox culture that envelops us, we risk becoming numb, freezing our faces into one all-purpose mask.

Modern advertisers sell us our sense of well-being; we buy "nanoseconds of happiness" with each new gadget or brand that comes along.[1] Constant overstimulation makes it difficult for us to know the difference between immediacy of feeling and depth of emotion, vulgarizing "that which is most intensely personal."[2] Television "reality" shows are scripted; houses and bodies beg for public makeovers; troubled families parade their spoiled and out-of-control children for all to see, while the rest of us participate as voyeurs. "Issues entertain-

1. Darrin M. McMahon, "Nanoseconds of Happiness: You're Going to Love Your iPhone, Until the Next Gizmo Calls," *The Washington Post*, 24 June 2007, sec. B, p. 2.

2. Don E. Saliers, "Liturgy and Moral Imagination: Encountering Images in a TV Culture," in *Musicians for the Churches: Reflections on Vocation and Formation*, Yale Studies in Sacred Music (New Haven: Institute of Sacred Music at Yale University, 2001), pp. 47-50.

ment"[3] allows us to substitute vicarious feeling for action by watching movies: consider *Schindler's List* on the Holocaust, *Blood Diamond* and *Hotel Rwanda* on genocide in Africa, *Slumdog Millionaire* on poverty, and *A Mighty Heart* on global terrorism.[4]

At every turn we are confronted with "bling," the pop word of excess for expensive jewelry, cars, shoes, and diamond-studded "grilles" for the teeth of the rich and famous. We fixate on America's Next Top Model and the next American Idol, while multitasking endlessly. Scientists question whether multitasking teens will be able to develop depth knowledge and analytical skills.[5] We are "all wired up, with no time to wind down," living in an age of "broken boundaries and unbroken days . . . reachable at all times" but feeling more disconnected than ever.[6] This is not true for everyone, however. Not everyone has access to the Internet, let alone to a computer. The United States faces a "digital divide"[7] that splits along economic, ethnic, and geographic lines. The urban poor, people in rural areas, and blacks are more likely not to have Internet access.

---

3. Laurel A. Dykstra, *Set Them Free: The Other Side of Exodus* (Maryknoll, N.Y.: Orbis Books, 2002), p. 76.

4. The latter has been criticized by one of Danny Pearl's colleagues as underscoring "how cheap and manufactured our quest for heroism has become." Pearl was the Southeast Asia bureau chief for *The Wall Street Journal* who was captured and beheaded in Pakistan in 2002. Pearl's widow, Mariane, wrote the book upon which the movie is based for her son, so that he would know that his "father was not a hero but an ordinary man." Paramount Studios, however, promoted the movie with a call to nominate "the most inspiring ordinary hero" and win a trip to the Bahamas. See Asra Nomani, "A Mighty Shame: It's the Story of Our Search for Danny Pearl. But in This Movie, He's Nowhere to Be Found," *The Washington Post,* 24 June 2007, sec. B, p. 1.

5. Lori Aratani, "Teens Can Multitask, But What Are Costs?" *The Washington Post,* 26 February 2007, sec. A, p. 1. Neuroscientists argue that "a central 'bottleneck' exists in the brain that prevents us from doing two things at once." See "Hang Up and Drive" in *Vanderbilt Magazine,* Spring 2007, pp. 22-23. The regions of the brain responsible for this bottleneck have recently been identified.

6. Catie Getches, "Wired Nights: All Wired Up, with No Time to Wind Down," *The Washington Post,* 17 October 2004, sec. B, pp. 1-2. DeNeen Brown asks, "Has anybody else noticed this growing revolution of robotic voices and machines supplanting much of the casual human contact we once had?" These voices include those of GPS devices, airport walkways, and grocery store self-checkouts. See "The Machine Speaks and We Cry Out," *The Washington Post,* 25 November 2007, sec. M, pp. 1, 6.

7. Jose Antonio Vargas, "Binary America: Split in Two by a Digital Divide," *The Washington Post,* 23 July 2007, sec. C, pp. 1, 3.

The young people of "Generation Me," born in the 1970s, 1980s, and 2000s, do their own thing without seeking the approval of others, with the encouragement of Dr. Phil and Rick Warren.[8] Their self-focus leads to anxiety, depression, and loneliness. Repercussions from living in a "cheating culture"[9] are now being felt at many levels, from presidential cabinet appointments to sub-prime loans, sports, and academe. Fueled by the fear and insecurity rooted in our "winner take all" society that lavishly rewards the best, we do whatever is necessary to win, including cheating. The Center for Academic Integrity reports that 70 percent of students admitted to cheating and declares that ours is a "growing culture of academic dishonesty."[10] Former TV anchor Dan Rather observes that as a nation we are addicted to fake news and celebrity gossip; he warns that "broadcast news, and journalism generally, should not be a sedative. It should be a wake-up call."[11]

We as pastors and lay leaders are called to challenge this pervasive cultural script by rescripting our interactions with one another and with biblical texts. We want to minister with authentic and life-giving words to people who hunger and thirst for exactly that. We want to give voice to those stories that get lost in our modern shuffle. To dig deeply into life experience in order to open ourselves to God's intention for wholeness is to challenge a world that deals superficially with what it means to be human. So we turn to a foundational text of our faith: the Bible as the Living Word of God. Secular culture measures us by what we own and how we look and pushes us toward autonomy and isolation from one another. In contrast, the Bible proclaims that our hu-

---

8. Jean M. Twenge, *Generation Me: Why Today's Young Americans Are More Confident, Assertive, Entitled — And More Miserable Than Ever Before* (New York: Free Press, 2006). Twenge refers to Dr. Phil's *Self Matters: Creating Your Life from the Inside Out* (New York: Free Press, 2001) and Rick Warren's *The Purpose-Driven Life: What on Earth Am I Here For?* (Grand Rapids: Inspirio/Zondervan, 2001). In the March 2005 issue of the *Ladies' Home Journal,* Warren advised, "Accept yourself. Don't chase after other people's approval. . . ." Robert Putnam, the author of *Bowling Alone: The Collapse and Revival of American Community* (New York: Simon & Schuster, 2000), speaks of "civic disengagement" that fractures community.

9. See David Callahan, *The Cheating Culture: Why Americans Are Doing Wrong to Get Ahead* (New York: Harcourt Books, 2004).

10. "Academic Dishonesty," in *Lex Collegii: A Legal Newsletter for Independent Higher Education* 30, no. 4 (Spring 2007): 1.

11. Tom Shales, "Dan Rather Takes on Network News with His Tart Remark," *The Washington Post,* 13 June 2007, sec. C, p. 8.

manity is rooted in covenant relationship with God and leads us toward community.[12]

Biblical texts remind us of our identity as God's beloved people even as we know ourselves through periods of wandering, grief, and rebellion as well as pain, joy, and thanksgiving. By helping people to see how their individual stories intersect with biblical stories,[13] we engage in the most basic forms of pastoral care and biblical interpretation. When we feel connected to biblical stories, the Bible can give us words for the journey through the cacophony of our world. Sometimes the text gives us words that we may not otherwise have had. Sometimes the text affirms what we already deeply know to be true. Sometimes the words challenge our current world or personal situation.

In our global and secular world, we cannot assume that everyone has some familiarity with biblical texts.[14] How can we engage in biblically enriched pastoral care in such a context? Much of the Hebrew Bible is a great story, with emotionally available characters, dramatic plots, and witty wordplays. These stories resonate with us because they hold up a mirror to who we are or show us who we can become, whether or not we belong to a church. As David Gunn and Danna Fewell point out, "If we realize that the world of the Bible is a broken world, . . . then we might start to see more clearly our own broken world. . . . And who knows? Maybe we shall find ourselves called to be the agents of change."[15] Like de-fragmenting a computer, connecting people to biblical stories can gather the fragments of their lives and open up within them more space to be all that God wants them to be.

---

12. Walter Brueggemann, *Theology of the Old Testament* (Minneapolis: Fortress Press, 1997), pp. 450-54.

13. Charles Gerkin, *An Introduction to Pastoral Care* (Nashville: Abingdon Press, 1997), p. 112.

14. According to Jean Twenge, Generation Me is "not very religious. Only 18 percent of 18-to-29-year-olds attend religious services every week," and college freshmen with no religious preference doubled from 1985 to 2003. See Twenge, *Generation Me,* p. 34. This fits with larger cultural trends. According to a 2006 Gallup Poll, 28 percent of Americans believe that the Bible is literally true, a figure down 10 percent from 1976; 19 percent called it an "ancient book of fables." Literal belief in the Bible was higher among older people and those with the lowest levels of education. The Bible seems to have "lost its position of cultural prominence." See "Fewer in U.S. Take Bible Literally," *The Washington Post,* sec. B, p. 9.

15. David Gunn and Danna Fewell, *Narrative in the Hebrew Bible* (New York: Oxford University Press, 1993), pp. 3, 205.

If we trust "the contagion process of story generation,"[16] biblical stories can help us to identify and transform unhealthy individual stories, even for those who aren't familiar with the Bible. Pastoral care givers are challenged to make these stories come alive for those receiving care.

Pastoral care and counseling, at its heart, is about storytelling. Stories center the pastoral care encounter, offering points of reflection for self-perception and understanding. Pastoral care givers do not engage in "extreme makeovers" of the psyche, but rather help organize and frame our understanding of ourselves,[17] the world, the way we speak about it, and the way we relate to God. The dynamics of storytelling as a key to self-definition and as a relational bridge were powerfully illustrated to Denise at a denominational evangelism conference she attended a few years ago that featured a workshop on how to talk about faith. The focus was not upon the how-to of making disciples, but rather upon answering this question in pairs: "Why are you a Christian?" We were surprised to learn in the plenary debriefing that instead of using theological declarations or categories, we answered the question by telling our stories to one another. Our stories often included references to biblical texts and characters. We listened, laughed, and cried. The stories of our experiences of God and of community formed the core of our Christian self-identity and bound us together in that workshop. Our shared stories were "privileged and imaginative acts of self-interpretation"[18] that invited our pastoral caring of one another.

Biblical texts invite us to play[19] with our stories in order to look imaginatively at our lives. We do not completely "re-author"[20] our stories, because remnants of the old stories still linger. We play into or image ourselves into new stories so that the older ones seem to lose their

16. Edward P. Wimberly, *Using Scripture in Pastoral Counseling* (Nashville: Abingdon Press, 1994), p. 10.

17. Christie Cozad Neuger, *Counseling Women* (Minneapolis: Fortress Press, 2001), pp. 52-54. See also Paul Chilcote, "Grace upon Grace: Charles Wesley as Spiritual Mentor," *The Circuit Rider* (Sept./Oct. 2006): 7. Chilcote argues that Wesley knew that "faith is by its very nature autobiographical" and so he solicited spiritual narratives from those in the Wesleyan Revival.

18. Herbert Anderson and Edward Foley, *Mighty Stories, Dangerous Rituals: Weaving Together the Human and the Divine* (San Francisco: Jossey-Bass, 1998), p. 5.

19. Michael S. Koppel, "Playing Church: Toward Critically Creative Pastoral Practices," *Pastoral Psychology* 55, no. 4 (March 2007): 431-40.

20. Edward Wimberly, *Recalling Our Own Stories: Spiritual Renewal for Religious Caregivers* (San Francisco: Jossey-Bass, 1997), p. 4.

power. New, healthier stories are written over the older ones, like a pa-limpsest.[21] As pastoral care givers, we need to help birth new stories through a process of asking questions.[22] The questions encourage a re-organization of experience and a recognition of the problems that can arise when our "core narrative thickens over time."[23] This thickening can block some of our experiences from being confirmed because they conflict with this core narrative that we have created.

QUESTIONS FOR REFLECTION
- How is the Bible a Living Word for you?
- What does the Bible have to say to people in our contemporary cul-ture?
- How does our culture challenge our connection with biblical texts?

The Bible as a Foundational Site for Excavation

The image of the Bible as a foundational site for excavation can offer us clues for what we can expect in the process of connecting our stories to the biblical stories. To say that the Bible is a foundational text of the Jewish and Christian faiths can suggest the image of concrete — some-thing hard and durable that can support the weight of whatever is built on top of it, especially when the concrete is reinforced with steel. We might assume that the Bible is foundational for faith because it's like concrete; on the contrary, it is highly porous and severely gapped.[24] The Bible is foundational because we give it the power to "story"[25] our lives — that is, to organize our human experience in relation to God. As the

21. "Think of the book of Esther as a kind of palimpsest: a story is written, then erased, and then a new story is written over the old, erased one." Vashti is erased, and Es-ther and Mordecai move into her space, but Vashti is not erased entirely. "She will haunt the rest of the story." Timothy Beal, *The Book of Hiding: Gender, Ethnicity, Annihilation, and Esther* (New York: Routledge, 1997), p. 29.

22. Michael White and David Epston, *Narrative Means to Therapeutic Ends* (New York: W. W. Norton & Co., 1990), pp. 17-18.

23. Beal, *The Book of Hiding*, p. 54.

24. Daniel Boyarin, *Intertextuality and the Reading of Midrash* (Indianapolis: Indiana University Press, 1990), p. 16. *Midrash* is the biblical interpretive process developed by the rabbis for reading between the lines. *Midrash* comes from the Hebrew root *drsh*, which means to seek, search, or inquire.

25. Wimberly, *Using Scripture in Pastoral Counseling*, p. 15.

Bible becomes a Living Word in our practice of biblical interpretation and pastoral caring, we need to understand that:

1. The process will be messy, even somewhat chaotic. We will get our hands dirty. The biblical story gets in our eyes and under our fingernails. We are messing with real "stuff" here — the stories, patterns, denials, betrayals, cover-ups, and unexpected discoveries of life as we sift through dirt, rocks, and broken pottery shards, both within the human text and within the biblical text. Doing this work seems to complicate our lives. Sometimes we will be left covered with dust because what we encounter simply baffles or stumps us. Sometimes we will rejoice in a major "find," seeing what had been previously hidden. Pastoral care givers and biblical interpreters alike will, it is hoped, exhibit "a tolerance for the untidy."[26]

2. We will uncover many layers of experience, both our own and those of others. Communities of faith have passed on biblical texts and interpretations, and families have inherited patterns and processes from generation to generation.[27] The past can be seen as "layered" experience in both the psychological and the biblical sense. Just as archeologists excavate tells (uninhabited mounds formed by repeated human occupation evident in layers built on top of layers, called strata), pastors and care givers can "unlayer" personal experience in stages. In this way, people can encounter the memory long ago experienced and yet buried from conscious awareness. Biblical interpreters can read between the lines of biblical texts to uncover layers of meaning through the experiences of their own lives.

3. The process will require an ability to work with a variety of tools. Archeologists may try to excavate complete buildings and walls on a wide scale, or expose details in a stratum, such as small figurines or pieces of jewelry. In order to get at the many layers of the biblical story and of our story, we may need a sledgehammer to break through denial or stereotypical interpretations of texts. In order to clarify what we're feeling or to reveal biblical nuances, we need only a brush. Agility in pastoral work and biblical interpretation means we know when and how to use these different tools to their maximum benefit.

4. We will engage in a communal experience. We really can't dig by

---

26. Wimberly, *Using Scripture in Pastoral Counseling*, p. 15.

27. Edwin H. Friedman, *Generation to Generation: Family Process in Church and Synagogue* (New York: Guilford Press, 1985).

ourselves; we dig in the company of others — past, present, and future — as we relate our stories to the biblical stories. An interdisciplinary team will be needed to analyze what we find in all of its variety, the big items and the small. Archeologists need historians, ceramicists who know pottery forms, osteologists who analyze burial remains, paleo-botanists who analyze plant remains, and washers to clean the pottery shards, in order to understand the human experience behind the biblical text. So, too, we need both sound biblical interpretation and pastoral care sensibilities to work together in constant conversation to cultivate the Living Word as a source for our pastoral caring of one another.

As pastoral care givers engaged in the process of excavation, we become skilled at refraining from rejecting as valueless what we initially discover. In moving through the layers of story, we observe with wonderment rather than rejection. We are like "scavengers"[28] who collect, extract, and cleanse what is discarded for the sake of survival and nurturing of life. Like gold prospectors,[29] we assume that gold is to be found. It may be hidden, or we may have mined similar territory previously, but we believe that it is, in fact, there if we remain open and alert. In Jungian terms, this gold is the internal coalescing of the fragments of the psyche.[30]

Pastoral ministers serve as companion guides in this process of mining or archeological excavation. If we take our role seriously, we will identify the pastoral care assumptions and conceptual guidelines we bring both to the interpretation of "living human documents"[31] and to biblical texts, and the linkage between them. We must also stand ready to help others understand what they find in themselves as well as in the biblical stories, taking care not to expose some layers too quickly or ignore those they would rather leave undisturbed. A challenge for the companion guide is to pay attention to the delicate balance needed.

28. Valerie DeMarinis in Robert C. Dykstra, *Images of Pastoral Care: Classic Readings* (St. Louis: Chalice Press, 2005), p. 9.

29. This metaphor was suggested by Candyce Loescher, a student in our Hebrew Bible and Pastoral Care Practices class at Wesley Seminary in the fall of 2006.

30. Carl Jung, *The Collected Works of C. G. Jung*, vol. 12, *Psychology and Alchemy*, trans. G. Adler and R. F. C. Hull (Princeton: Princeton University Press, 1980).

31. Anton T. Boisen, "The Living Human Document," in Dykstra, *Images of Pastoral Care*, pp. 22-29.

QUESTIONS FOR REFLECTION

- What story do you like to tell about yourself? What title would you give it?
- What story about yourself do you tend to cover up? Why? What would it take to excavate this story? What title would you give this story?

The Hebrew Bible/Pastoral Care Connection

Pastoral care givers have an intuitive sense that the Bible and pastoral care can be enriched by one another, but they often find themselves floundering as they try to bring the two together. This is not surprising, given the complexity of the relationship and the disconnects that have too often plagued it. In order to bring the two together, we must excavate our underlying assumptions about the Bible and the goals of pastoral care.[32] There was a time in the mid-twentieth century when the Bible did not play a central role in pastoral care and counseling.[33] Pastors wanted to be seen as professionals along with psychiatrists and social workers,[34] so they borrowed psychiatric and behavioral science language and avoided theological and biblical language as much as possible. They assumed that the Bible had little to say and was even embarrassing when used in pastoral care situations. This approach, unfortunately, compartmentalizes the horizontal (human) and vertical (transcendent) aspects of our life.

During my (Denise's) year-long extended unit of Clinical Pastoral Education in 1986, as I began my first year of teaching at Wesley Seminary, I experienced such compartmentalization. I had wanted to use the Hebrew Bible, and especially the psalm laments, in my pastoral caring for patients. However, when we discussed our verbatim reports in class, we usually ran out of time before we reached the last item on the

32. For an examination of anthropological assumptions shaping Bible/care intersections, see Denise Dombkowski Hopkins, "Biblical Anthropology, Discipline of," in *Dictionary of Pastoral Care and Counseling*, ed. Rodney Hunter (Nashville: Abingdon Press, 1990), pp. 85-88.

33. Paul Pruyser, *The Minister as Diagnostician* (Philadelphia: Westminster Press, 1976).

34. See, for example, James Glasse, *Profession: Minister* (Nashville: Abingdon Press, 1968).

list: "What biblical texts or theology did you use in your pastoral encounter with this patient?" It seemed to me that this question was really no more than an afterthought, when in fact the Bible needed to be
a significant dialogue partner with the experiential aspects of our encounter with our patients.[35] In the last two decades, CPE programs
have moved toward embracing fruitful intersections between the Bible
and pastoral care.

In many ways, CPE reflected what was going on in local churches
which saw themselves as part of a "professional service economy."[36]
Rather than being a "community of mutual relations," churches offered services to laypeople. Pastoral care became one more "commod-
ity," and pastors burned out because they thought that they represented God as "the Perfect Service Provider, the one professional who
can meet all needs."[37] This may still be true especially in small towns,
where, as one of our students pointed out, "the preacher" is the only
show in town, the only other social agency being the fire station.

QUESTIONS FOR REFLECTION
- In what ways do you use the Bible in your pastoral care practices? If
you do not, why not?
- In what ways has the Bible been used in the care that you have received? Was it helpful, hurtful, or ineffectual?

GROUP EXERCISE
On a scale of one to ten, are you more comfortable with excavating
the human text (10) or the biblical text (1)? Designate one end
of the room as "ten" and the other as "one" and place yourself
along the continuum to reflect your response. Discuss your
positions afterward.

---

35. See Larry Graham, *Care of Persons, Care of Worlds: A Psychosystems Approach to Pastoral Care and Counseling* (Nashville: Abingdon Press, 1992). Graham, among others, criticized the CPE model for being too non-theological and too focused on the subjective aspects of experience.

36. Roy Steinhoff-Smith, *The Mutuality of Care* (St. Louis: Chalice Press, 1999), p. 13.

37. Steinhoff-Smith, *The Mutuality of Care*, p. 15.

Healing the Disconnects

Facilitating connections between biblical texts and human texts does not often come easily to many care givers. What a loss, given how enriching such connections can be. One reason for the disconnect is the long-standing separation in theological education between the "classical" and the "practical" disciplines — that is, between biblical studies and pastoral care; they rarely talked to one another.[38] This is often true on the biblical side of the divide, where a bit of arrogance comes into play when it comes to pastoral care. Michael and I are attempting to heal the divide by proposing a new group, The Bible and Pastoral Theology, in the Society of Biblical Literature, an organization founded in 1880 to foster critical biblical interpretation. We invite our readers to join us in this endeavor.

This book intends to encourage a conversation between the Bible and pastoral care that we believe can shape transformative pastoral care practices and biblical interpretation. Meaningful pastoral care practice needs to emerge from and remain in conversation with the foundational texts of the Judeo-Christian faith. As one of those texts, the Hebrew Bible[39] draws us in and shapes our caring of one another. Rather than creating a list of Bible passages that we link to pastoral care situations, Denise and I aim to expose the multivalence or layers (strata) of both biblical text and human text with their resulting tensions, ambiguities, and complexities. Both biblical interpretation and ministerial care practices can be enriched as a result.

Another disconnect between pastoral care and biblical interpretation comes from the insistent focus upon the historical-critical method as the primary method of interpretation. The historical-critical method aims to uncover the context of a biblical passage by investigating the religious, social, political, economic, and historical circumstances or context out of which the text emerged. Overlapping disciplines have developed to answer certain questions about the context of the biblical text, among them: What is the original wording of the

---

38. See Stephen Clark, *From Athens to Jerusalem* (Oxford: Clarendon Press, 1984).

39. We as authors use the term "Hebrew Bible" rather than "Old Testament" to remind Christians that the first part of our canon, written originally in Hebrew, is also scripture for the Jewish faithful. The adjective "old" in "Old Testament" often carries destructive baggage that can, unconsciously, lead to negative assessments of this part of our canon as "worn out," "superseded," "inferior," and so on.

text (textual criticism)? What is the type or form of the text that helps to communicate its meaning (form criticism)? How do the literary features of a text help to communicate its meaning (rhetorical criticism)? How and why has a text been edited (redaction criticism)? How does the canonical position of a text or book shape its meaning (canonical criticism)? By asking these questions, interpreters can see that the Word of God has been spoken in concrete times in particular places to specific groups and individuals living in the ancient world. The Bible is not simply the timeless word of God hanging out in the universe; it is the Word of God in human words. This recognition guards against making the Bible say whatever is convenient.

However, all these "isms" can strike terror into the heart of pastors and care givers who dare to draw upon biblical texts in pastoral care situations. Practitioners may think that only "experts" can interpret texts. After all, the historical-critical method assumes that by asking the "right" questions, the text can claim its own voice and integrity and reveal its "objective" meaning, one that everyone can embrace. Each person asks the same question and gets the same answer. The problem with this assumption is that one reading becomes normative for everyone, whether or not it squares with someone else's experience. Also, how do we know that we as readers are asking the "right" question? Questions emerging out of different experiences will shape interpretation differently. Dominant readings can function to mute or deny questions and interpretations from the margins of power and thereby support a kind of cultural imperialism.[40]

A good example of this kind of "objective" reading that assumes a consensus about the meaning and function of a biblical text is offered by Jacqueline Grant. She argues that black women cannot accept terms that others accept without question, such as servanthood, to describe their relationship with God. She insists that in the United States, "servanthood, . . . in effect, has been servitude." African-American women have been the "servants of the servants." To prevent language from covering over oppression, she urges Christians to reconsider servant language in favor of more inclusive discipleship lan-

40. See William Meyers, "The Hermeneutical Dilemma of the African-American Biblical Student," in *Stony the Road We Trod: African-American Biblical Interpretation,* ed. Cain Felder (Minneapolis: Fortress Press, 1991), and *Reading from This Place: Social Location and Biblical Interpretation in the United States,* ed. Fernando Segovia and Mary Ann Tolbert (Minneapolis: Fortress Press, 1995).

guage.[41] An interpretive process that honors human experience as a dialogue partner with the biblical text affirms that we all bring gifts as interpreters to biblical texts. This affirmation echoes the notion that pastoral care is not condescension but mutuality: "Care is not what experts do, but what all of us do."[42]

To make matters worse, the historical-critical method failed to allow possibilities for pastoral care taking place in the very process of interpretation. In the name of "objectivity," the historical-critical method valued reason over body and feeling. This claim to objectivity kept the biblical story at arm's length from the interpreter's own story and experience.[43] "Objectivity" cannot be attained in either biblical interpretation or the pastoral care process. In pastoral caring, "therapeutic neutrality is seldom, if ever, possible. When we listen, we interpret, whether we want to or not."[44] Keeping the biblical story at arm's length from the interpreter blocks the efforts of the pastoral care giver to connect the biblical and the human text.[45] How do we react to one another when the biblical text we are encountering together exposes, challenges, or comforts us? Biblical texts can help all of us become more critically reflective of our own stories — the gaps, the cover-ups, the image-making (idolatry). With the biblical text as a mirror of ourselves, we can become critically aware of what's happening and of how God's Holy Mystery may be moving through it all. Such an encounter presents fertile ground for formation in Bible study groups.

41. Jacqueline Grant, "The Sin of Servanthood and the Deliverance of Discipleship," in *A Troubling in My Soul: Womanist Perspectives on Evil and Suffering*, ed. Emilie Townes (Maryknoll, N.Y.: Orbis Books, 1993), pp. 199-218.

42. Steinhoff-Smith, *The Mutuality of Care*, p. 1.

43. Bruce C. Birch, "Old Testament Narrative and Moral Address," in *Canon, Theology, and Old Testament Interpretation*, ed. G. Tucker, D. Peterson, and R. Wilson (Philadelphia: Fortress Press, 1988), pp. 84-85.

44. Anderson and Foley, *Mighty Stories, Dangerous Rituals*, p. 47.

45. The historical-critical method developed out of the assumptions of modernism: truth is written down, universal, timeless, and true for all people in all places at all times. By contrast, post-modern assumptions about truth stress that it is oral, local, contextual, and pluralistic; this different way of knowing is very unsettling for many. See Walter Brueggemann, *Texts Under Negotiation: The Bible and Postmodern Imagination* (Minneapolis: Fortress Press, 1993). In the post-modern context, we can no longer assume that we all understand biblical texts in the same way, or even that we are familiar with the biblical stories at all.

QUESTIONS FOR REFLECTION

- Have you been encouraged to interact with biblical texts out of your own experience? Why or why not?
- What process of interpretation do you use with the Bible? Outline the steps that you follow.

Roadmap to Community

"Storying" our lives in conversation with biblical texts invites us into a "de-centered" way of being, a beneficial corrective to much of popular American culture that puts the "me-self" at the center of existence. In becoming de-centered, we learn to interact with the world as if we ourselves were not the center of existence — which we aren't! In so doing, we are ever so subtly or even abruptly opened to an expanded worldview. We envision new story possibilities. Our personal and church stories are re-shaped in not-yet-imagined ways as we step into the challenging world of the Bible. De-centering gives the care receiver an opportunity to step back and identify with a biblical character as well as to view and evaluate that character. This provides distance for seeing, naming, and acknowledging behavior that would normally occupy the center and spill over into the pastoral space. Room is left to see and hear differently. Sometimes we need to be jolted into de-centered hearing. This was the case for riders on the metropolitan area subway in Washington, D.C., who were lulled into ignoring a tired announcement about doors opening and closing. Now they're treated to a snappy new message: "Step back! Doors closing. Please stand clear of the doors." Despite complaints, it did get their attention.

A de-centering, perspective-shifting dynamic is at work in the parable of the ewe lamb in 2 Samuel 12. Nathan the prophet delivers God's word in a parable to King David after his murder of Uriah and his rape of Bathsheba. In Nathan's story there is a rich man with many herds and a poor man with one little ewe lamb; the rich man slaughters the ewe lamb to feed a guest. David is incensed by the rich man's action and calls for his punishment. In verse 7, Nathan tells him, "You are the man!" David comes to see himself in the parable and, to his credit, accepts his guilt. Nathan was no fool. Using the parable helped him avoid both directly confronting David and arousing David's defensiveness. The parable possibly saved Nathan from a fate similar to Uriah's.[46]

De-centering ourselves and our stories offers soul healing as we reclaim the therapeutic nature of the text in community.[47] Today we receive physical therapy in order to restore physical movement after an injury; drug therapy to halt disease processes in the body; psychotherapy to restore emotional health and well-being. In these instances, therapy is understood as a remedy to a problem of physical injury, bodily disease, or psychological or emotional disturbance. The root meaning of the word *therapy,* which comes from the Greek word *therapeia* and relates to the Greek verb *therapeuo,* is to "wait upon." "Therapy was (and is) a service done to the sick."[48] When we read the biblical stories and share our stories in community, we engage in a healing process as we serve and wait upon the text and one another. This process destabilizes and reorganizes our understanding of sick/healer; care giver/care receiver; and subject/object. Usual divisions and distinctions become blurred.

Sharing our stories around biblical texts in groups provides a *window* as well as a *mirror* as we grow in faith.[49] A group serves as a window, and the window lets in more light with the presence of theological, gender, ideological, economic, and ethnic diversity. A group functions as a window as we can begin to see the world and our faith through diverse perspectives. It's like wearing many different pairs of glasses. To view the group as a window into the world is to appreciate the existence of many faith-filled perspectives. The church at its best nurtures and encourages these different "theological worlds."[50] A group serves also

46. See John Dominic Crossan, *The Dark Interval: Towards a Theology of Story* (Niles, Ill.: Argus Communications, 1975), for his discussion of myth and parable as polar opposites. Myth mediates and reconciles opposites, while parable challenges and unsettles reconciliation.

47. We as authors suggest storytelling and story sharing serve some of the same purposes (goals) of the therapeutic environment: democratic process, the confrontation of reality, permissive tolerance of disturbed behavior, and egalitarianism. See J. Fog and J. Gilmore, "Therapeutic Community," in *Dictionary of Pastoral Care and Counseling,* pp. 1273-74.

48. www.medterms.com/script/main/art.asp?articlekey=10897.

49. Leif Vaage, "Learning to Read the Bible with Desire: Teaching the Eros of Exegesis in the Theological Classroom," *Teaching Theology and Religion* 10, no. 2 (April 2007): 91. Vaage suggests that the biblical text "may even be a funny mirror, reflecting back an image of ourselves from surfaces that are decidedly uneven."

50. To identify the worlds within your faith community, see W. Paul Jones, *Worlds within a Congregation: Dealing with Theological Diversity* (Nashville: Abingdon Press, 2000).

as a mirror. We begin to see reflections of ourselves in submerged, subjugated, or dominant story strands of others. As we listen and share in groups, we might come to see ourselves more clearly as whole and yet fragile creatures with both strengths and weaknesses.

To view the group as a mirror is to see the reflection of others in ourselves and to forge the bonds of community. For Latinos/as, the community is a powerful healing agent; Latinos/as have "learned that it is by relying on each other that we are able to overcome the obstacles that form part of our daily living."[51] Similarly, Homer Ashby recognizes that the survival of African-Americans is in jeopardy and that "without a collective community there can be no transmission of a healthy sense of self-esteem or self-worth." African-American community as mirror functions as a "counterbalancing force" against negative messages from the dominant culture.[52]

A Hearing-Healing-Heeding Community

A multifaceted, intercultural care approach to congregational Bible study assumes that groups serve more than one purpose,[53] appropriately fulfilling what we call a *hearing-healing-heeding* function.[54] This phrase points to dynamics in the encounter between the text and our stories: (1) *hearing* cultivates mutual teaching and learning and invites rational as well as nonrational insights; (2) *healing* fosters integration of self into community (though it isn't appropriate to call forth details that might overexpose participants); and (3) *heeding* calls the group forward in faithful and engaged action that follows from collaborative study rather than a preconceived agenda.

51. R. Esteban Montilla and Ferney Medina, *Pastoral Care and Counseling with Latino/as* (Minneapolis: Fortress Press, 2006), p. 45.

52. Homer Ashby Jr., *Our Home Is Over Jordan: A Black Pastoral Theology* (St. Louis: Chalice Press, 2007), p. 9.

53. Groups can serve many purposes: task/work groups; guidance/psychoeducational groups; counseling/interpersonal problem-solving groups; psychotherapy/personality reconstruction groups. See M. Corey and G. Corey, *Groups: Process and Practice* (Pacific Grove, Calif.: Brooks/Cole Publishers, 1987), pp. 9-17.

54. We, the authors, appreciate the connections between our model and clergy education's focus on integrating the cognitive, practical, and normative apprenticeships of ministry. See C. Foster, L. Dahill, L. Golemon, and B. Tolentino, *Educating Clergy: Teaching Practices and Pastoral Imagination* (San Francisco: Jossey-Bass, 2006).

Guidelines for Such a Community

1. Establish a covenant of care: set the group ground rules up front and return to them regularly
2. Engage in communal reflection: identify connections in the group and in contemporary culture
3. Maintain confidentiality: keep the stories of the group in the group
4. Share stories: respect the revealing/concealing dynamic without pressuring
5. Call for a response in daily life: commit to embody the learning

The Road Map process for biblical interpretation[55] supports hearing-healing-heeding in groups. The Road Map is undergirded by these three assumptions: (1) the Bible is a collection of testimonies that are historically and culturally relative, shaped by the people and times out of which they emerged; (2) the perspective of every reader is also historically and culturally relative, shaped by the reader's social location (class, gender, ethnicity, sexual orientation, physical and mental ability, economic/political/social status); and (3) while no one reading of the text can claim special privilege, neither does any reading of it function in isolation from other persons and communities.

Our interaction with a biblical text is influenced, in part, by our experiences in the world.[56] Certain "speed bumps" in a biblical text grab our attention and push our emotional buttons. To pretend that they don't so that we can be "objective" robs the story of its power. Also, we may not all share the same speed bumps or have the same buttons pushed. While no single interpretation can claim precedence over any other, neither does any one function in isolation from other interpretations and communities. This approach allows room for intersections between the Bible and pastoral care to surface, creating a liminal or threshold space in which new perspectives are shaped. Biblical texts "read" us and invite us into a larger story, one that expands our own worldview.

---

55. Frederick Tiffany and Sharon Ringe, *Biblical Interpretation: A Road Map* (Nashville: Abingdon Press, 1996). This is the interpretive process we follow at Wesley Theological Seminary.

56. See "How the Bible Is Read, Interpreted, and Used" in *New Interpreter's Bible,* vol. I (Nashville: Abingdon Press, 1994), pp. 33-213. These articles by various authors treat interpretation in Jewish and Christian traditions, contemporary methods of reading the Bible, and reading the Bible from different social locations — as African-Americans, Asian Americans, Hispanic Americans, Native Americans, and women.

The Road Map unfolds in five interrelated steps:

1. *Begin the journey at home.* We need to probe the social location of the reader and of the reading community. This is not simply a check-list, but a process of uncovering the contexts which shape our questions and the way we read the texts.
2. *Encounter the biblical text.* We must pay attention to feelings and re-actions that the passage evokes and to the "speed bumps" that slow us down. (We — Denise and Michael — often begin with this step because it seems to draw readers out more readily, and connects them more easily to step 1.)
3. *Read the biblical text closely.* We need to notice literary features, structure, and differences in text translations.
4. *Read the biblical text contextually.* We need to locate the passage in its literary and social context.
5. *Engage the biblical text, other readers, and our communities.* It is impor-tant to bring our engagement with the text into dialogue with other readers to discern the various messages of the text.

Clearly, steps three and four are rooted in the historical-critical method, while steps one, two, and five move us beyond that method to consider how the text matters to us and our faith communities. As these steps are taken, stories that need to be told are heard, and pasto-ral caring can take place. Usually a character, word, or event in the text triggers a memory, an emotion, or a story which the reader begins to organize and reflect upon in conversation with the biblical text and other readers. The goal is to help readers clarify their own personal feel-ings in relation to texts, not to have readers adopt the same perspec-tives and feelings as the biblical character. The facilitator of the Road Map process does not control the process. She or he must be as open and vulnerable to the text as the other readers. The facilitator reminds the group about boundaries, making certain to anchor observations and feelings in textual details. Otherwise, we as readers run the risk of making the text say whatever we want it to say or confirming what we already believe.

QUESTIONS FOR REFLECTION
- Reflect on an experience of being jolted into de-centered listening. What happened?

- What surprises or challenges you about the Road Map?
- How does the Road Map shape or shift your interpretation of the Bible?
- With what biblical character do you most identify? Why? How might the Road Map give you a different angle of vision on this character?

The Bible as Answer Book

Several years ago, a bumper sticker read, "Find help FAST . . . in the Bible pages." Bumper stickers are today's proverbs, pithy sayings that sum up experience and guide us to successful living. Some might applaud the way in which this bumper sticker publicly proclaims the centrality of the Bible in everyday life. However, Michael and I question its assumption that the Bible is an answer book or a manual that helps people move directly and quickly to the problem at hand. "Biblical counseling" is one example of this view. Advocates of this approach claim that "scripture is sufficient to answer comprehensively the deepest needs of the human heart."[57] The literal interpretation of Scripture often goes hand in hand with this approach, ignoring the interpretation inherent in any "application" of Scripture to life. Interpreters must be careful about claims of biblical authority. When too much authority is invested in the biblical text itself or in a particular translation of the text, Christianity becomes "a book-centered religion rather than a God-centered one."[58]

When lists of chapter and verse are generated for issues such as divorce, grief, conflict, healing, and so on and simply "applied" (such a mechanical term!) to a problem, the Bible becomes a "prescription" for

---

57. David Winfrey, "Biblical Therapy," *Christian Century*, 23 January 2007, pp. 24-27. This definition, quoted by Winfrey, comes from school officials from Southern Baptist Theological Seminary in Louisville, which no longer participates in CPE programs. The *Journal of Biblical Counseling* follows this argument and rejects the competing theories of psychology. See also Ed Hindson and Howard Eyrich, *Totally Sufficient: The Bible and Christian Counseling* (Rosshire, Eng.: Christian Focus Publications, 2004); Jeffrey Watson, *Biblical Counseling for Today* (Nashville: Thomas Nelson, 2000); and Steven Waterhouse, *Life's Tough Questions: What the Bible Says About . . .* (Amarillo, Tex.: Westcliff Press, 2005).

58. Bruce Birch and Larry Rasmussen, *The Bible and Ethics in the Christian Life* (Minneapolis: Augsburg Publishing House, 1989), ch. 8.

"fixing" the problem.[59] This "moral instructional use"[60] of the Bible can influence negatively the pastoral encounter. The care giver expresses "oughts" and "shoulds" in a directive care process in which both the Bible and the care giver have absolute, objective authority. This approach "can make children of counselees" and frustrate their growth toward their full human possibilities.[61]

Job's friends illustrate the authoritarian use of Scripture in a pastoral care situation. In their so-called dialogue with Job, they were determined to convict Job of sin rather than listen to him. Their arguments with him grew out of the Wisdom theme of the Two Ways, which says that the righteous are rewarded and the wicked are punished. (This is also known as the theory of act/consequence.) They reasoned that Job must have done something to deserve his suffering. As Eliphaz insists, "Think now, who that was innocent ever perished? . . . As I have seen, those who plow iniquity and sow trouble reap the same" (4:7-8). They offer up several corollaries of act/consequence, including these: suffering is temporary, so be patient (8:20-21); suffering either leads you to repentance (8:5-7) or it is disciplinary (5:17; cf. Heb. 12:6), both of which are good for you. One of them, Zophar, even goes so far as to insist that Job isn't getting as much as he deserved! (Job 11:6b). With friends like that, who needs enemies?

Also, the repeated use of rhetorical questions by Job's friends serves to shut down any real conversation. Zophar, for example, asks "Can you find out the deep things of God?" (11:7) as a way to assert the mystery of suffering and the experiential limits of human knowledge. How can one respond to a question whose answer (No!) is already obvious to the one asking? The friends' attack simply pushes Job into hurling his own rhetorical questions back at them — "Is my strength the strength of stones, or is my flesh bronze?" (6:12) — and at God, with a bitter parody of Psalm 8:3-4: "What are human beings, that you make so much of

59. In *God and the Rhetoric of Sexuality* (Philadelphia: Fortress Press, 1978), Phyllis Trible distinguishes between prescription and description in Genesis 3: God describes the consequences of the disobedience of the man and the woman in the garden of Eden, but does not prescribe a punishment. God's judgments against them are culturally conditioned and not divine "oughts." They describe how things are rather than prescribe how they should be (p. 128).

60. Donald Capps, "Bible, Pastoral Use and Interpretation of," in *Dictionary of Pastoral Care and Counseling*, pp. 82-85.

61. Wimberly, *Using Scripture in Pastoral Counseling*, p. 12.

them, . . . visit them every morning, test them every moment? Will you not . . . let me alone until I swallow my spittle?" (7:17-19). Unfortunately, God fires God's own list of rhetorical questions at Job when God appears in the speeches from the whirlwind in Job 38–41: "Where were you when I laid the foundation of the earth?" (38:4); "Have you entered the storehouses of the snow?" (38:22); "Is it by your wisdom that the hawk soars?" (39:26). I (Denise) have a button that reads "Do rhetorical questions annoy you?" I wear it whenever I teach a Bible study on Job. Rhetorical questions do not allow for a response. What's worse, they encourage defensiveness. Asking them is often the worst thing we can do in a pastoral care situation.

The best thing that Job's friends did for him was to sit with him for seven days and seven nights in empathic silence when he was on the dung heap (2:13). Sitting with Job in silence without either making sense of the situation or explaining to him what he did "wrong" (in 1:1 the narrator makes it clear that he was "blameless and upright") was certainly challenging. Reflective and compassionate listening[62] is exactly what's needed in such a situation. Reflective listening and presence do not mean simply *not* saying something, as one sits stirring with all kinds of thoughts and suggestions to offer. Reflective listening requires the ability to sit with another person, mirroring speech and nonverbal cues from the other. The three friends showed mirroring behavior when they wept, tore their robes, and threw dust on their heads (Job 2:12) — all traditional acts of mourning in the Ancient Near East. They mirror and thus comfort Job, who has reacted to his calamities in 1:20 by tearing his robe, shaving his head, and falling on the ground.

A pastoral presence requires an emptiness of mind *(kenosis),* in the sense of attending patiently and carefully to what is actually happening with the other person. In such presence we recognize the fear and anxiety that may be stirred within us as the other speaks or does not speak. Cultivating an ability to listen means that we become increasingly comfortable with silence. Not simply a mere absence of speaking words, silence makes us available to the other person and to the movement of God's Spirit. Listening presence requires a bracketing of our own tendency to judge, explain, or justify. By practicing this presence, we can

---

62. In *Listening for the Soul: Pastoral Care and Spiritual Direction* (Minneapolis: Fortress Press, 2000), Jean Stairs speaks of listening as acts of obedience, intimacy, receptivity, hospitality, focus, and soul inquiry (pp. 15-35).

begin to let go of our need to defend ourselves or God as we sit with another person in pain.

Questions for Reflection

- In what ways do you use the Bible as an answer book?
- Have you experienced the equivalent of Job's friends in your life? Explain. How did this experience feel?
- Can you think of a time when your mirroring activity brought comfort to someone else or when someone else's mirroring activity comforted you?

Pitching the Platitudes

When we as care givers don't practice mutual and attentive listening, we are more likely to speak platitudes, engage in moral exhortations, and offer proof texts for complex problems. One of our students in class had experienced the harm inflicted by this sort of sloppy "care." Her father had died when she was only six, and a family friend had insisted that her mother must have done something "bad" to deserve his death. For this student, the Bible became a weapon that cut deeply into her psyche.

Similarly, when diagnosis labels primarily from the outside — e.g., he has clinical depression; she has an anxiety disorder — it can also function as a harmful weapon in pastoral and clinical care. Instead, diagnosis should function as a temporary marker, as a spur for gathering further information to navigate painful situations. Care givers can often gather this information in storytelling and listening. However, when we care givers encounter unsettling feelings in our own stories or those of others, we may be pushed to platitudes as a defensive cover-up of those feelings.

Michael and I offer a working definition of a platitude: a superficial comment that stifles further story exploration. When someone uses platitudes, it is usually a temporary means of reassurance and comfort. Over time, however, platitudes as a form of self-talk can close off access to lived experience or to what's actually going on inside. Whether said to self or others, platitudes often block soul healing.

As care givers we need to pay particular attention to the negative aspect of platitudes. Intended as positive affirmation, they can have the boomerang effect of reinforcing negative images and disempowering people from constructing their own meaningful narratives. Among other things, platitudes can short-circuit grieving processes. So what to do? When Denise and I feel the urge to utter a platitude, we decide to pitch it in the virtual trash can! We list some common platitudes below.

> It could be worse.
> There are more fish in the sea.
> She is in a better place.
> God needed another angel.
> Look on the bright side.
> There's more of you to love.
> There, but for the grace of God, go I . . .
> Only the good die young.

GROUP EXERCISE
- Add to the list of platitudes above. Then discuss how to avoid using them.

Avoiding "Selective Storying"

Pastoral care givers need to avoid the unhelpful practice of "selective storying"[63] of our own stories as well as of the biblical stories. We choose our favorite stories to make ourselves look good or to avoid discomfort. We all do this. This choosing makes us less available to the other. We need to remember that "in a counseling relationship, *there is nowhere to hide.*"[64] This tendency to create a canon within a canon of stories is echoed by the biblical traditioning process itself,[65] as well as by the imposition of theological categories upon the multi-faceted Bible. How else do we arrive at the categories of Creation, Fall,

63. In *Using Scripture in Pastoral Counseling,* Wimberly defines "storying" as "organizing human experience using stories" (p. 15).

64. Neil Pembroke, *The Art of Listening: Dialogue, Shame, and Pastoral Care* (Grand Rapids: Wm. B. Eerdmans, 2002), p. 169. Citing the counseling work of Irvin Yalom with an obese woman, Pembroke notes how the pretense of presence and compassion and hiding one's negative reactions to a care receiver can reinforce that person's low self-esteem and expectations.

65. In *Torah and Canon* (Philadelphia: Fortress Press, 1972), James A. Sanders describes the Bible as "a glorious mess of adaptability."

Covenant, and Sin? The overarching narrative isn't the whole story. Tension is created by those bits and pieces that don't seem to fit — the remnants, the recovered artifacts, the submerged localized traditions or customs that have been covered over. The remnants of a tradition have a way of pulling at us, of refusing to disappear. Sometimes our images of God or of ourselves override the biblical stories.

Are there "negative" biblical stories that should be off-limits to care receivers who would "twist" and "distort" them, as Edward Wimberly suggests?[66] These are precisely the stories that attract and that merit lingering reflection. How comforting to know that even cheating, lying, demanding Jacob is transformed in his encounter with God (see Chapter Two), and that power, ironically, resides in the negative thinking of the psalm laments (see Chapter Six).

Care givers need to remember that the Hebrew Bible does not provide "a coherent and comprehensive offer of God" but only "hints, fragments, vignettes."[67] In Israel's plurivocal testimony about God, core testimony and countertestimony resist organization. Core testimony makes basic claims about God over time, rooted in transformative verbs such as *save, deliver, command, create, lead.* This is the God of covenant, doxology, and presence. Countertestimony is rooted in Israel's lived experience of absence and silence. This is the God of exile, lament, and theodicy (literally, in Greek, "God's justice"). Tension between core testimony and countertestimony characterizes Israelite faith, and is echoed by the Good Friday/Easter dialectic of Christian tradition. Some desperately want the sense that Sunday resolves Friday, but "liturgically, both claims linger."[68]

For most of us, neither is our sense of self as coherent and comprehensive as we would like to believe. Culturally and psychologically, we tend to favor the dominant story and smooth over unresolved tensions and remnants. This can be particularly challenging for people who stand on the margins, since their stories are primarily countertestimony to begin with. Pastoral care givers need to recognize this tension in relationship with the biblical stories, within themselves, and in care receivers.

66. Wimberly, *Using Scripture in Pastoral Counseling,* p. 126.
67. Brueggemann, *Theology of the Old Testament,* p. 117.
68. Brueggemann, *Theology of the Old Testament,* p. 401.

A QUESTION FOR REFLECTION

- What is your core testimony about God? What is your counter-testimony?

TAKE-AWAY POINTS

Biblical texts enter into our care giving when we do the following:

1. Honor the Bible as a source for wholeness in our fragmented world.
2. Know biblical texts well enough ourselves to use them, yet not so well that we think we have exhausted their meaning or that there is only *one* meaning to be discovered. We need to do our "good enough" Bible homework.
3. Practice "the art of holding on loosely" — that is, of avoiding taking control of the story and allowing those in care "freedom to move about, to think, imagine, and feel for themselves what it would be like to be living in a different kind of story."[69]
4. Listen for "touch points" in stories that we can help connect to biblical stories, and vice versa.
5. Pay closer attention to details of biblical and human stories.
6. Embrace the messiness of the Bible/pastoral care process. We need to be prepared to get our hands dirty.
7. Practice mutual and attentive listening. We might learn to count to ten before jumping in with a response.
8. Avoid rhetorical questions that can be perceived as judgmental.
9. Recognize that the Bible is not an answer book.
10. Note the multivalence or layers of both the biblical text and the human text; both contain many stories and voices.
11. Create space in each day to unplug (cell phone, e-mail, TV, iPod) from our distracting culture.
12. Listen to books on tape or expert storytellers such as Garrison Keillor to become more familiar with the storytelling and listening process.
13. Distinguish mirrors from windows.

69. Donald Capps, *Living Stories: Pastoral Counseling in Congregational Context* (Minneapolis: Fortress Press, 1998), p. 205.

CARE PRAYER

God of All Connections,

You write us into existence and co-author all stories. We study and pray together aware of your holy authorship throughout many generations. Gather us into respectful and sensitive community, eager to excavate the many layers of our stories and the biblical stories. Prompt us to ask curious questions of the texts and of one another. Open us gently to mystery of the unknown when we become fearful of stories we hear and defensive of stories we need to tell. Cultivate in us an urgent expectancy as we dig deeply into your Word and into the stories of our lives. Give us the courage to hold one another in love as we encounter differences of opinion and impasses of understanding, and spark us to dance with delight as we stumble upon nuggets of pure gold. Amen.

Chapter 2

Telling Our Stories and the
Relational Aspects of Storytelling

Rick's Story

Rick visited Mary in the nursing home every week in his role as volunteer chaplain. Suffering from multiple sclerosis, Mary had been bound to a wheelchair for the last two years. During each visit, Rick would ask Mary if she ever felt like lamenting. Her answer was always silence, or "No." Patiently each week, he would read a psalm of lament to her and ask his question, because he sensed that she was holding deep pain inside. Finally, one day, she looked at him and answered, "Every day in this wheelchair," and her laments came pouring out.[1]

•   •

Silence

Cultivating pastoral availability[2] asks that we develop a capacity for patience and silence. The human soul, connected as it is with the heart of

1. Story told by Rick Cauthern, a student in our fall 2006 class on the Hebrew Bible and pastoral care practices at Wesley Theological Seminary.

2. In *The Art of Listening: Dialogue, Shame, and Pastoral Care* (Grand Rapids: Wm. B. Eerdmans, 2002), Neil Pembroke argues that availability and confirmation are the *"two fundamental moments in the ministry of care."* Availability involves the reception of and belonging to the other. Confirmation means establishing a relationship with the other to help him/her reach fullest potential (p. 7).

God, does not always move in predictable, timely ways or express itself in readily understandable language. Many of us grope our way to expression. Some of us are stubborn, fearful, or hesitant. Being with people in pastoral care, whether individuals or groups, asks that we make ourselves available for whatever needs to happen in the moment, just as Rick made himself consistently available through his presence with Mary.

When we as care givers become more comfortable with dwelling in patient silence, then whatever people share, whenever and however they choose to share, we'll be ready to listen. The patient, silent waiting of Job's friends in Job 2:11-13 set the stage for his gut-wrenching lament in chapter 3, reversing the passive acceptance of his calamities in chapters 1–2. We develop the capacity for tolerating, and perhaps even reveling in, silence because it can nurture storytelling and story listening in unimaginable ways. Silence is the poised and sustained ability to be present in and with whatever is, even the slowly emerging chaos of the "unstory."[3]

For many of us, though, silence may not come easily or naturally. It needs regular tending and encouragement.[4] Silence is not so much the absence of words and thoughts as it is a fullness of presence. Creating space for silence is as individual as each of us is. We suggest to our students that they cultivate habits that make silence possible within the regular patterns and rhythms of ministry. Care givers who cultivate silence as a habit of mind and being hopefully will avoid falling into the trap of finishing another's sentences, completing the narrative with their own vision of its next steps or its ending, or unhelpfully projecting their own stories onto the other.

A QUESTION FOR REFLECTION
- How comfortable are you with silence?

PRACTICES FOR CULTIVATING SILENCE
- Walking the labyrinth
- Engaging in times of centering prayer

---

3. In *The Incredible Woman: Listening to Women's Silences in Pastoral Care and Counseling* (Nashville: Abingdon Press, 1996), Riet Bons-Storm speaks of the "unstory" of abused women that precedes the telling.

4. John Savage, unfortunately, only devotes one paragraph to the "skill" of silence in *Listening and Caring Skills in Ministry: A Guide for Groups and Leaders* (Nashville: Abingdon Press, 1996), p. 98.

- Taking regular retreat days (or half days)
- Contemplating wildlife, a garden, or a sunrise first thing in the morning
- Allowing "quiet times" with God
- Breathing deeply and slowly

Speaking and Listening

As people of God caring with and for each other, we tell and listen to stories because both practices reflect the activity of God in whose image we are made. We can all too easily image God as the Divine Orator commanding creation into existence by sheer force of the spoken word ("and God said, 'Let there be . . .' and there was . . ."). However, we do not so easily image God as the Divine Listener, taking in and reflecting on creation. It is the omniscient narrator in Genesis 1 who declares at the end of each day of creation, "And God saw that it was good"; God does not speak these words. On the seventh day, God rests (literally, *shabbat,* "ceases") and says nothing at all. We hear only the narrator. Speaking and listening are linked in this creation story. When grounded in silent awareness, these practices allow the Living Word to be heard by both speaker and listener.

Through speaking and listening, we engage in creative acts reflective of the creative activity of God and come to recognize the authoring power inherent in both processes. To author our stories is to give voice to them, to name and put words to that which was originally formless. Authoring places us as subjects in our own stories, rather than making us objects of a story told about us. When we practice "good enough listening,"[5] we make space for others to share their stories and claim this power for themselves. When we "hear into speech"[6] the voiceless, we bear witness to God's presence in them. We also help to set boundaries for the chaos that swirls around them, just as God's speaking creation into being set boundaries for, but did not eliminate, chaos present in

5. This phrase came from Pamela Couture, in a response to a paper at The Society for Pastoral Theology annual study conference in San Juan, Puerto Rico, June 14, 2007.

6. Nelle Morton, *The Journey Is Home* (Boston: Beacon Press, 1985), pp. 127-28. Morton speaks out of women's experience of a "depth hearing that takes place before the speaking — a hearing that is far more than acute listening" and evokes new speech from the one heard. This is the hearing of empowerment and Pentecost.

the beginning. The Hebrew word *tehom* symbolizes this chaos. It means "the deep." These chaotic waters appear also in Psalm 104:9: "You set a boundary that they [the waters] may not pass, so that they might not again cover the earth." Chaos is not merely negative, but serves as the raw material of creation. It is full of potential.

Listening offers a gift to the storyteller that says, "You're real — you matter," at a time when the person in crisis questions his or her worth and identity. This is especially true for women. As a cross-racial team of female scholars argues, "Each person holds subjective 'truths' . . . women need to tell our stories among ourselves and get used to hearing our own voices."[7] This kind of listening is modeled on the biblical testimony of a God who has ears to hear and eyes to see those who are suffering, as in the call of Moses in Exodus 3:7-9: "I have observed the misery of my people who are in Egypt; I have heard their cry on account of their taskmasters. Indeed, I know their sufferings." Also, God is petitioned frequently to see and hear in the Psalms (e.g., Psalm 35:22; Psalm 51:1-2).

Everyone should be allowed to tell her or his own story. My (Denise's) uncle, for example, loves to tell the story of his hospitalization and emergency gallbladder surgery in minute, graphic detail. Sometimes he even needs to be restrained from showing his laparoscopic scars. This telling helps him to make sense of a frightening experience and deal with fears about his present health.[8]

QUESTIONS FOR REFLECTION

- When have you experienced God as Divine Orator or Divine Listener in your life?
- Reflect on a time when your story wasn't listened to. How did that make you feel?

---

7. Marsha Foster Boyd and Carolyn Stahl Bohler, "Womanist-Feminist Alliances: Meeting on the Bridge," in *Feminist and Womanist Pastoral Theology*, ed. Bonnie Miller-McLemore and Brita Gill-Austern (Nashville: Abingdon Press, 1999), p. 193.

8. In *Listening and Caring Skills in Ministry*, John Savage calls this a "rehearsal story" that retells a past incident of pain in order to inform listeners of what is going on in the present (pp. 84-89).

Co-Authoring

Our stories are not ours alone, but involve many co-authors, including God.[9] We as pastoral care givers "must become grounded in the Living Word in order to bring the Living Word to others."[10] We must begin the process of grounding by acknowledging a fundamental anthropological principle, namely, that God gives human life meaning. We are not autonomous and self-actualizing. Instead, we are defined by our relationship with God who has called us into covenant with God and one another.[11] Through our life-giving and life-defining relationship with God, nurtured by intentional practices, we author our healthiest stories. God's role as co-author of our stories is introduced in Genesis 1, at the very beginning of the Bible. If we pay attention to the literary or rhetorical features of this chapter, we can recognize clues to God's co-authorship. The pattern for day six, when humans are created, is different than the pattern followed for the other days of creation. It is longer, and on this day God speaks more than the narrator.[12]

Only humans are made in the image of God (Gen. 1:26),[13] and only

9. Herbert Anderson and Edward Foley, *Mighty Stories, Dangerous Rituals: Weaving Together the Human and the Divine* (San Francisco: Jossey-Bass, 1998), p. 19.

10. This comment was made by student Sue Walters during our fall 2006 class on the Hebrew Bible and pastoral care practices at Wesley Theological Seminary. See Pamela Cooper-White, *Shared Wisdom: Use of the Self in Pastoral Care and Counseling* (Minneapolis: Fortress Press, 2004). She lists five steps for self-care that we need to take before we can care for others. See also John Savage, *Listening and Caring Skills in Ministry: ". . . you can enter the pain of another only at the level you can enter your own"* (p. 96).

11. Denise Dombkowski Hopkins, "Biblical Anthropology, Discipline Of," in *Dictionary of Pastoral Care and Counseling*, ed. Rodney Hunter (Nashville: Abingdon Press, 1990), pp. 85-86.

12. Robert Alter, in *The Art of Hebrew Narrative* (New York: Basic Books, 1981), notes important characteristics of biblical narrative: it is concise and the plot is central, so that we must pay attention to every word; direct speech and dialogue predominate over description; repetition can slow the plot, create suspense, and provide emphasis; the narrator is omniscient, reliable, and unobtrusive; narrative patterning — for example, inclusion or brackets (repeated phrases at beginning and end) can progress or balance episodes; word choice is careful, artful, and purposeful. See also Peter Miscall, "Introduction to Narrative Literature," in *New Interpreter's Bible,* vol. 2 (Nashville: Abingdon Press, 1998), pp. 540-41.

13. See Pamela Cooper-White, *Many Voices: Pastoral Psychotherapy in Relational and Theological Perspective* (Minneapolis: Fortress Press, 2007), pp. 38-66. She proposes characteristics of human beings as part of divine creation: good, vulnerable, embodied, alike

they are given dominion (Gen. 1:26-28). For some interpreters, the dominance of language on the second half of day six offers the most important clue about who we are as humans created in God's image. Ours is a likeness that invites conversation and relationship. We can respond to God's call and commission. The royal use of "image" in the Ancient Near East is democratized here. All human beings, male and female, and not just kings, "mirror God to the world."[14] "Image" suggests the capacity for relationship rather than something physical. Church leaders can often spend too much time and energy "protecting inaccurate self-images"[15] when genuine relationships need to be the focus. Our movement toward authentic self-knowledge invites feedback from others, reflection, and learning from mistakes, all within the context of our relationship with God.

God as interested and curious co-author seeks us out and invites us to tell our stories, often by asking questions. After the disobedience in the garden, God the Questioner asks the man, "Where are you?" (Gen. 3:9). The rest of the Bible can be seen as an extension and commentary on this question,[16] which is echoed by Jesus in Luke 19:10: "For the Son of Man came to seek out and to save the lost." Care givers can model themselves after the Divine Questioner by asking open-ended questions. This point is illustrated poignantly by a woman at an Alzheimer's conference, who told part of her story. For fifteen years she had cared for her mother-in-law, who had Alzheimer's, and she was now caring for her husband, who had the same disease and had been diagnosed with it relatively young, at age 54. She shared that "it would

---

and unique, intrinsically rational, multiple, fluid/in process, loved, loving. See also Leroy Howe, *The Image of God: A Theology for Pastoral Care and Counseling* (Nashville: Abingdon Press, 1995), pp. 27-37, "Human Beings in the 'Image of God.'"

14. B. Birch, W. Brueggemann, T. Fretheim, and D. Petersen, *A Theological Introduction to the Old Testament,* 2d ed. (Nashville: Abingdon Press, 2005), p. 43.

15. Lovett Weems, "Leaders Know Themselves," in *Leading Ideas,* 12 April 2006. In this online newsletter of the Lewis Center for Church Leadership at Wesley Theological Seminary, Weems notes that John Wesley modeled self-examination as a regular practice, first daily, and then every Saturday. See also Linda S. Hileman, "Keeping Up Appearances," *Circuit Rider,* March/April 2007, pp. 14-15. She argues that the case of Mary and Matthew Winkler (she shot him to death in 2005; he was a pastor, and no one knew they had a problem) shows how pastors and their families are so good at "focusing on everyone else's problems and neglecting [their] own."

16. William B. Oglesby Jr., *Biblical Themes for Pastoral Care* (Nashville: Abingdon Press, 1980), p. 46.

mean a lot to my husband if people said something, asked how he was. But they say nothing. He wants them to know what he's going through." She wanted conference participants to know that the disease was affecting them both. They yearned for questions that would evoke their respective stories.

God persists in questioning in Genesis 3:11 — "Who told you that you were naked? Have you eaten from the tree of which I commanded you not to eat?" Unfortunately, the man and woman in the garden answer by passing the buck of responsibility. Their story conceals more than reveals.[17] With this cover-up, they further distance themselves from God and from one another. When our stories conceal, we may be trying to protect something we think is important. Concealing stories may be either destructive or life-giving. For example, a pastor in our jointly taught class chose Eli in 1 Samuel 2 as the biblical character with whom he most identified. "We would all like to picture ourselves as Samuel, young, full of promise, and blessed by God," he says. "In truth, we are all much more like Eli: flawed, blind to the sins of those around us (and our own), never hearing God's call on our lives directly. . . . For all his failings, he does the one thing that he was put in place to do: to recognize the call of God to another — to Samuel — and to help Samuel answer that call." Eli accepts God's judgment on him and his family with dignity, and helps us to see that "we all have a special role (however unlikely) to play in God's story."[18]

Care givers do well to heed the caution not to press too quickly by asking too many questions. We can learn to listen loosely and recognize that many stories exist on many levels simultaneously. Attentive listening surfaces questions for both care giver and receiver. We must also know our own stories well. In D. W. Winnicott's terms,[19] biblical stories themselves can be considered transitional objects (that which mediates psychic and external realities, helping us to recognize where "I" end and "the other" begins), like a blanket or a teddy bear in childhood. Both pastoral care givers and receivers relate to this object, but often in differing ways. Considering the Bible as a transitional object helps us

17. Anderson and Foley, *Mighty Stories, Dangerous Rituals,* pp. 7-12. When stories conceal, we exercise self-deception. When they reveal, we allow ourselves to be vulnerable.

18. This is a journal entry from Michael Smith, a United Methodist pastor in upstate New York, who participated in our September 2006 class.

19. D. W. Winnicott, *The Maturational Processes and the Facilitating Environment* (New York: International Universities Press, 1965).

to name the powerful energy, both conscious and unconscious, that gets stirred up in our encounter with it.

Attentive listening can create positive silence that allows stories to surface naturally rather than be coerced. In Genesis 4, however, we are introduced to a different kind of silence, a negative silence. By questioning an angry Cain in verses 6-7, God gives him the opportunity to tell God what's wrong: "Why are you angry, and why has your countenance fallen?" Cain, however, chooses not to answer God, not to tell his story, and in this treacherous and hate-filled silence, he kills his brother Abel (v. 8). These texts suggest that our silence with God can negatively shape speech and actions toward our brothers and sisters.[20] Telling and listening to stories generate healing power because stories reconnect us with others and with God, and call us from self-absorption, alienation, and radical skepticism.[21]

In his silence, Cain refuses God's invitation to tell his story. Cain does not allow God to co-author a positive story with him, which might have prevented Abel's murder. Without a co-authored story, Cain also damages himself: "In killing Abel," Norman Cohen explains, "Cain actually killed a part of himself."[22] In killing his brother, the shepherd, he becomes Abel: Cain the farmer must now wander the earth. Nevertheless, we can read verse 13 — "Is my sin too great to be forgiven?" — with the rabbis of the Talmud as an expression of Cain's repentance.[23] Then we see

---

20. This insight comes from David C. Hopkins, Professor of Archaeology and Biblical Interpretation at Wesley Theological Seminary. We, the authors, note also that Abel does not speak to Cain, who perhaps needed some comforting. See the children's book written by Sandy Eisenberg Sasso and illustrated by Joani K. Rothenberg: *Cain and Abel: Finding the Fruits of Peace* (Woodstock, Vt.: Jewish Lights Publishing, 2001). This book raises questions about positive ways of dealing with anger and rejection.

21. Daniel Taylor, *The Healing Power of Stories: Creating Yourself through the Stories of Your Life* (New York: Doubleday, 1996).

22. Norman J. Cohen, *Self, Struggle, and Change: Family Conflict Stories in Genesis and Their Healing Insights for Our Lives* (Woodstock, Vt.: Jewish Lights Publishing, 1995), p. 52. "Abel is truly Cain's other side," Cohen says (p. 42). Six times in four verses (Gen. 4:8-11), the narrator tells us that Abel is Cain's brother.

23. In many Bibles *'avon* is translated as "punishment," but it can often mean "sin." *Neso* is often translated "to bear" but more often means "to forgive or pardon." The Talmud is a commentary on the Mishnah (an anthology of legal statements covering different topics produced by the rabbis of the second century c.e.). There is a Jerusalem Talmud (dating from the third to the fourth centuries c.e.) and a Babylonian Talmud (produced in the third to the sixth centuries c.e.). See Shaye Cohen, *From the Maccabees to the Mishnah*, 2d ed. (Louisville: Westminster John Knox, 2006).

that Cain accepts responsibility for his actions and reconciles with his past to move into a new future of family and city-building. He affirms for us "our potential for goodness,"[24] and models how we may be called into a different future when we allow God to co-author our story.

QUESTIONS FOR REFLECTION

- What story, from daily life or from the Bible, is important to your identity? Do you have a sense of what it reveals or conceals about you?
- Think of a time when you needed someone to ask you a question in order to prompt your story. Did they ask, or didn't they? What was this experience like for you?
- When have you been called into a different future?
- Have you experienced different kinds of silences in your life — for example, angry silence, contemplative silence, chaotic silence? What moved you from this silence to story?

Stories on the Road to Healing

Often we have to tell a story many times until we don't hurt anymore. Even through many cathartic retellings, pain still lingers. Consider the story Denise told at the beginning of one class session:

Frustrated with the seemingly endless amount of paperwork related to the institutional care of her mother, who has Alzheimer's disease, and the adamant refusals of her father to seek further assistance for his own declining mental and physical health at home, Denise feels the emotional weight of coordinating care for her elderly parents, who live in upstate New York. Her only brother drowned accidentally thirty-one years ago, leaving Denise as the sole care giver for her parents. Remembrance of her brother and grief over his death are never far from consciousness these days as she attends to the health and life challenges of her parents. This particular day — more so than others — presented a cascade of parental challenges that triggered Denise's feelings of exasperation, desperation, futility, and grief. She shared the difficulties openly and

---

24. Cohen, *Self, Struggle, and Change*, pp. 61-62. Cohen also argues that the mark on Cain's forehead does not label him an outcast. The term used for "mark" is *'ot*, which is used in the Bible as a sign of covenant with God, as are the Sabbath, circumcision, and the rainbow after the Flood.

honestly with the class, and then concluded with the words, "Now I feel better." Michael responded by saying, "But you don't have to."

It often hurts to care and to offer acts of care with love in situations like this one. Sometimes our efforts seem pointless. We feel exhausted by the sheer drudgery of meeting institutional requirements, and even more by the deeply rutted patterns of family relationships that may be only minimally changeable, if at all. We silently ponder forbidden thoughts: wondering if we're doing all we can; hoping for death rather than prolonged and lingering suffering; secretly wishing that it would all just go away. We only have control over our story and responses, and too often that doesn't feel like enough. We tell the story anyway to lift the weight that we carry and to feel relief. We may actually feel better, because sharing our stories releases emotional energy and does "feel good."

While "feeling good" may be the result of our telling, it would be an additional burden to "require" ourselves to feel good. Difficult life situations cannot be smoothed over by one telling of the story. Neither care givers nor care receivers ought to be burdened with this requirement. Christian pastoral care givers offer the caring presence of God in Christ as we sit with people experiencing difficult emotions. We sit through as many tellings as are needed in order to live into the healing that God intends for all of creation. As care receivers, we may say "I feel better now" because we are appreciative of someone listening, or because we feel relief in sharing the details and emotions of our story. However, if "I feel better" expresses our desire not to burden someone with our stories, then we run the risk of stifling those stories and blocking our own healing.

As care givers, our job in story-listening is *not* to try to make people feel better. When we communicate to care receivers that they must, we actually signal our own need to feel better. We want closure, or we want to "fix" what's wrong. The Bible cautions us that such closure is not always possible. The parable of the prodigal son and his brother in Luke 15:11-32, for example, leaves us hanging at the end. We do not know how, or even if, the two brothers will get along with one another and with their father.

Similarly, Psalm 6 moves pain away from the center of the psalmist's experience. This change of focus gives relief, but the pain is not resolved. This psalm is actually not a penitential lament, as it has traditionally been classified, but an angry lament. It does not include a confession of sin and a recognition that the psalmist's sin has caused her/his suffering. Instead, Psalm 6 moves from the pain of God's punitive anger ("O LORD, do not rebuke me in your anger"; v. 1), to grief ("every night I flood my bed with tears"; v. 6), to protest "Depart from me, all you workers of evil"; v. 8). It leaves unanswered initial questions about pain's cause and purpose. Juxtaposing God as judge with God as caring healer allows "a place for irreconcilable ways of thinking about God's part in the experience of pain."[25] The psalm ends with a confession of trust that asserts a future rescue: "All my enemies shall be ashamed" (v. 10). The psalmist continues to suffer, awaiting God's future deliverance.

QUESTIONS FOR REFLECTION

- In pastoral care situations, do you feel a responsibility to make the care receiver feel better? Why?
- Do you feel it is your responsibility as a care receiver to make your care giver feel better? Why?

Confronting Our Negative Stories

Michael's Story

When I received word that my teacher at Yale, Letty Russell, had died fifteen months after being diagnosed with cancer, I reflected upon her death. I recalled Letty's memorable phrase "gossiping the Gospel." To gossip the Gospel assumes that the Bible is a book of stories handed on from generation to generation and that storytelling is a central aspect of the biblical tradition. To assert that the Bible is a story book is not to say that it is fictional. Rather, it is to insist that theological insights and testimony are offered up in its stories. As Letty writes, "The Bible is both Scripture and Script. As Scripture it is a record of what God has done and is doing in and through the lives of people and their history. We study the Bible to understand how God acts so that we can partici-

---

25. Kristin Swenson, *Living through the Pain: Psalms and the Search for Wholeness* (Waco, Tex.: Baylor University Press, 2005), p. 87.

pate in those actions on behalf of humanity. Our participation as Christians makes the Bible Script . . . that stretches back . . . to creation [and] . . . forward into our own life stories and beyond, as we join together with others in the continuing struggle toward a new creation in which God makes all things new!"[26]

•   •

"We study the Bible to understand how God acts" — these are Letty's words. She would also say that we read the Bible so that it can also read us. We encounter the biblical stories because we yearn to know God and to be known by God. This encounter often brings us to a challenging place. In knowing God and ourselves, we come face-to-face with glorious as well as shadowy truths. Much is revealed in the encounter between our stories and the biblical stories. Consider Jacob's story, for example. Genesis 32–33 presents another installment of the "brother problem"[27] that began with Cain and Abel, continued with Isaac and Ishmael, Jacob and Esau, and then plagued Joseph and his brothers. Jacob, who had cheated Esau out of his birthright and their dying father's blessing (Gen. 25:19–34:27), and had fled to escape his brother's wrath, is on his way back home to Canaan when he learns that Esau is coming to meet him with four hundred men!

To enter into this story, Denise and I suggest that you avoid reading the text silently or listening passively as one person reads the text for the entire group. The text invites us to take it more seriously than that. Since the Bible does not come with stage directions or a director, we are all forced to make decisions about how to read this text. How we read it matters. Every pause, every whisper, every change in tempo or volume communicates meaning. Reading the text begins our interpretation and embodiment of it.[28] People will pay more attention to this

26. Letty Russell, *The Future of Partnership* (Philadelphia: Westminster Press, 1979), p. 22.

27. Frank Frick, *A Journey Through the Hebrew Scriptures,* 2nd ed. (Belmont, Calif.: Thomson/Wadsworth, 2003), p. 132.

28. Tracy Radosevic, "MULLing the Biblical Text," *The Journal of Biblical Storytelling* 11 (2001): 67-77. Radosevic's acronym urges us to master (not memorize), understand, live with, and link personally with the story. Her whole body becomes involved with the story — her gestures, voice, and so on. See also Kenneth R. Parker, "Story-embodying," *The Journal of Biblical Storytelling* 5 (1995): 85-88. (The Web site for the Network of Biblical

biblical story when a cast of characters tells it, and the readers themselves will discover elements they had previously missed. To read these two chapters, you will need someone to be the narrator, Jacob, the collective speaker for the messengers, the man/God who wrestles, and Esau. Once the reading is finished, begin with step two of the Road Map given in the preceding chapter. What "speed bumps" (details in the text that give pause or push emotional buttons) pop up from the reading?

When Michael and I engage this text in workshops, readers often point to the mystery of reconnections as a speed bump; we don't know why Esau, instead of killing Jacob, runs to meet him, embraces him, kisses him, and weeps (Gen. 33:4). Many register their dislike for Jacob; they see Jacob wrestling with God and demanding a blessing as another example of the lying Jacob who betrayed his dying father and his brother and cheated his uncle Laban. Jacob never totally loses his personality, despite his new name.[29] Even after he and Esau have reconciled, Jacob declines Esau's request to travel with him, promises to meet him in Seir, and winds up in Shechem instead (Gen. 33:12-20). Some are sympathetic because of the mark that Jacob carries away from the wrestling — his limp — because they bear marks of their own wrestling with God. Others feel sorry for Jacob because he's simply living up to the name he has been given in a kind of self-fulfilling prophecy. A few see the positive value of wrestling for blessing rather than expecting that blessing to simply be served up on a silver platter. Many take comfort in God's coming to Jacob when he is most alone, by himself on the banks of the Jabbok River. He has just sent all of his family and possessions away to the other side (Gen. 32:22-24). Still others wonder if Ja-

---

Storytellers can be found at nbs@nbsint.org.) Also, see *The Storyteller's Companion to the Bible* series edited by Michael Williams (Nashville: Abingdon Press, 1991-), and L. Gregory Jones, "Embodying Scripture in the Community of Faith," in *The Art of Reading Scripture,* ed. Ellen F. Davis and Richard B. Hays (Grand Rapids: Wm. B. Eerdmans, 2003), pp. 143-59. Jones argues that "we have failed to attend adequately to the task of actually reading and embodying the texts themselves," which is essential for scriptural imagination (pp. 145-46).

29. The name Jacob means "the one who supplants," which conjures up his birth story. He was born holding on to his brother's heel, trying to pull him back so that he could be the firstborn. His new name, Israel, means "the one who strives with God." Jacob becomes an eponym for the people Israel — that is, his name and character embody/symbolize the name and character of Israel.

cob's terror (Gen. 32:7) at the prospect of meeting his brother has something to do with his own shame and/or guilt because of his past.

By imaginatively stepping into the textual gaps and by paying attention to its key rhetorical features, we can explore Jacob's shame as well as our own. Jacob reminds readers that we are not always our "best" selves in the midst of conflict. Shame "exposes" us to the "deeper" terrain of human selfhood such as negative stories from our past, threats to our present, and fears about the future. We find Jacob in a liminal (in between, neither here nor there) space at the Jabbok River, poised on the threshold of new possibilities in terms of his self-understanding, his relationship with his brother Esau, and his future with God. In this space, alone, exposed, and vulnerable, stripped of what has defined him in his pirated role as the firstborn, Jacob faces his flawed self and the gap between who he is and who he could be. He is morally shamed.[30] Ironically, his shame affords him the opportunity to assess and edit the personal and familial myths[31] that have contributed to his false self and to shape a story more in line with God's call upon his life.

Shame can be positive by helping us to maintain boundaries for appropriate behavior.[32] Shame can also be negative in that it makes us feel deficient, flawed, and inferior — in short, not "good enough." Shame relates to who we are; guilt relates to what we do. Intense shame can make us feel small, incapacitate us, or lead to overcompensation, a feeling of inferiority, or a feeling of superiority. In this sense, shame is "a failed wholeness."[33] In Korean culture, shame often resides in *han,* described as "the slow death of the spirit" and "boxed-in hope."[34] Shame silences

30. Pembroke, *The Art of Listening,* p. 156. Perhaps Jacob realizes that he is not the person he thought he was as he sits alone by the Jabbok River.

31. Edward Wimberly, *Recalling Our Own Stories: Spiritual Renewal for Religous Caregivers* (San Francisco: Jossey-Bass, 1997), p. 4. Wimberly defines myth as *"the beliefs and convictions that people have about themselves, their relationship with others, their roles in life, and their ministry."* He offers a list of questions to help readers uncover the personal, familial, marital, and ministerial myths by which they operate.

32. Marie Fortune, *A Sacred Trust: Boundary Issues for Clergy and Spiritual Teachers,* video (Seattle: The FaithTrust Institute, 2003). Respecting the sanctity of the self helps to maintain proper boundaries.

33. J. McClendon, quoted in Pembroke, *The Art of Listening,* p. 8.

34. Andrew Sung Park, *From Hurt to Healing: A Theology of the Wounded* (Nashville: Abingdon Press, 2004), p. 10. *Han* can exist on both the individual level (where it is expressed by anger, bitterness, and helplessness) and the communal level (where it is an in-

stories. Shame is difficult to talk about and listen to, and telling often produces more shame as it is re-experienced in the telling.[35] We allow culture to silence our shame for the sake of our popularity. Ironically, shaming has gone public in the media's dogged pursuit of revealing all — consider *Celebrity Rehab* and other TV "reality" shows.

Physical signs of shame include lowering the gaze, covering the face, blushing, talking softly, or staying quiet.[36] Shame is experienced as feeling heavy, small, or exposed. One tries to escape or hide from the uncovering or exposure of shame.[37] The biblical book of Esther has been called the "book of hiding."[38] The name Esther comes from the Hebrew root *str,* meaning "to hide." Esther hides her Jewish identity in the Diaspora until she is forced to reveal it for the sake of her people. During the Jewish festival of Purim, the book of Esther is read and everyone wears masks to symbolize this theme of hiding.

Shame appears much earlier in the Hebrew Bible in the story of the man and woman in the garden of Eden. Before their disobedience, they are "not ashamed" (in Hebrew, *lo' 'arumim;* Gen. 2:25). After their disobedience, they hide their nakedness from God and one another behind fig leaves. God makes a covering for the human couple to keep them from re-experiencing their shame every time they see themselves naked. God acts as the refuge for their shame and ours; God does not require that we cover up with fig leaves. The psalmists turn repeatedly to God as refuge, one of the two main metaphors for God in the book of Psalms.[39]

---

ternalized collective memory of victims handed down from generation to generation). See also Chung Hyun Kyung, *Struggle to Be the Sun Again* (Maryknoll, N.Y.: Orbis Books, 1990). Kyung describes *han* for Korean women as a "lump" in their spirit; true feelings are "stuck" inside and breed either resentment and anger or resignation (p. 42).

35. Donald Capps, *The Depleted Self: Sin in a Narcissistic Age* (Minneapolis: Fortress Press, 1993).

36. *Self-Conscious Emotions: The Psychology of Shame, Guilt, Embarrassment, and Pride,* ed. J. Tangney and K. Fischer (New York: Guilford Press, 1995), p. 7.

37. Thomas Scheff, *Microsociology: Discourse, Emotion, and Social Structure* (Chicago: University of Chicago Press, 1990).

38. Timothy K. Beal, *The Book of Hiding: Gender, Ethnicity, Annihilation, and Esther* (New York: Routledge, 1997).

39. William Brown, *Seeing the Psalms: A Theology of Metaphor* (Louisville: Westminster John Knox, 2002), p. 16. The other metaphor is God as a path or a way, which leads to God as refuge. Ironically, Michael and I note, God is accused of hiding in the psalms of lament — for example, "Why do you hide your face?" (Ps. 44:24) and "How long will you hide your face from me?" (Ps. 13:1).

QUESTIONS FOR REFLECTION

- When have you been in a liminal (in between) or threshold situation? What do you remember about it?
- Think back to a time when you experienced shame in your life. How did you internalize this shame?
- In terms of the embodiment of shame, reflect on your prayer posture. When someone says, "Let us pray," what do you do? Bow your head? Close your eyes? Kneel? Why? What kind of prayer would you pray in such a position? One of thanksgiving? Petition? Praise? Angry lament?
- Who are you when you pray?

Roles and Scripts

Because Jacob's self is an "embedded selfhood" rather than a solitary self existing in a vacuum, we need to explore the scripts that shape him and the roles he plays to keep the family system intact. The roles we play tend to keep systems and patterns in a predictable place. Our families, cultures, and religious traditions all influence the way we see ourselves and others see us. Common roles and their accompanying scripts include the following:

The Succeeder: the one whose accomplishments bring recognition to others

The Attender: the one who reads and responds to everyone's needs

The Failure/Underachiever: the one who acts irresponsibly and gets blamed for failure

The Cheerleader: the one who applauds others' successes and keeps them going during down times

The Overseer: the distant one who watches over everyone else

The Saint: the morally pure one who removes his or her self from the stains of the world

The Pleaser: the one who does what everyone else wants

The Good Child/Overachiever: the one who acts respectfully and responsibly, taking on the role of authority

The Sacrificer: the one who always gives up self for the benefit of others

The Perfectionist: the one whose standards often exceed realistic
  expectations
The Connector: the one who helps build community by keeping
  the lines of communication open
The Victim: the one who doesn't expect anything better
The Loser: the one who isolates herself or himself because of distrust of the world

These roles and their accompanying scripts may seem written in stone,
but they're not. Though we are all significantly shaped by these narrative scripts, we also change them through script-sorting and script-
shaping. We engage in this process of self-differentiation[40] through reflective introspection and conversation. This can lead us to see more
clearly our true nature as beloved creations of God.

GROUP EXERCISE
What other roles and scripts can you identify in your life? Add
  them to the list above.

From the moment we are born, we step into a narrated world.
Stories preceded our births and will follow our deaths. Our families
told stories about us before they even knew us. They held ideals, fanta-
sies, expectations, and roles for who we would become. These stories
helped to shape our becoming. We are not separate from the stories
that our families have told about us. Though they don't fully capture
"who" we are, they do give shape and meaning to our world. These stories allow us to interpret events and ourselves. Sometimes the negative
stories we inherit can't be shaken. They cling like prickly burrs. I
(Denise) remember vividly the story my mother told me repeatedly
about my birth: My father's mother chastised him for not "being a
man" because his firstborn was a daughter and not a son. I believe that
this story pushed me to embrace early in my life the scripts of the Succeeder, the Good Child/Overachiever, the Attender, and the Perfectionist (the bane of church leaders everywhere). I also now recognize the
profound negative effect this story had upon my father.

---

40. See Roberta M. Gilbert, *Extraordinary Relationships: A New Way of Thinking about
Human Interactions* (Hoboken, N.J.: Wiley Press, 1992).

- What scripts do you imagine Jacob was wrestling with at the Jabbok River?

Wrestling

To explore Jacob's scripts, we return to Genesis 25 and his birth story. Jacob was grasping and ambitious, even in the womb (Gen. 25:19-26), and his name, meaning "the one who grabs by the heel, supplants," reflects that aspect of his character. Jacob's dealings with his brother and uncle suggest that he had internalized the shame embedded in his name. This sheds light on his later reunion with his brother. Perhaps his sending a sequence of servants with gifts ahead of him to undercut his brother's wrath is an expression not only of his deceitful self, but of this shame. He conjectures, "I may appease him with the present that goes ahead of me, and afterwards I shall see his face; perhaps he will accept me" (Gen. 32:20). His wrestling with God seems to diminish his shame, for following this encounter, Jacob himself goes on ahead of his servants and family as Esau approaches him (Gen. 33:1-3).

Jacob's deceptive nature seems to run in the family. Some would say that "the apple doesn't fall far from the tree" and that Jacob is simply fulfilling the family legacy. After all, it's Jacob's own mother, Rebekah, who comes up with the detailed plan for tricking Isaac into blessing him instead of Esau (Gen. 27:1-17).[41] And Jacob and his uncle Laban try to out-cheat one another (Gen. 29:15–31:21). Even Jacob's wife, Rachel, deceives by stealing her father Laban's household gods (Gen. 31:19). The narrator of the story attempts to blame the brothers' conflict on Esau: Esau "despised his birthright" (Gen. 25:34) and "made life bitter for Isaac and Rebekah" (Gen. 26:34-35). But this probably reflects Israel's long-standing historical enmity with Edom. Esau's name may be the first ethnic joke in the Bible, one that pushes Esau to make bad decisions because his self-esteem has been damaged by his name. (Esau means "hairy," and he becomes the ancestor of Edom, which means

---

41. Susan Niditch argues that Rebekah is a "trickster," a marginalized woman who uses mockery, humor, and deception in a man's world to achieve power and success, usually through her male children. See *Women's Bible Commentary,* exp. ed. with the Apocrypha, ed. C. Newsom and S. Ringe (Louisville: Westminster John Knox, 1998), pp. 22-23, 28-29.

"red." Esau is born hairy and red; see Genesis 25:25, 30.) Persons prone to shame expect poor treatment, as Esau did — reflected in his selling his birthright for some stew. Persons prone to shame might also react aggressively, like Jacob, the "mama's boy," did when he deceived his blind, dying father.[42]

The narrator tells us that Isaac and Rebekah responded to Jacob and Esau with different scripts: "Isaac loved Esau because he was fond of game; but Rebekah loved Jacob" (Gen. 25:28). Isaac's love for Esau seems conditional, while Rebekah's love for Jacob is unconditional. "Divided brothers, divided parents, divided love supply all the ingredients for trouble."[43] We know about family divisions from our own stories. One pastor who took the class observed, "I identify with Rebekah as the mother of Jacob and her need to intervene in his life, and I am challenged by Rebekah as the mother of Esau. I judge her for helping one child at the expense of the other, but I can relate to this as the mother of three sons, one with learning disabilities."[44] How ironic that only when Jacob assumes a disguise and impersonates Esau does his father come to know him. Jacob "figuratively leaves his mother's womb and enters the real world of engagement with others."[45] While bringing Isaac food, he passes through a liminal space, the opening to Isaac's tent. Jacob is offered an opportunity to know himself when Isaac responds to Jacob's presence in the tent with *hineini* (Gen. 27:18).[46]

The positive power of shame emerges out of Jacob's self-imposed solitariness and his wrestling with himself, Esau, and God.[47] Jacob fi-

---

42. Pembroke, *The Art of Listening*, p. 139. Denise and I suggest that both Esau and Jacob are probably experiencing inherited identity shame (p. 152).

43. Phyllis Trible, "Beholding Esau," in Norman H. Cohen, *Hineini in Our Lives: Learning How to Respond to Others through Fourteen Biblical Texts and Personal Stories* (Woodstock, Vt.: Jewish Lights Publishing, 2003), p. 171.

44. Cynthia Hill, student journal, Wesley Theological Seminary, September 2006.

45. Cohen, *Hineini in Our Lives*, pp. 40-41.

46. Cohen, *Hineini in Our Lives*, p. xi. In the fourteen passages in which this word is found, it can have various meanings: the ability to be present for and receptive to the other (Gen. 27:18), the readiness to act on behalf of the other (Gen. 27:1), or the willingness to sacrifice for someone or something higher (Gen. 37:13). From this word we can learn about who we are as we function in our relationships.

47. In *Godwrestling* (New York: Schocken Books, 1978), Arthur Waskow asks why God uses the plural "men" when God gives Jacob a new name, Israel, in Genesis 32:28: "for you have striven with God and with men [humans — NRSV]." Who are the other "men" besides God (who is referred to as "a man" in 32:24, and "the man" in v. 25)? Waskow sug-

nally comes to terms with himself. This prepares Jacob for his encounter with Esau, when they finally meet, embrace, and kiss (Gen. 33:4) on their way to restoring the interpersonal bridge[48] between them. As Miroslav Volf observes, opening arms to one another issues an invitation, creates a space for the other, and suggests completeness.[49] Both must desire embrace without coercion. The text indicates that it is Esau, not Jacob, who runs, embraces, and kisses. The only act the narrator describes that Jacob and Esau share is weeping. Commingled tears can be agents of healing. But it may be that they don't fully embrace after all, since Jacob doesn't keep his promise to meet Esau in Seir (Gen. 33:12, 14, 17) and winds up in Shechem instead. It looks as if their wrestling will continue. God models for care givers the kind of persistent wrestling presence that can lead to at least the beginnings of embrace and move us one step closer to healing.

God as wrestler suggests that we as care givers need to listen long enough so that we know with what and with whom the care receiver is wrestling. Jacob is also a wrestler who gives care receivers permission to struggle with their shadow side, since he faces God "*in* the wound, in his own need to supplant, in his grieved sense of having been supplanted by fate — by God."[50] Jacob models the process of individuation, "the process by which a person becomes fully the individual he or she can be."[51] But in this process, the past is not obliterated. Before Jacob is

---

gests that the men were Esau, since seeing Esau was like seeing God's face (Gen. 33:10), and Jacob himself (p. 7). Jacob wrestled his own fear and hatred of Esau.

48. In *Shame: The Power of Caring* (Cambridge: Schenkman Publishing Co., 1980), Gershen Kaufman uses the gerundive "interpersonal bridging" in the caring relationship to describe the gradual movement from shame-based defensive strategies to vulnerability and openness (p. 145), but it makes sense here.

49. Miroslav Volf, *Exclusion and Embrace: A Theological Exploration of Identity, Otherness, and Reconciliation* (Nashville: Abingdon Press, 1996), p. 100. The four movements of embrace include opening the arms, waiting, closing the arms, and opening them again. Embrace requires repentance, forgiveness, making space in oneself for the other, and healing of memory.

50. Walter Wink, "Wrestling with God: Psychological Insights in Bible Study," in *Psychology and the Bible: A New Way to Read the Scriptures*, ed. H. Ellens and W. Rollins (Westport, Conn.: Praeger, 2004), p. 11. Wink argues that this wrestling becomes "a paradigm for the relation of psychology to theology, the capacity to see our 'fate' (our neuroses, our genetic givens, the accidents of birth and location, and the damage done to us by others) as divinely appointed encounter and task" (p. 14). See also D. Andrew Kille, "Jacob: A Study in Individuation," in Ellens and Rollins, *Psychology and the Bible*, pp. 66-82.

51. Kille, "Jacob: A Study in Individuation," p. 67.

given his new name, Israel, the man requires Jacob to identify his old self (Gen. 32:27); "one cannot simply repress the past; it must be included and transformed in the new."[52]

This reality is affirmed in a moving exploration by Ellen Frankel and Herb Levine of the broken tablets of the Torah[53] mentioned in Deuteronomy 10:1-2. There, God tells Moses, "Carve out two new tablets of stone like the former ones. . . . I will write on the tablets the words that were on the former tablets, which you smashed, and you shall put them in the ark." The rabbis pounce on the ambiguity of the word *them* and suggest that both the whole and the broken tablets were placed in the ark. The authors suggest that "it is up to us to make a new set of whole tablets, a mosaic composed of fragments from the past and emerging patterns of our own time."[54]

The use of the word *face* three times in Genesis 32–33 tells readers something about what script is shaped in a liminal, threshold space. This threefold repetition mirrors the steps in Jacob's process from persona, to presence, to possibility. The first occurrence, in Genesis 32:20, shows a Jacob wearing a mask of shame and deceit as he tries to bribe Esau with gifts sent ahead. The second occurrence, in Genesis 32:30 ("So Jacob called the place Peniel, saying, 'For I have seen God face to face, and yet my life is preserved'"), reveals a Jacob with a dawning awareness of his own brokenness, more fully present to himself, to Esau, and to God. It's as if God flipped a light switch. The third occurrence, in Genesis 33:10, is directed to Esau: "For truly to see your face is like seeing the face of God." This shows Jacob more open to possibility. He expresses an almost primal hunger for connection.[55]

---

52. Kille, "Jacob: A Study in Individuation," p. 78.

53. Torah is usually translated as "law" because of the Septuagint, the Greek translation of the Hebrew Bible, which offers the Greek *nomos* for the Hebrew *torah*. However, *torah* comes from a root meaning "to throw" or "to cast," and more accurately means "instruction" and "guidance."

54. Ellen Frankel and Herb Levine, "The Broken Tablets and the Whole: An Exploration of Shavuot," *Kerem: Creative Explorations in Judaism* 7 (5761/2001): 82.

55. Lewis Parks, "Small Churches as Healthy Family Systems," *Leading Ideas: A Resource for Church Leaders,* 14 February 2007, churchleadership.com/leading ideas/leaddocs/ 2007/070214_article.html. In this e-letter of the Lewis Center for Church Leadership, Parks suggests that in a healthy small church, "there is the ability to name and face, rather than deny . . ."; "God's deliverance is experienced in the breaking of negative family legacies and the beginning of new and positive ones"; and "members and leaders are growing in self-awareness, including awareness of the assets and liabilities of their birth order."

Bill's Story

With tears in his eyes, Bill, a local pastor, shared the connection he had just made. "I'd never noticed it before; it never meant anything to me before today." We had been wrestling with Jacob's story in Genesis 32–33 that morning in West Virginia. Pastors, clinical social workers, and pastoral counselors had gathered for an all-day workshop on the intersections of the Bible and pastoral care. I (Denise) posed this question: What was the significance of the repetition of the word face *three times in this story? Bill shared this with us: "My wife and I had struggled for years to have children. We adopted one of two twin girls when she was three. When they were ten, the girls met for the first time. My daughter had waited for this moment for a long time, and we weren't sure how she would react when she actually saw her twin sister. To my joy and amazement, she turned to me with eyes wide with discovery and exclaimed, 'She has my face!' My daughter became whole at that moment."*

•   •

Wrestling is soul work in which we simultaneously hold on and let go. God and Jacob wrestle until daybreak, but Jacob will not let go until God blesses him (Gen. 32:24-26).

QUESTIONS FOR REFLECTION

- With what scripts do you wrestle? Chart your own family genogram to help you find out. A genogram is a family map, somewhat like a family tree, but focused more on roles and relationships. In doing this exercise, pay attention to people who have had the most influence and the least influence upon you.
- Reflect on the quality of relationships in the map, noticing whether they are particularly close or distant. Identify your roles, as well as those of others, on the map.
- Talk about your map in a small group, noting what surprised you and what you learned about yourself and others.
- What is your persona or mask? How would you begin to remove this mask on the way to more life-giving possibilities in your relationships with yourself, others, and God? What are you holding on to, and what keeps you from letting go?
- How does Genesis 32–33 help you to challenge these scripts?

Bibliodrama

Bibliodrama offers us another way to encounter this Genesis text.[56] Bibliodrama is a modern form of *midrash,* an ancient method of Jewish biblical interpretation (from the Hebrew verbal root *drsh,* meaning "to seek, inquire"). It is a text-centered process that encourages improvisation rather than acting. Participants are invited to enter into the story by speaking in the first person as a character from within the story. Five minutes of warm-ups help to prepare participants to engage the text. We (Denise and I) suggest a spectrogram that allows a group to register a range of responses to the following questions by physically standing and placing themselves on an imaginary line from 1 to 10:

1. The Bible has the power to shape my life or has little relevance for my life.
2. When it comes to conflict, do I meet it head on or run in the opposite direction?
3. In my relationship with God, do I like to wrestle or quietly accept?
4. When I experience shame, do I lash out at others or wish to disappear?
5. When dealing with the past, do I repress and bury it or do I explore and learn from it?

Once these warm-up exercises have been completed, participants can engage in the Bibliodrama after the leader sets the stage: "Let yourself imagine that you are Jacob all alone on the bank of the Jabbok River. Esau is coming to meet you with four hundred men. What are you feeling right now?" In a recent workshop Michael and I conducted, the imaginative responses to this question revealed many issues that the participants themselves were struggling with in their own lives:

I'm terrified.
I feel guilty.
Been there, done that — I'll get out of it because I always do.
My number may be up this time.
I'm feeling very alone.

56. Peter Pitzele, *Scripture Windows: Toward a Practice of Bibliodrama* (Los Angeles: Alef Design Group, 1997).

What have I started?
What will it cost me this time?
I just want to go home.
Have I explored all of my options?
I'm a survivor — my mother taught me well.
I did what I needed to do.
I don't care if I lose everything as long as I come out OK.
God has always protected me.

A question for reflection after the Bibliodrama allowed participants to ponder the feelings that arose as they voiced Jacob's character: What keeps me from experiencing God's presence in my life? Powerful responses included the following: holding on to past hurts; busyness that takes me in many directions; wearing blinders that prevent me from being open to new possibilities; being uncomfortable with God's presence; self-centeredness and preoccupation; restlessness about the future; overstimulation by the secular world; previous failure to pray; not wanting that much intimacy; procrastination; lack of humility; taking God's presence for granted; operating out of expectations that others have of me as clergy.

Bibliodrama prompted our students to enter into Jacob's story in a way that drew them deeper into that story and their own. Because they had "become" Jacob in their role-playing, they unwittingly exposed aspects of their own negative stories. As observers of this interaction, we noted a kind of shock that surprised the participants when they spoke as Jacob. Denise and I recommend Bibliodrama because it can create a safe-enough space for becoming aware of those aspects of our stories that we might otherwise keep hidden.

TAKE-AWAY POINTS

1. Know your own story so that you can listen attentively to the stories of others.
2. Pay attention to language and tone that capture our attention in both biblical and human texts.
3. Differentiate among different silences in both biblical and human texts.
4. Practice listening more often if you happen to be a "speaker," and practice speaking more often if you happen to be a "listener."

5. Refrain from making people "feel better" and from smoothing over tensions in biblical texts.
6. Don't be afraid of wrestling. Embrace and risk wrestling with God, biblical texts, yourself, and others.
7. Notice what triggers shame in yourself and others.
8. Identify the primary roles and scripts that govern your life.
9. Imagine different possibilities for life in community.
10. Allow yourself to move from persona, to presence, and then on to possibility.

CARE PRAYER

O God of our boundary places,

Help us to be open to the possibilities that are often hidden inside the spaces in which we find ourselves: between the security of the known and the fear of the unknown; between what has been and what will be; between our shame and our glory. Call us from our shadows into the light of the wholeness that you intend for us. May we reflect that light in our ministries of caring. Amen.

Chapter 3

God Images and Pastoral Images

Loretta's Story

My image of God? God was the bearded old man with a magnifying glass in one hand and a sledgehammer in the other — watching every move and ready to strike. I lived in a truly graceless environment. Yet God was also the Lap that my Little One, my child self, crawled up into. As God's lap-child I found a measure of comfort that kept me from falling into an inescapable abyss. God as Protector is not the God I've experienced existentially, but it is the God to whom my heart clings.

•   •

According to a recent poll conducted by the Pew Forum on Religion and Public Life, 92 percent of people in the United States believe in God or a universal spirit, including one in five of those who identify themselves as atheists; 79 percent believe in miracles; and 68 percent say they believe in angels and demons.[1] Before we congratulate ourselves on our religiosity, we would do well to heed these words: "It is not enough to say that one believes in God. What is important finally is the *kind of*

---

1. See Jacqueline L. Salmon, "Most Americans Believe in Higher Power, Poll Finds," *The Washington Post*, 24 June 2008, sec. A, p. 2. Salmon is reporting on the results of The Religious Landscape Survey, one of the largest polls ever conducted; 35,000 adults were interviewed. See also Greg Peterson, "God on the Brain: The Neurobiology of Faith," *Christian Century*, 27 January 1999, pp. 84-88. Discussing the "God-spot" in the human brain, Peterson argues that "God is something that is experienced, not argued about."

God in whom one believes. Or, to use different language: metaphors matter."[2] Who is God for the people in this survey? Respondents described a range of images: a supernatural being, a vivid divine presence, a spirit within each one of us.

Ask and Tell

Our usual tendency as pastoral leaders is to tell people how we see God. We unwittingly do this more often than we realize, probably because it is done so often to us. Perhaps we think that this is what a pastoral leader does. Perhaps we want to privilege our view of God. Shifting this dynamic can be beneficial. In asking an open-ended question from the opposite end of the God/human relationship — that is, asking how God sees us or how we see ourselves before God — we create a powerfully vulnerable exercise. In Loretta's telling about God, she saw an old man with a sledgehammer, ready to strike. By asking who she was before God, she saw the opposite: an inviting Lap who welcomed her as a lap-child needing protection.

This imaginative exercise fosters a sense of wondering and pondering together. It short-circuits the unhelpful inclination to explain, beyond a reasonable measure, how or who God is. One curriculum resource for Christian education suggests teaching children to engage in theological reflection by starting their statements about God with the phrase "I wonder. . . ."[3] Children might respond with "I wonder how God created so many different kinds of animals," or "I wonder what God's favorite color is." This instructional method encourages children to use their own imaginations to spark thoughtful wonder about God. Michael and I suggest that adults can also learn to plumb images with such an open-ended and curious perspective.

God images emerge from the unconscious mind as well. It requires something of us, however: a willingness to let the images reveal themselves, and to see in the images a reflection of the Divine that we both seek and fear. These images of God come in myriad ways, most often in

2. Terence E. Fretheim, *The Suffering of God: An Old Testament Perspective* (Philadelphia: Fortress Press, 1984), p. 1.

3. See godlyplay.com. Godly play was developed by Jerome Berryman to cultivate the spirituality of children. See *Godly Play: A Way of Religious Education* (San Francisco: HarperSanFrancisco, 1991).

symbols and images from dreams, works of art, scenes from film, and the Bible. The distinction between conscious and unconscious image is a subtle one. Distinguishing characteristics of the unconscious image include surprise, bewilderment, delight, and fear. A coming-to-consciousness image seeks us out, finds us, and grabs hold of us so that we cannot but see differently.

We (Denise and I) understand that images serve a projective function as they illumine aspects of how we see the Divine. But we reject the Freudian notion that God images are mere illusion, wishful thinking based on an infantile need for a reality that does not actually exist.[4] Scholars of psychology and religion have investigated the complex interrelationship between God images and human well-being.[5]

We build on these studies in a way that acknowledges and affirms the commitment of religious communities to know the Holy Reality within and beyond imagination and projection. We also affirm the attempt to consider other images of the Holy and of ourselves that might expand, contract, challenge, or affirm our God image, our worldview, and the resulting implications for ministries of care. The Hebrew Bible, as central to Jewish and Christian faith traditions, provides a source for *imago Dei* and pastoral identity. It suggests possibilities and challenges for God-human and human-human relationships. Pastoral leaders bear responsibility for exercising power and authority with language and imagery that leads to shalom (wholeness, well-being) for all people.

Michael and I operate with certain assumptions about God images and encourage pastors and care givers to outline their own assumptions in conversation with their faith communities. Our assumptions about God images are as follows:

> God images cast the Divine in living metaphors recognizable to human faculties, such as reason, intuition, emotion.
> God image-making and representation occur before, during, and after verbal development, which means that sometimes we can talk about them and sometimes we can't.

---

4. Sigmund Freud, *Future of an Illusion,* trans. W. D. Robson-Scott (New York: Liveright, 1949).

5. See "God Image Handbook for Spiritual Counseling and Psychotherapy: Research, Theory, and Practice," *Journal of Spirituality in Mental Health* 9, no. 3/4 (2007).

God images can be enriched in trusting faith groups by thoughtful reflection and appropriate storytelling.

God images are influenced by positive as well as negative experiences in families, congregations, and society.

God images can stimulate theological conversation in community about core beliefs.

God images ought never be used in congregations as a tool for clinical diagnosis.

God images reveal only part of how we view and understand the Holy.

GROUP EXERCISE

First, generate a list of adjectives and nouns or draw pictures to describe how God sees you — that is, how do you imagine that God experiences you?

Next, generate a list of adjectives and nouns or draw pictures to describe how you image God. Are your adjectives and nouns mostly core testimony (what we believe is true of God all the time) or countertestimony (questions about God prompted by lived experience)?

Do the two lists/pictures match up? Why or why not?

Share your work with a partner or the whole group.

God Images and Concepts

A rich and growing body of literature addresses the formation of God images within us and how these images contribute to health and well-being.[6] We (Denise and I) refer to conscious and unconscious images of God, whereas other researchers have distinguished between God im-

---

6. Resources include the "God Image Handbook for Spiritual Counseling and Psychotherapy" cited above, and the following counseling and pastoral volumes: Ana Maria Rizzuto, *The Birth of the Living God: A Psychoanalytic Study* (Chicago: University of Chicago Press, 1979); Carroll Saussy, *God Images and Self-Esteem: Empowering Women in a Patriarchal Society* (Louisville: Westminster John Knox Press, 1991); M. Kathryn Armistead, *God-Images and the Healing Process* (Minneapolis: Fortress Press, 1995); Larry Kent Graham, *Discovering Images of God: Narratives of Care among Lesbians and Gays* (Louisville: Westminster John Knox Press, 1997); Carolyn Bohler, *God the What?: What Our Metaphors for God Reveal about Our Beliefs in God* (Woodstock, Vt.: Skylight Paths Publishing, 2008).

ages and God concepts.[7] A God concept, according to Louis Hoffman, is "largely conscious and rational, based upon what a person is taught about God, and influenced by such things as religious teachings of parents, spiritual leaders, and religious texts."[8] Many people connect God concepts with abstract thought. In contrast, a God image emerges from complex "emotional, experiential, and unconscious" dynamics.[9] Many people connect God images with experience. The terms "God concepts" and "God images" are often used interchangeably in research literature. Rather than adhering to precise definitional categories, we strongly suggest that pastoral leaders remain open to what can be learned from others about who God is. Both God concepts and God images — or, as we have called them, conscious and unconscious God images — can hold insights about God.

Early experiences with primary care givers (parents and other guardians) have significant and lasting influence upon our images of God. Images can substitute for parental experience that we did not have in childhood, so that an image of God becomes the wished-for loving parent. Images can also correspond with the nature of interpersonal relationships, so that a person with a secure self-image will have an image of God that reflects this sense. Of course, our own experience is probably a complex interplay of family, gender, social, and cultural factors. Images are not only influenced by what we have received, but also by how we act when we become parents. Parents can replicate positive or negative God images through the socialization process with their children.[10]

Like the angels that ascend and descend the ladder in Jacob's dream (Gen. 28), something of the Divine moves between our concepts of God and our images of God, between the known and the unknown world, between conscious and unconscious processes. This ladder reminds us that "we ascend toward God one step at a time. . . . Sometimes

7. See particularly Louis Hoffman, "A Developmental Perspective on the God Image," in *Spirituality and Psychological Health,* ed. Richard H. Cox, Betty Ervin-Cox, and Louis Hoffman (Colorado Springs: Colorado School of Professional Psychology, 2005), pp. 129-50.

8. Hoffman, cited in Christopher Grimes, "God Image Research: A Literature Review," *Journal of Spirituality in Mental Health* 9, no. 3/4 (2008): 12.

9. Hoffman, cited in Grimes, "God Image Research," p. 12.

10. See Grimes, "God Image Research," pp. 19-24 for the theoretical expansion of these family-of-origin and culture-of-origin dynamics.

we slip and miss a step, falling back. . . . Most people do not leap toward God in one great burst of enthusiasm."[11] The angels stepping up and down the ladder connect above (the vertical) with below (the horizontal — that is, Jacob's sleeping body stretched out on the very ground that he will inherit). It is sleep that makes Jacob aware of his unconscious self, of the angels and of God. "His sleep, therefore, is far from static."[12]

Like Jacob, when we awake with new insights about God and our vision for how and where we may be called in our lives, then we can mark this place with an appropriate ritual (just as Jacob poured oil on the stone). Such ritualizing recognizes the presence of God that infuses both concept and image, and simultaneously defies confinement. Jacob "went on his journey" (Gen. 29:1), and so must we also take a journey to know God in, through, and beyond the images. Pastors tend this thin place where image meets concept, knowing the power and possibility for transformational growth in faith.

GROUP EXERCISE
Reflect upon early experiences with primary care givers. How do these experiences shape your God images? How do they support or challenge your images, both conscious and unconscious?

God Images and the Bible

For many of us, the Bible has shaped our image of God in powerful ways. Almost all of the language about God in the Bible is metaphorical, "because human language can never speak adequately about divine reality."[13] *Metaphor* comes from the Greek: *meta* means "trans" or "across" and *phor* is from *pherein*, meaning "to carry." A metaphor "carries across" or transfers meanings from one thing to another. Meta-

11. *Etz Hayim: Torah and Commentary*, ed. David Lieber (New York: Jewish Publication Society, 1999), p. 166. This commentary is a product of the Conservative Movement in Judaism.

12. Aviva Gottlieb Zornberg, *The Beginning of Desire: Reflections on Genesis* (New York: Doubleday/Image Books, 1995), p. 191.

13. Elisabeth Schüssler Fiorenza, *Jesus: Miriam's Child, Sophia's Prophet* (New York: Continuum Books, 1994), p. 161.

phors help us to speak imaginatively of a lesser-known thing in terms of a better-known thing. Using metaphor, we evoke and organize associations and embrace new understandings.[14] Some biblical metaphors for God come from the natural world: God is an eagle (Deut. 32:11) or a rock (Psalm 31:2-3). Most metaphors for God come from the human sphere of emotion and family and societal roles; it is anthropomorphic language.[15]

The Bible, however, is not gender-neutral. That the Bible is male-centered is reinforced by the fact that of a total of 1,426 biblical names, 1,315 are those of men. Women's names comprise only about 8 percent (111) of the total.[16] Only two women in the Bible have books named after them — Ruth and Esther — and only two in the Apocrypha: Susanna and Judith. Women in the Bible are either not named at all or named in connection with a male who has power over them, such as a father or a husband. Consider these examples: "Deborah, a prophetess, wife of Lappidoth" (Judges 4:4); "Bathsheba, daughter of Eliam, the wife of Uriah the Hittite" (2 Sam. 11:3); "his [Zechariah's] wife was a descendant of Aaron, and her name was Elizabeth" (Luke 1:5). In John 8:3, "a woman who had been caught in adultery" doesn't even have a name. In a dictionary of women in the Bible, the section of unnamed women is twice as long as that of named women.[17]

Men who shaped Hebrew Bible texts showed little interest in women's roles, even though women were essential to the basic unit of society. This basic unit was the family household, an economic and biological unity. Women not only bore and raised children; they also made clothing, household vessels, and implements, worked in the fields, and processed and prepared food. Readers can glimpse women's contributions in the portrait of the capable wife in Proverbs 31:10-31. She makes clothes, "provides food for her household," and "considers a field and buys it." Women's domain was primarily the private realm of

14. William P. Brown, *Seeing the Psalms: A Theology of Metaphor* (Louisville: Westminster John Knox Press, 2002), pp. 3-14.

15. Fretheim, *The Suffering of God*, p. 6.

16. Carol L. Meyers, "Everyday Life: Women in the Period of the Hebrew Bible," in *Women's Bible Commentary*, expanded ed. with the Apocrypha, ed. Carol A. Newsom and Sharon H. Ringe (Louisville: Westminster John Knox Press, 1998), pp. 251-59.

17. Carol Meyers, general editor, *Women in Scripture: A Dictionary of Named and Unnamed Women in the Hebrew Bible, the Apocryphal/Deuterocanonical Books, and the New Testament* (Boston: Houghton Mifflin, 2000).

home and family. However, the Hebrew Bible focuses on mainly male — that is, public — aspects of life such as government, war, the economy, and worship;[18] God images mirror and shape that focus. Even archeologists became obsessed with the artifacts of male life, such as monumental buildings like palaces and fortresses, weapons of battle, and stables. The widely popular Indiana Jones movies express this archeological fascination well. Not until the 1980s did the focus begin to shift to uncovering the material environment of daily life: houses, tools, dietary indicators, technology. Unfortunately, these artifacts are not "gender noisy."[19] They do not reveal the gender of the persons who used them.

KINGAFAP God Images

Speaking about God is not simply a matter of being "politically correct." Elizabeth Johnson insists that "the way in which a faith community shapes language about God implicitly represents what it takes to be the highest good, the profoundest truth, the most appealing beauty. Such speaking, in turn, powerfully molds the corporate identity of the community and directs its praxis."[20] Biblical God images are shaped by the male-centeredness of the Bible. If we survey metaphors for God in the male-centered Hebrew Bible, we find that they are overwhelmingly male. God is a warrior, an aggrieved husband, an enthroned king, a father. Why? Because these biblical texts were produced and compiled primarily by males whose experience of God was shaped by their own roles in society. The male-centeredness of the Bible illustrates one of the assumptions of the Road Map for biblical interpretation (discussed in Chapter 1) — namely, that every biblical text has a context. It also reveals the ideology — that is, "the worldview or set of beliefs shared by members of a group" — that the Bible embraces. Julia O'Brien analyzes this ideology in the prophetic books. She argues that "when the Prophetic Books call God King, Father, and

18. Philip King and Lawrence Stager, *Life in Biblical Israel* (Louisville: Westminster John Knox Press, 2001), pp. 49-58.

19. Meyers, "Everyday Life," p. 252. In *Did God Have a Wife? Archeology and Folk Religion in Ancient Israel* (Grand Rapids: Wm. B. Eerdmans, 2005), William G. Dever disagrees with this assessment (p. 239).

20. Elizabeth A. Johnson, *She Who Is* (New York: Crossroad, 1992), p. 4.

Husband, they reveal the privilege granted to human kings, fathers, and husbands."[21]

Brian Wren has shown how biblical male images of God are taken up in Christian hymnals. He speaks of the KINGAFAP God metaphor, an acronym for "King-God-Almighty-Father-Protector."[22] The KINGAFAP God is aloof, transcendent, powerful, and in control. As such, he mirrors the domination of males over females in society. In Korean culture, for example, patriarchal God images combine with Confucian teachings about women submitting to male figures in their lives to shape negatively the identity and self-worth of Korean Christian women.[23] If we are created in God's image, as Genesis 1 declares, we run the risk of valuing men as more God-like when the predominant biblical image of God is male. And there are related issues. For both women and men with abusive or absentee fathers, it may become difficult to enter into an intimate relationship with a father-God figure.[24] For some people with disabilities, a powerful male God suggests that "physical disability is a travesty of the divine image."[25]

KINGAFAP images of God in the Hebrew Bible can reinforce the dualism of modernity described by Rebecca Chopp. Modernity is divided into two domains which are, at their root, gendered: the public or primary domain, and the private or secondary domain. The public domain is that of the man, and the private domain is that of the woman. These domains are divided by a set of values and tasks. The public, male domain is "objective, scientific, exchange-oriented." Within it, man is autonomous, competitive, aggressive, and powerful. The private, female realm "is the realm of all the public rejects: the affections,

21. Julia M. O'Brien, *Challenging Prophetic Metaphor: Theology and Ideology in the Prophets* (Louisville: Westminster John Knox Press, 2008), p. xvii.

22. Brian Wren, *What Language Shall I Borrow? God-Talk in Worship: A Male Response to Feminist Theology* (New York: Crossroad, 1989).

23. Simone Sunghae Kim, "A Korean Feminist Perspective on God Representation," *Pastoral Psychology* 55 (2006): 35-45.

24. Pierre Balthazar, "How Anger toward Absentee Fathers May Make It Difficult to Call God 'Father,'" *Pastoral Psychology* 55 (2007): 543-49. Balthazar studied youth in the Caribbean, many of whom grew up with absentee or abusive fathers. One young man asked, "How can I call God 'Father' when I do not know what a father is?" A study by Christina Lambert and Sharon Kurpius, "Relationship of Gender Role Identity and Attitudes with Images of God," *American Journal of Pastoral Counseling* 7, no. 2 (2004): 55-75, found that perceptions of God are related to gender attitudes.

25. Nancy Eiseland, *The Disabled God* (Nashville: Abingdon Press, 1994), p. 70.

relationships, caring, and physicality."[26] These are devalued. Pushing Chopp's argument, we can see the irony in the centrality of the public-domain KINGAFAP image in Christian life when our culture has assigned the private-domain values of caring and feeling to Christianity. One task of pastoral care could be to help care receivers understand this gendered dualism and script new stories for their lives.

Though pastors may not always be aware of it, biblical images of God inform both what pastors believe and how pastors relate to persons in a pastoral situation. Male images of God can contribute to and reinforce a hierarchical ordering of human life, and vice versa. We can't help but move from human images to God images because, after all, we are human. Ann Ulanov suggests the movement from God to human, or what she calls meeting images from the other side.[27] Such movement can challenge seeing God in just one way — for example, as the KINGAFAP God. This image of God can support the model of care giver as powerful and knowledgeable, and of care receiver as lacking power and knowledge. Under the influence of these images, we run the risk of practicing a pastoral care of "condescension": the one who has gives to the one who lacks. We do well to remember that "care is not what experts do, but what all of us do."[28] Good pastoral care grows out of a mutuality in which all participate and receive from each other. Care is our responsiveness to one another, the way we attend to one another.[29]

26. Rebecca Chopp, "Writing Women's Lives," *Memphis Theological Seminary Journal* 29 (Spring 1991), 3-13.

27. Ann Ulanov, *Picturing God* (Boston: Cowley, 1986), p. 179.

28. Roy SteinhoffSmith, *The Mutuality of Care* (St. Louis: Chalice Press, 1999), p. 1. The paradigmatic biblical text for such mutuality of care is Mark 7:24-30, the story of Jesus and the Syrophoenician woman, who is the star of the story. She initiates the turns of the plot; because of her, Jesus changes his mind. The story shifts focus from the retreating, irritable, and cruel Jesus to the vital and smart woman committed to saving her daughter. It is the woman who "heals Jesus of his isolation" (p. 20). Jesus discovers that healing is not something that flows out of him that he does to the woman. Rather, "healing happens in a meeting in which all participate fully" (p. 20). All are changed in the meeting — Jesus, woman, daughter. This reading echoes Rita Nakashima Brock's interpretation of the woman with the issue of blood in Mark 5 in her book entitled *Journeys by Heart: A Christology of Erotic Power* (New York: Crossroad, 1988). This woman teaches Jesus that power is not for Jesus to possess; it is only power when it is shared.

29. This point was made many years ago by William Oglesby, *Biblical Themes for Pastoral Care* (Nashville: Abingdon Press, 1980), p. 40.

GROUP EXERCISE
Page through your church hymnal and notice how God is described. What adjectives and nouns are used to talk about God? Do you notice any KINGAFAP language?

What other images of God are expressed in these hymns?

The Suffering God

Images of the suffering God in the Hebrew Bible challenge KINGAFAP images of God. Laments of a neglected God in the Hebrew Bible showcase divine suffering.[30] God suffers because of the people's rejection of God as Lord. God's memories of the divine relationship with Israel shape God's suffering and grieving in the present, as we see in Isaiah 1:2-3; Jeremiah 2; 3:19-20; Psalm 81:8; and Hosea 11:1-9. God's open-ended questions of lament leave the future open, as in Jeremiah 4:14; Hosea 6:4; and Jeremiah 5:7-9. These questions are not simply rhetorical but are meant to evoke Israel's response for redemption. God also suffers with the people who are suffering, as in Exodus 3:7-8, in which God "knows" in the sense of "experiences" (see also Judges 2:18). God acts with empathy as a mourner in Amos 5:1-2, in which God uses the first-person singular (see also Jeremiah 48:31-32 and Jeremiah 9:17-18). Finally, God suffers for the people, often at divine cost. For example, God grows weary of the people's sins (Isa. 1:14; 7:13; 43:23-24), practices divine restraint (Isa. 48:9; Ezek. 20:21-22; Ps. 78:38), and experiences divine humiliation (1 Sam. 4–6; Ps. 78).

Consider in this connection the experience of Sister Ruth, formerly a Catholic campus minister in a northern California college town who deeply enjoyed serving students, faculty, and administration. Sister Ruth shared her contemplative gifts in community by working in partnership with others on social justice issues. When the Bishop of the Diocese decided that a woman shouldn't be a leader in this particular ministry site, Sister Ruth was rightfully angry and hurt. One night she had a dream in which she saw a tear suspended in space. She reflected on this image in her waking life and during times of prayer, eventually coming to new insight and awareness about God and herself. For Sister Ruth this dream image symbolized not her own

---

30. For what follows, see Terence Fretheim, *The Suffering of God,* pp. 107-48.

grief, but the grief of God. This image subtly shifted her view of the situation she was facing.

God as Shepherd, Servant, Aggrieved Husband

Another traditional biblical image of God is God as shepherd and people as sheep or God's flock. This pervasive image can be found in Psalm 23, Ezekiel 34, and Jeremiah 23, as well as in Gospel testimony about Jesus — for example, John 10:11. Book titles in the pastoral care field reflect fascination with this shepherd/flock image, beginning with Seward Hiltner's *The Christian Shepherd: Some Aspects of Pastoral Care*.[31] Shepherd images focus on the skill, tenderness, self-sacrifice, and courage of the shepherd. As powerful as the shepherd image of care has been for many, Marsha Foster Boyd rejects this image as white, male, linear, and fraternal. She suggests the image of "empowered cojourner" as more appropriate for African-American women in pastoral care. She also critiques Henri Nouwen's concept of the "wounded healer," for "to dwell on the wounds that need to be healed for African-American women keeps them debilitated, keeps them disempowered."[32]

Similarly, womanist Jacqueline Grant calls for a reconsideration of servant language in theology and pastoral care, since African-American women have been the "servants of the servants" in slavery and domestic service. In the United States, she insists, "servanthood . . . has been servitude," never properly recognized. So that language doesn't camouflage oppressive reality, Grant urges Christians to reconsider servant language in favor of inclusive discipleship language.[33] Here again, one

31. Seward Hiltner, *The Christian Shepherd: Some Aspects of Pastoral Care* (Nashville: Abingdon Press, 1959). See also Alastair Campbell, "The Courageous Shepherd," in *Images of Pastoral Care: Classic Readings,* ed. Robert C. Dykstra (St. Louis: Chalice Press, 2005), pp. 54-61. In *Shepherd Leadership: Wisdom for Leaders from Psalm 23* (San Francisco: Jossey-Bass, 2003), Blaine McCormick and David Davenport argue that the church leader as shepherd meets needs, knows the valley, comes alongside, uses the right tools, transforms conflict, removes irritants, shares a positive vision, and cultivates loyalty.

32. Marsha Foster Boyd, "Womanist Care: Some Reflections on the Pastoral Care and the Transformation of African-American Women," in *Embracing the Spirit: Womanist Perspectives on Hope, Salvation, and Transformation,* ed. Emilie Townes (Maryknoll, N.Y.: Orbis Books, 1997), pp. 197-203.

33. Jacqueline Grant, "The Sin of Servanthood and the Deliverance of Disciple-

of the assumptions of the Road Map for biblical interpretation comes into play: every reader has a context that shapes his or her reading of the text; this context shapes God images as well.

The biblical image/metaphor of God as aggrieved husband surfaces prominently in the prophets — especially Hosea 1-3, Jeremiah 2 and 13, and Ezekiel 16:46-63 and 23:1-49. In this metaphor, Israel is portrayed as a sexually promiscuous wife or brazen whore who deserves punishment from her wronged and patient husband, God. The marriage metaphor embraces God's (the husband's) violence against Israel (the wife). This violence is always portrayed in sexually violent terms: rape, beating, humiliating exposure of private parts, and mutilation. Feminists and social workers alike have pointed, for example, to the clear pattern of domestic violence against Hosea's wife, Gomer, in Hosea 1-2, a pattern of tension/explosion/honeymoon. The husband/Hosea/God isolates the wife/Gomer/Israel: "Therefore I will hedge up her way with thorns; and I will build a wall against her, so that she cannot find her paths" (2:6). Physical and psychological punishment follows. Hosea/God takes away Gomer's/Israel's food and clothing and humiliates her: "Now I will uncover her shame in the sight of her lovers" (2:10; cf. Jer. 13:22, 26). In Hosea 2:14-15, God initiates a nostalgic honeymoon: "Therefore, I will now allure her, and bring her into the wilderness, and speak tenderly to her. . . . There she shall respond as in the days of her youth. . . ." Unfortunately, the Revised Common Lectionary for Year C includes only the anticipated honeymoon of 2:14-23, and leaves out the violence of the earlier verses in chapter 2.

The prophets use such language to force their male audience to realize that Israel's pending destruction was deserved punishment from God. The "shock value" of these metaphors is intended to provoke "an emotional response" and lead to change.[34] Renita Weems challenges the "fatal attraction" of this God/husband metaphor: "Only those who had a certain relationship with power could appreciate some of the assumptions" in this metaphor.[35] These texts are negative in very different ways for men and women. Women are forced to read as men would in order to

---

ship," *A Troubling in My Soul: Womanist Perspectives on Evil and Suffering,* ed. Emilie Townes (Maryknoll, N.Y.: Orbis Books, 1993), p. 200.

34. O'Brien, *Challenging Prophetic Metaphor,* p. xvii.

35. Renita Weems, *Battered Love: Marriage, Sex, and Violence in the Hebrew Prophets* (Minneapolis: Fortress Press, 1995), p. 41.

salvage a positive message about God. Weems rightfully challenges readers to break the hold such texts have over us, first "by claiming our rights as readers to differ with authors, and second, by deciding as readers, especially those marginalized by the texts, whether the worlds that the authors place us in are indeed worth inhabiting."[36]

Julia O'Brien goes further. Rather than occurring as exceptions, she says, troubling prophetic marriage metaphors operate pervasively out of patriarchy, both in the biblical world and in the world of its interpreters. We have internalized gender scripts around modern ideologies of romantic marriage. Disturbingly, "the patriarchal assumptions of Hosea's metaphor are so familiar to many of us that they remain invisible."[37]

We (Michael and I) suggest reading these texts as a mirror reflecting our own violent, patriarchal tendencies. We read these texts as descriptive (showing what is), rather than prescriptive (proclaiming what ought to be).

GROUP EXERCISE

Skim the Hebrew Bible for images of God. (The book of Psalms and many prophetic books offer vivid images.)

Which images most closely capture your understanding of God? Which challenge your understanding of God?

Share what you've found with the group.

Female Images of God

The Hebrew Bible does offer female images of God, but these are not nearly as numerous as male images, and often have been ignored. We do well to remember that uncovering female images of God requires not only looking at a few biblical texts but also re-examining the nature of biblical interpretation itself and our notion of biblical authority. Beginning with Eve, women in the Hebrew Bible have symbolized evil, sin, and death. As the biblical texts were being shaped, their gender symbol-

36. Weems, *Battered Love,* p. 10. Gale Yee has raised the issue of using the metaphor to justify a husband's physical abuse of his wife in her commentary on Hosea in "Hosea," in *Women's Bible Commentary,* pp. 207-15.

37. O'Brien, *Challenging Prophetic Metaphor,* p. 71. She also warns that "feminist critique, if taken seriously, makes traditional ways of doing theology with the Prophets extremely difficult, if not impossible" (p. 29).

ization was connected with disastrous foreign policy decisions by men, issues of ethnicity and colonialism, and disparities in social and economic class.[38] Again, as the Road Map for biblical interpretation assumes, every biblical text has a context, and so does every reader.

The text's context interacts with our context as readers, as we see in centuries of damaging, stereotype-generating interpretation of Genesis 2:18: "Then the LORD God said, 'It is not good that the man *[ha'adam]* should be alone; I will make him a helper as his partner.'" Traditional interpretations have considered woman as inferior because she is created second, for the sake of man. She is his little woman, walking two steps behind; she is the weaker sex, tempted by the snake (Gen. 3), often needing a firm, disciplinary hand. Some denominations today cite this verse and others in Genesis 2–3 to deny ordination to women.

When we examine this verse, we see that the Hebrew for *helper* is *'ezer,* which is a masculine noun often used of God as helper, especially in the Psalms. See, for example, Psalm 70:5: "Hasten to me, O God! You are my helper *['ezer]* and my deliverer." And see Psalm 121:1: "I lift up my eyes to the hills — from where will my help *['ezer]* come? My help *['ezer]* comes from the LORD, who made heaven and earth." Further, the prepositional phrase *kenegdo* in Genesis 2:18 modifies the noun *'ezer* in a way that points to the mutuality of the pair rather than to isolation and hierarchy. Literally, the phrase means "over against him." The phrase "a helper over against him" is better translated as "counterpart."[39] The animals that God parades past *ha'adam* do not suffice as counterparts.

Many female figures in the Bible have been exemplars for the image of women in society at particular times. For example, Judith in the Apocrypha, who cut off general Holofernes' head, was praised for her courage and godliness when the church was threatened by persecutions in the first century C.E. (1 Clement 55) and later honored for her celibacy by Tertullian (160-230 C.E.) and by Ambrose of Milan (339-396 C.E.) in support of a celibate priesthood. Luther called the story of Ju-

---

38. Gale A. Yee, *Poor Banished Children of Eve: Woman as Evil in the Hebrew Bible* (Minneapolis: Fortress Press, 2003). Yee understands texts as ideological products of social praxis, which is itself shaped by politics and culture. But see O'Brien's critique, *Challenging Prophetic Metaphor,* pp. 46-48.

39. See Phyllis Trible, *God and the Rhetoric of Sexuality* (Philadelphia: Fortress Press, 1978), pp. 72-75, 88-94. Trible argues that these misogynist interpretations violate the rhetoric of the story. She translates verse 18 this way: "I will make for it a companion corresponding to it."

dith "a serious and brave tragedy." Yet Victorian England objected to Judith's morals because she dressed up to seduce Holofernes and got him drunk before she cut off his head. Judith forces us to confront the presuppositions about gender that we bring to the text.[40] From these divergent interpretations, we learn more about Judith's interpreters and their contexts than we do about Judith herself.

Second Isaiah, who prophesied a word of comfort to the exiles in Babylon in the sixth century B.C.E., speaks of God with female birthing imagery, as in Isaiah 49:15: Can a woman forget her nursing child, or show no compassion for the child of her womb? Even these may forget, yet I will not forget you." The love of God the Divine Mother transcends even a human mother's love. Isaiah 42:14 declares, "For a long time I have held my peace . . . now I will cry out like a woman in labor, I will gasp and pant." This image is embedded within a hymn of creation (42:5-17) that celebrates God as the author of a new creation for the exiles, who will be redeemed. God is described as a midwife in Isaiah 46:3-4: "[You] have been borne by me from your birth, carried from the womb; even to your old age . . . I will carry you. I have made, and I will bear; I will carry and will save." In Isaiah 45:9-10, God as potter, father, and mother brooks no challenge to the divine intent to save Israel. Compare Jeremiah's negative use of childbirth imagery to symbolize pain and death so that the exiles will come to accept their responsibility for their situation: "For I heard a cry as of a woman in labor, anguish as of one bringing forth her first child, the cry of daughter Zion gasping for breath, stretching out her hands, 'Woe is me! I am fainting before killers!'" (Jer. 4:31).

Third Isaiah, who prophesied to the community of return after the Exile, picks up Second Isaiah's female images for God in Isaiah 66:13: "As a mother comforts her child, so I will comfort you; you shall be comforted in Jerusalem." Feminist scholars speculate about the abundance of positive female imagery in Second Isaiah.[41] They suggest that the loss of kingship, temple, and homeland led the group clustered around Second Isaiah to seek comforting God metaphors in the one social unit that was still intact: the family. This means that images were drawn from the domestic sphere of marriage, childbirth, and mother-

---

40. Denise Dombkowksi Hopkins, "Judith," in *Women's Bible Commentary,* pp. 279-85. See also interpretations of Mary Magdalene in scholarly literature, theater, poetry, and film.

41. Susan Ackerman, "Isaiah," in *Women's Bible Commentary,* p. 176.

hood. Another possibility is that these female images correspond to a temporary increase in female status during the Exile, since so many men had been lost. Denise and I suggest a World War II parallel: "Rosie the Riveter," who went to work in the factories while the men were away at war. Goldie Hawn and Kurt Russell starred in the movie *Swing Shift*, which showcased this theme.

In Matthew 23:37, Jesus compares himself to a mother hen: "Jerusalem, Jerusalem, the city that kills the prophets and stones those who are sent to it! How often have I desired to gather your children together as a hen gathers her brood under her wings." Jesus also takes on the role of public mourner here, a role traditionally assigned to women (cf. Matt. 28:1 and Mark 16:1-2 — the women at the empty tomb — and Jer. 9:17-19, in which God calls the "mourning women," the "skilled women," to come and "raise a dirge over us").[42]

Archeological and scriptural evidence challenges us to wonder whether or not the Israelites always viewed God as male. Jeremiah 7:18 mentions worship of the Queen of Heaven: "The fathers kindle fire, and the women knead dough, to make cakes for the queen of heaven" (cf. Jer. 44:15-28). The Queen of Heaven provided women with a deity who offered them protection and prosperity, as Jeremiah 44:17-18 attests: "We used to have plenty of food, and prospered"; when they stopped worshipping her, they "lacked everything" and perished "by the sword and by famine." Scholars are not certain about the identity of the Queen of Heaven. She may combine features of two or more fertility goddesses of the ancient Near East such as Ishtar, Astarte, Asherah, Isis, Ma'at, Inanna, and Anath, who were local manifestations of the cosmic mother goddess and also divine consorts.[43] Archeologists

42. Michael and I also suggest a connection between Rachel in Jeremiah 31:15-22, where she mourns her children, and Matthew 2:18, which quotes Jeremiah 31 in the context of Herod's massacre of the innocents. In the context of Romans 8:22, Paul uses birth pains negatively as a metaphor for the chaos that precedes the dawn of a new age: "the whole creation has been groaning in labor pains until now." Yet he also speaks positively in Galatians 4:19 of himself as experiencing labor pains with the Galatians who are being birthed as Christians, and in 1 Thessalonians 2:7 he likens his care for the Thessalonians to a nurse's tender care for her own children.

43. See Philip King and Lawrence Stager, *Life in Biblical Israel* (Louisville: Westminster John Knox Press, 2001), p. 350, and William Dever, *Did God Have a Wife?* p. 236. Scholars disagree about whether a disc-shaped object held by female terra-cotta figurines is a round loaf, a plate, a sun disc, or a frame-drum or tambourine. Dever argues for a mold-made cake (p. 234).

have found thousands of terra-cotta fertility figurines in Israel, including Jerusalem, that date from the tenth to the sixth centuries B.C.E. Pillar-shaped figurines from the eighth and the seventh centuries were discovered in private homes in Jerusalem, not in sanctuaries.[44] These mother-goddess figurines, naked with heavy breasts, were probably used as good-luck charms for conception and childbirth.

Bill Dever, the dean of American archeology, argues that traditional biblical scholarship has been "reluctant" to acknowledge the centrality of the goddess Asherah to the religious practice of most people in ancient Israel.[45] This popular or "folk" religion, centered in the family, penetrated Jerusalem worship. It came to clash with the official "book" religion of the Deuteronomists, who regarded it as "pagan." Thus, King Josiah "reformed" worship by destroying all the high places and removing all the Asherah from the Jerusalem temple. These "reforms" of Josiah are recounted in 2 Kings 23. When this recounting is pieced together with other texts in Deuteronomy and with numerous condemnations of idolatrous practices in the prophets, we have what Dever terms an "inventory" of folk religion practices. He asks, ". . . why would later reforming priests and prophets condemn these things so vociferously *unless they remained popular* in Israelite religion? The reformers knew what they were talking about when they protested. Why haven't *we* caught on until recently?"[46]

Lady Wisdom

As we argued above, wisdom is the search for God-given order in the world. In Hebrew, the word for wisdom is *chokmah;* in Greek, it is *sophia.*

44. King and Stager, *Life in Biblical Israel,* p. 348. Perhaps Israelite religion appropriated several aspects of the Canaanite cult, including the identity of Israel's god as El, the chief god of the Canaanite pantheon, whose consort was Asherah. Perhaps Asherah simply personified God's more "feminine" attributes; see Dever, *Did God Have a Wife?* p. 236.

45. *'asherah* occurs more than forty times in the Hebrew Bible. Traditionally, the word has been translated as referring only to a wooden pole or a tree-like object, but Dever insists that they are "stand-ins" for Asherah the goddess rather than idols (*Did God Have a Wife?* p. 223). Hilltop shrines with tree groves were common throughout the ancient world.

46. Dever, *Did God Have a Wife?* p. 215. See also p. 237: ". . . their inclusion implies that the *majority* of people, not just an easily ignored minority, were doing them . . . principally doing them in a family context, where women played a highly significant role."

Both of these words are feminine nouns. Proverbs 1–9 personifies wisdom as a woman; she is Lady Wisdom or Woman Wisdom. "She exists both as a person who speaks and as cosmic reality."[47] Lady Wisdom is a bit like Mother Nature or Mother Church. In Proverbs 1–9, she embodies all of the positive roles of women as wives, mothers, and wise women in Israelite society.[48] Her "evil twin" is Woman Stranger or the Foreign Woman, whose temptations lead to death. She embodies all the negatives that men fear about women: the scolding wife/mother, the widow, the adulteress, the prostitute, and the uppity woman. Think about the movies *Fatal Attraction* and *Basic Instinct* here. These fears brings out the misogyny of the sages.[49] Some have suggested that the figure of Woman Wisdom may indicate the survival of goddess worship within the later monotheistic structure of Israelite theology. The wisdom traditions of Mesopotamia and Egypt were sanctioned by goddesses: Ma'at in Egypt and Nisaba in Sumer, or a Canaanite fertility goddess developed from the Sumerian Inanna or Semitic Ishtar.

Woman Wisdom or Lady Wisdom has power in the male-dominated Israelite society. In Proverbs 1:20-21, Woman Wisdom stands on a street corner in the busiest part of the city, the place usually reserved for judges, prophets, and prostitutes. We are presented with an ancient version of *Trading Spaces* (a once-popular television show): she is at work in male public spaces of power. This is extraordinary. In verse 23 she demands

47. Raymond C. Van Leeuwen, "Proverbs," in *New Interpreter's Bible*, vol. 5 (Nashville: Abingdon Press, 1997), p. 96. Van Leeuwen notes that some see Wisdom as a poetic personification of the attribute by which God created the world (Prov. 3:19-20; Ps. 104:24; Jer. 10:12), while some think she is a hypostasis, or independent personal being, or even God in female imagery.

48. Carole Fontaine, *Smooth Words: Women, Proverbs, and Performance in Biblical Wisdom*, JSOT Supplement Series 356 (Sheffield: Sheffield Academic Press, 2002). As "household sage," woman was manager, teacher, counselor, maid, healer, and mourner. Sages don't often mention daughters and sisters, perhaps because of their liminal social status. The exception is Ben Sira in the Apocrypha. See also Masenya Madipoane, *How Worthy Is the Woman of Worth? Rereading Proverbs 31:10-31 in African-South Africa*, Bible and Theology in Africa, 4 (New York: Peter Lang, 2004). Madipoane argues that a *Bosadi* (ideal "womanhood" in Northern Sotho, serving men's interests) approach to this text shows that it contains elements of both liberation and oppression.

49. See Carol Fontaine, "Proverbs," in *Women's Bible Commentary*, pp. 53-160, and Claudia Camp, "Wise and Strange: An Interpretation of the Female Imagery in Proverbs in the Light of Trickster Mythology," *Semeia* 42 (1988): 14-36. See also Naphtali Gutstein, "Proverbs 31:10-31: The Woman of Valor as Allegory," *Jewish Bible Quarterly* 27, no. 1 (2005): 36-39. Gutstein argues that this text extols the virtues of Wisdom personified.

that her male audience "pay attention." The end result will be positively life-giving: "those who listen to me will be secure and will live at ease, without dread of disaster" (v. 33). Veiled in her rhetoric are elements of eroticism and men's longing for her. In Proverbs 3:16 she conjures Ma'at, the Egyptian goddess of justice. She holds the symbol for long life, the *ankh* (an elongated cross with a loop at the top), in one hand; in the other, she holds a symbol of power: "Long life is in her right hand; in her left hand are riches and honor." A recent bumper sticker echoes this theme: "ankh [symbol] if you love Jesus."

Woman Stranger is a nasty woman; she is compared to an adulteress. Like the fertility goddesses who descended to the underworld in ancient myths, her paths lead down to death (Prov. 2:16-19). Proverbs 5 is saturated with warnings about the loose woman who uses seductive language and leads men to ruin. Verses 3-4 declare, "For the lips of a loose [strange] woman drip honey, and her speech is smoother than oil; but in the end she is bitter as wormwood, sharp as a two-edged sword." As the negative counterpart to wisdom, she suggests a male audience and perhaps a post-exilic context of conflicts over ethnic purity and the issue of survival.[50]

Finally, in Proverbs 8, Lady Wisdom praises herself and describes her role in creation, in the style of Egyptian gods and goddesses like Re, Isis, and Ma'at. Kings obtain and keep their positions through her (vv. 15-16), just as Ma'at is the power behind Pharaoh's throne. In 1 Kings 3, God gives Solomon the gift of wisdom to legitimate his reign. Proverbs 8:22 has given rise to great argument. The NRSV translates this verse as "The LORD created me at the beginning of his work." The word *created* is *qanani* in Hebrew, from the root *qanah,* meaning "to acquire, possess, create." The Septuagint uses the Greek verb *ktizo,* meaning "create," while other Greek texts use *ktaomai,* meaning "to procure, acquire, get."

Depending upon the translation, Woman Wisdom is either a sexually conceived child of God or a pre-existent entity whom God acquires in order to begin creation. They carry out the ordering of the universe together. Both have Egyptian parallels: Ma'at is both the

---

50. In *Poor Banished Children of Eve,* Gale Yee argues that the "Other Woman" must be viewed within the wider sociopolitical context of Persian Yehud. Persian tributary demands created a stratified society that exacerbated returnee/native divisions. Exiles returning from Babylon married into the native population to secure land for production. Woman Wisdom thus represented the "acceptable" insider woman to marry, while the Other Woman symbolized the attractive outsider woman who was unacceptable (p. 158).

child of the creator god and the master plan he uses in his work.[51] Lady Wisdom declares in 8:35, "Whoever finds me finds life." These are the words of a saving god. We hear echoes of these words in other places — for example, the *logos* in the prologue to the Gospel of John (see also Job 28; Sirach 1:1-10; 24:1-19; Wisd. of Sol. 7:22–8:1; Matt. 11:19; 23:34-36; Luke 11:49). Wisdom has moved beyond mere representations of divine powers to function as a symbol expressing humankind's experience of God as creator, giver of life, judge, and provider. In Sirach 24 of the Apocrypha (200 B.C.E.–100 C.E.), wisdom praises herself and describes her search for a resting place. Sirach identifies her with the Torah, "the book of the Covenant of God Most High." She becomes stabilized and permanent in a time of religious and social chaos and challenges to Jewish identity during the second century B.C.E. under the Hasmoneans.

In the Hebrew Bible, God's compassion is linked to the womb (in Hebrew, *rechem*). The plural of *womb (rechamim)* forms the abstract idea of compassion, mercy, and love; a good translation would be "womb-love." The adjective for *merciful* is *rachum,* and the verb meaning "to show mercy" is *rchm.* So we can see that compassion roots itself in a metaphor, in the movement from a better-known, physical organ of the female body to a lesser-known mode of being, from the concrete to the abstract.[52] Men can also participate in the journey of this metaphor, even though *womb* is a woman's organ. When Joseph, for example, sees his brother Benjamin for the first time, he weeps, "because his *rechamim* yearned for his brother" (Gen. 43:30). In Psalm 103:13, the metaphor extends to a father and to God: "As a father has compassion for his children, so the LORD has compassion for those who fear him." In Isaiah 46:3-4, God reassures the exiles: "Listen to me, . . . all the remnant of the house of Israel, who have been borne by me from your birth [*beten*

---

51. In *Wisdom's Friends: Community and Christology in the Fourth Gospel* (Louisville: Westminster John Knox Press, 1999), Sharon Ringe argues that God discovers her. She is the prototype or model of God's work. She is the partner and shaper of God's work and vice versa; they are interdependent. Ringe argues that wisdom's feminine personification "surely collided with Jesus' male identity" (p. 44).

52. Trible, *God and the Rhetoric of Sexuality,* p. 33. In this connection, Trible cites the story of King Solomon and the two harlots who claim the same child (1 Kings 3:16-28). The biological mother gave up her child rather than see it cut in two "because her *rechamim* (compassion) yearned for her son." Only after this does the word *mother* appear in the story.

means "womb"], carried from the womb [*rechem*]; even to your old age I am he, even when you turn gray I will carry you" (cf. Isa. 49:13). In Jeremiah 31:20, God consoles a weeping Rachel over the loss of her children: "Is Ephraim [another name for Israel] my dear son? . . . I still remember him. Therefore . . . I will truly show motherly compassion [*rachem 'arachamenu*] upon him."[53] Our Korean students tell Denise and me that *jung* corresponds to this womb-love; it is a deep-seated loyalty, love, and closeness.

A QUESTION FOR REFLECTION
- Can you conceive of God as a compassionate God of womb-love? As a woman? Why or why not?

Image Idolatry

Conceiving of God in gender-inclusive terms, as female and as male, may be difficult for some people, while for others it may be a matter of theological and psychological survival. Our efforts to project what we desire God to be surely do not change who God actually is. Yet through this projection process, we intuit more clearly what we cannot yet see. The Divine Self will be revealed to those who dare confront the eruption of a different reality. Our pastoral work is to help people to recover, reclaim, and integrate the many faces and attributes of God's being. Such efforts allow us to take up into ourselves (introjection), as women and men, those aspects of God's being that we ourselves need for growing up into the fullness of who we have been created to be. As Ann Ulanov reminds us, "In the life of the spirit, we expect to wake up out of our shadowy state of consciousness to a clear perception of God. But, as Bernard of Clairvaux says, at an advanced stage we go to sleep, falling into darkness as the only suitable non-interfering reception of God's working within us."[54]

In a sense, the Second Commandment both binds and frees us with regard to images that take the place of God (idols). This prohibition forbids us to give our allegiance to objects that masquerade as God's pres-

53. Trible, *God and the Rhetoric of Sexuality*, p. 45. The NRSV translates the verse this way: "Therefore I am deeply moved for him; I will surely have mercy on him."
54. Ulanov, *Picturing God*, p. 19.

ence, thus freeing us up for full relationship with God. "You shall not make for yourself an idol [in Hebrew, *pesel*], whether in the form of anything that is in heaven above, or that is on the earth beneath, or that is in the water under the earth. You shall not bow down to them or worship them; for I the LORD your God am a jealous [passionate] God" (Exod. 20:4-5; Deut. 5:8-9; cf. Exod. 20:23; Lev. 19:4; Deut. 27:15).

For Israel, *pesel* meant "a carved, shaped, or poured three-dimensional representation of God."[55] This commandment distinguishes between God the Creator and God's creation. Walter Harrelson gets at this distinction when he asks this question: "How can any created reality, no matter how sublime, do justice to God's transcendent character, God's mystery, God's beauty and glory?"[56] Also, God created human beings in God's image (in Hebrew, *tselem*) and likeness *(demuth)*. Genesis 1:26 suggests that we, not idols, are meant to represent God on earth as agents and reflections. The first two commandments remind us that God always transcends our images. Similarly, Deuteronomy 4 insists in its interpretation of the Second Commandment that "the Lord alone determines how God shall be seen, revealed, known, and accessible."[57] Deuteronomy 4:12 declares: "You heard the sound of words but saw no form; there was only a voice." God makes God's self known through the word (cf. John 1).

Our human penchant to turn anything into an idol, including but not limited to images, reaches far back into history. After all, the impatient Israelites couldn't wait for Moses to return from the top of Mt. Sinai, so they built a golden calf and sacrificed to it (Exod. 32:1-6). What golden calves do we build as our idols today? Can we step faithfully into this danger zone without doing harm to ourselves? Can we image the image without concretizing, literalizing, or confining it? We need to be conscious of our binding and freeing of images.

---

55. Walter J. Harrelson, *The Ten Commandments for Today* (Louisville: Westminster John Knox Press, 2006), p. 33.

56. Harrelson, *The Ten Commandments for Today,* p. 34. For an exploration of the reason for this commandment, see pp. 33-35.

57. Patrick D. Miller, *The Ten Commandments,* Interpretation: Resources for the Use of Scripture in the Church (Louisville: Westminster John Knox Press, 2009), p. 51. Miller traces the trajectory of the Second Commandment and finds in it an economic dimension (silver and gold idols show off wealth); a political dimension (God "authorizes but also judges and destabilizes political authority," p. 57); and a theological dimension (theology "always teeters on the brink of idolatry," p. 58).

We (Michael and I) suggest that pastors and congregants can draw on the biblical texts as a resource for the process and content of God-image reflection or what we call faithful (ir)reverencing of the text. We reverence the text as we build on images and metaphors explicit in the biblical story or poem. Making images of God is a natural human endeavor. "Imagination," as Albert Einstein once said, "is more important than knowledge. Knowledge is limited. Imagination encircles the world."[58] Using our imaginations faithfully can enrich our sense of God. At times we also need to "irreverence" the text by challenging and disrupting problematic images (e.g., God as abusive spouse). Irreverence can help us to recognize when metaphors for God have become "literalized to the point that they exclude other metaphors for the same subject [and] they function as idols."[59]

Images call forth our knowing or unknowing, sometimes in whole but often in partial and obscure ways. We need to investigate these images with sufficient care and attention. And then we need to let go of them. Letting go of images in due time, no matter how powerful their claim on our psyche and soul, models necessary and faithful action. It is also a biblical injunction.

GROUP EXERCISE

Generate a list of idol images in your life and in our culture. Have you ever made God into an idol?

God Images and Context

Images of God from the Hebrew Bible reveal something about God, but not every image is beneficial for pastoral care. Some images of God may be toxic to the health of people and creation; these we must "irreverence." Yet even these images can play a positive role if they are

---

58. Einstein, as quoted in "What Life Means to Einstein: An Interview" by George Sylvester Viereck in *The Saturday Evening Post*, 26 October 1929, p. 117.

59. In *Seeing the Psalms*, William Brown says that ". . . an image can become an idol when its connotative force is mistaken for its denotative scope . . ." (p. 10). In *The Suffering of God*, Terence Fretheim speaks of a "controlling metaphor" that delimits other metaphorical possibilities and brings coherence to a range of thinking about God — for example, God's sovereignty and grace (p. 11). He also reminds us that the variety of biblical metaphors should keep us from literalism (p. 8).

used in the appropriate context. Kathleen O'Connor argues that in Jeremiah 2–9, for example, "images and metaphors about the deity tumble over and contradict each other," rendering the character of God "multiple and unstable."[60] In 2:1–4:2, God is the aggrieved divine husband whose rhetoric of shaming and blaming and broken-family metaphors invite our empathy and indict the Israelites: "Have you seen what she did, that faithless one, Israel, how she went up on every high hill and under every green tree, and played the whore there?" (Jer. 3:6). In 4:5–6:30 and 7:1-20, God is an avenging architect of war spouting a rhetoric of fear and terror: "I looked, and lo, the fruitful land was a desert, and all its cities were laid in ruins before the LORD, before his fierce anger" (Jer. 4:26). God is a weeping and vulnerable God in 8:18–9:22: "O that my head were a spring of water, and my eyes a fountain of tears, so that I might weep day and night for the slain of my poor people!" (Jer. 9:1). All of these images help the Israelite community face the disaster of Babylonian exile in the sixth century B.C.E. by giving the community language to voice its pain, and by assigning blame to the people so that the historical chaos they are experiencing is not seen as arbitrary.

In this light, these images of God function as coping and survival mechanisms: "The book defends God to help the community maintain continuity with its past and to keep God engaged in the present disaster."[61] Yet we know that survivors of child abuse also accept blame for their abuse, believing that they can change their future by changing their behavior.[62] This leaves the larger arrangement of relationships intact and allows the abuse to continue. We must take hold of these images of God with great care when working with abused individuals, lest

---

60. Kathleen O'Connor, "The Tears of God and Divine Character in Jeremiah 2–9," in *Troubling Jeremiah,* ed. Pete Diamond, Kathleen O'Connor, and Louis Stulman, JSOT Supplement Series 260 (Sheffield: Sheffield Academic Press, 1999), p. 387. Whereas O'Connor argues that these images contradict each other, Terence Fretheim argues that they are in tension with one another: anger and tears go together; divine judgment stands in the service of grace. See Fretheim, "The Character of God in Jeremiah," in *Character and Scripture,* ed. William P. Brown (Grand Rapids: Wm. B. Eerdmans, 2002), p. 214.

61. Kathleen O'Connor, "The Book of Jeremiah: Reconstructing Community after Disaster," in *Character Ethics and the Old Testament: Moral Dimensions of Scripture,* ed. Daniel Carroll and Jacqueline Lapsley (Louisville: Westminster John Knox Press, 2007), p. 88.

62. See Alice Miller, *The Drama of the Gifted Child: The Search for the True Self* (New York: Basic Books, 1981).

they reinforce their self-blaming and ongoing abuse.[63] Working with God images in pastoral care is a theologically creative and constructive process at the same time that it is a deconstructive, critical process, reflecting pastoral and theological courage and maturity.[64] Our (Denise and Michael's) theological claim is that the Living God relates intimately with all of creation, giving of the Divine Self and receiving all of creation. Therefore, an image of God that does not receive persons in their totality reflects a problematic or flawed image. Since God is inherently relational, images of God and care ought to reflect God's capacity for receiving and giving. Human identity is also cooperatively constructed and continually in formation. Images of God and care need to reflect this reality.

In her book *God Images in the Healing Process*, Kathryn Armistead advocates a pastoral perspective of imaging holy ground in the alliance between care giver and care receiver. She writes in the field of pastoral counseling, and suggests movements of discovering, surveying, being nourished on, and sharing the fruit from holy ground. Holy ground is a deeply biblical image (see Exod. 3:5). Armistead uses the imagery to suggest a way of being with people in crisis who seek the companionship of a caring counselor and, more importantly, the companionship of God.[65] This rich description captures the intimacy of connection at the heart of caring relationship, and reflects the environment we (Mi-

63. See David Blumenthal, *Facing the Abusing God: A Theology of Protest* (Louisville: Westminster John Knox Press, 1993). Blumenthal argues that "given Jewish history [the Holocaust] and family violence as our generations have experienced them, distrust is a proper religious affection, and a theology of sustained suspicion is a proper theology to have" (p. 257).

64. See Carrie Doehring, *Internal Desecration: Traumatization and Representations of God* (Lanham, Md.: University Press of America, 1993). Doehring argues, building on A. M. Rizutto, that "rigid, limited God representations represent a lower or frozen level of development" (p. 51). See also Larry Kent Graham, *Discovering God Images: Narratives of Care among Lesbians and Gays* (Louisville: Westminster John Knox Press, 1997). Graham reconstructs God images from the experiences of marginalized persons. Doehring's study illuminates the complex and often inextricably associated psychological and theological processes operative for those who have been traumatized or abused. Healing requires the sustained attention of a skilled professional. Pastors can provide environments and establish relationships of safety, remembrance, and mourning, and thus facilitate reconnection with ordinary life. These three stages of recovery are outlined in Judith Herman, *Trauma and Recovery* (New York: Basic Books, 1992).

65. M. Kathryn Armistead, *God-Images in the Healing Process* (Minneapolis: Augsburg Fortress Press, 1995).

chael and I) encourage for honoring God images. Standing and caring on holy ground calls us to participant observation[66] in community, wherein we help one another cultivate our primary and life-giving relationship with God.

God images work on us and we work on them in a circular relationship. God images work on us not simply psychologically or theologically from the top down. We do not act this way merely because that is how God is. We cannot, because God's identity cannot be reduced so simply. The texts of the Hebrew Bible give us not one but many views of God. We (Denise and I) see the relationship between us and our God images as a process of relation that constantly seeks to discover and name ways of acting that foster well-being. Carl Jung developed one method for enhancing this discovery. Known as "active imagination,"[67] this process helps people to engage in dialogue with unconscious material, such as dream images or symbols, in order to move toward consciousness. Whether through writing, drawing, daydreaming, or free association, this method can bring to the surface previously unknown or unrecognized aspects of selfhood. Identity, both God's and our own, is always in formation. We discover that relationships between us and our God images move interdependently, and that as we change, so do our images of God, and vice versa. Despite resistance from the accumulated debris of unhealthy images of God, we can come to embrace more life-giving images of God.

Group Guidelines for Reflection on God Images

1. Name the God images.
2. Wonder together about these images.
3. Inquire whether they build self-esteem/confidence or reduce self-esteem/confidence.
4. Offer alternative images to counter images that denigrate or destroy personal and communal confidence.
5. Wonder together about these images.
6. Welcome a multiplicity of images.

66. Harry Stack Sullivan, *The Interpersonal Theory of Psychiatry,* ed. Helen Perry and Mary Gawel (New York: W. W. Norton, 1953); Mary Clark Moschella, *Ethnography as a Pastoral Practice: An Introduction* (Cleveland: Pilgrim Press, 2008).

67. For further exploration of this method, see Carl Jung, *On Active Imagination* (Princeton: Princeton University Press, 1997).

Robyn's Story

One of my parishioners returned early from a holiday in Italy because she was ill. She discovered that she had end-stage ovarian cancer. As her pastor, I was horrified and frustrated that I didn't know how to fix her situation. When I went to visit her, I just cried at the edge of her bed and told her how sorry I was that I couldn't do anything to make her better. In her wisdom she replied, "You are not here to fix this. You are here so people do not have to go through things like this alone." After much processing, I have come to understand that I companion people on their journeys. My call as a pastor is not to fix, solve, or make things better. I realize now that because I saw God as the Great Fixer, I thought I needed to be a Great Fixer, too. When I think about who God is for me, I know that I also need to think about how I think God views me. One informs the other and vice versa.

•   •

Pastoral Identity and God Images

God images influence pastoral identity in direct and indirect ways. Sometimes we are conscious of the connection between the image we form of God and the practices of ministry in which we engage; sometimes we are not. Indeed, we can hold an image of God that contradicts our actions in ministry. Our true theological colors can seep out when we are least aware of it, as they did in Robyn's situation. For Robyn, a blunt and painful confrontation with a parishioner's diagnosis uncovered her assumptions about God and about herself, revealing her profound feelings of inadequacy when she measured herself against God as "the Great Fixer." Who could ever live up to such expectations of self in light of this God? We shrivel before such an image.

The parishioner herself offered care in the form of an alternative God image and care practice: "Your purpose is to be here as a companion," she said. Released from the image of a "fixing God" and all the internal demands of self that come with it, Robyn subtly and yet profoundly shifted her pastoral care to be present as a companion as she listened and responded to the true need of the moment. This story illustrates a process of theological construction, and affirms that pastoral identity can never be separated from relationships of caring community.

By "pastoral identity" we mean a person's sense of self as a care giver that is at once theologically and psychologically solid enough to withstand the inevitable pressures, demands, and crises of care giving as well as fluid enough to remain flexibly open to new ideas, awareness, and learning about God, self, and others. Our pastoral identity evolves so that we are able to care with composure within increasingly complex situations. In psychological terms, we need to be willing to know ourselves with a breadth and depth that allows for probing our histories, understanding our gifts and our wounds, and acknowledging our biases and preferences. In theological terms, we need to know how to speak about God with coherent language in conversation with the texts, doctrines, and history of church traditions. Pastoral identity embodies theology in our core; this theology shapes our engagement in concrete acts of care.[68] The connection with a community of faith keeps pastoral identity dynamic, in both positive and negative ways.[69]

God images do not immediately translate into pastoral identity and practice. They do, however, offer a valuable resource for pastoral and theological meaning-making. We can ask ourselves, "How does this image of God help or hinder my pastoral self-understanding? How does it help or hinder building trust-filled, caring relationships?"[70] Pastoral identity can be elusive and frustratingly difficult, for it seems that no metaphor or image can fully capture what occurs experientially. Ministry is also like this: it can be an extremely messy and unpredictable business. We may long for a sense of security in the midst of the chaos and contradictions. Images can creatively capture our deepest intuitions, challenge our narrow understandings of selfhood or

68. Joretta Marshall, "Toward the Development of a Pastoral Soul: Reflections on Identity and Theological Education," *Pastoral Psychology* 43, no. 1 (September 1994): 11-29.

69. Barbara Brown Taylor, *Leaving Church: A Memoir of Faith* (New York: HarperCollins, 2006). Taylor experienced a crisis of pastoral identity in her move from a large city church to a small rural church, but she found a spirituality of imperfection that led her to leave the pastorate and draw closer to identification with all of humanity.

70. See Carroll Saussy, *God Images and Self-Esteem.* Saussy argues that self-esteem is related to at least six major factors: (1) parental acceptance (which produces good enough foundational self-esteem), (2) an understanding of human life and our place in it (values), (3) satisfying relationships, (4) competence, (5) passion for life (vocation, purpose), and (6) self-acceptance (realistic perception of givens). Analyzing these six factors can help us to understand how our God images and our self-esteem are related.

God, and open up closed-off possibilities. Images from text and experience must be held up against other necessary givens in care ministry: church accountability structures that safeguard the health and well-being of all persons; ethical and legal standards between self and others; and norms of respectful interpersonal communication.

Images of Pastoral Care, a volume of historic and contemporary images of care edited by Robert Dykstra, makes a valuable contribution to pastoral theology and the practice of care. He argues that pastoral identity is necessarily unstable. We are "scavengers" who rummage through what others discard so as to embrace divergent strategies of care.[71] Dykstra suggests that we approach images such as wounded healer, wise fool, intimate stranger, agent of hope, midwife, gardener, moral coach, living human web, and self-differentiated Samaritan as evocative art that can inspire us and focus our ministry.[72] We all can engage such images in the manner of art critics, with a combination of appreciation and critical appraisal. Other approaches to our pastoral images include reverence (as one would contemplate an icon) and recognition of threat (e.g., the threat of a "graven" image that must be destroyed).[73]

Michael and I want to help pastoral leaders foster explicit connections between images of God encountered in the Hebrew Bible and practices of care, and regularly revisit and revise their interpretation of these images and care practices. Images can stimulate ongoing reflective analysis of strengths and limitations in ministry. They can leave care givers and care receivers, all of us pilgrims on the way, with further questions to ponder.

QUESTIONS FOR REFLECTION
- What associations can you make between your images of God and your pastoral identity?
- Is there a close correlation? What are some of the congruities? The incongruities?
- How does your image of God shape your pastoral identity positively? How does it shape your pastoral image negatively?
- Which of your pastoral behaviors are life-enhancing? Which are life-sapping?

71. Valerie DeMarinis, quoted in *Images of Pastoral Care,* p. 9.
72. Dykstra, *Images of Pastoral Care,* p. 12.
73. Dykstra, *Images of Pastoral Care,* p. 13.

- How does your image of God influence your self-esteem?
- How is your self-understanding as care giver enhanced by the complex interplay of many images?

Theological Construction of God Images

Pastoral theology revolves around an axis of deconstruction-construction-reconstruction, providing a discernible complementary or contradictory fit between an image of God and identity and practice in ministries of care. Deconstruction is often precipitated by a sense of things falling apart or no longer holding up as we thought. This is one sure sign that we are facing challenges to a myth we hold about God or ourselves. Construction is simply allowing ourselves to listen anew amid the rubble, even as we may have no idea what really needs to happen. We draw on inherent wisdom in the moment and workings of the Spirit. This construction may happen rather quickly after deconstruction, as it did for Robyn, with the realization dawning that the situation called for some new way of thinking and acting. Reconstruction is the intentional and deliberative stage of evaluating and critiquing the God image and resulting pastoral image in light of our experience, and our subsequent actions that enhance well-being for all.

Myth and Parable

If we examine carefully the images we hold of ourselves as care givers, we will inevitably discover the tension between perfection and realism contained within them.[74] This is the tension between myth and parable. Myth mediates and reconciles irreducible opposites — e.g., beauty and the beast — creating a sense of perfection. Myth gives us stability, which allows us to dream and makes room for optimism. Parable, on the other hand, creates contradiction where there was reconciliation. Parable challenges complacent security and acts as an agent of change. It doesn't al-

---

74. Herbert Anderson and Edward Foley, *Mighty Stories, Dangerous Rituals: Weaving Together the Human and the Divine* (San Francisco: Jossey-Bass, 1998), pp. 12-16. Anderson and Foley reference John Dominic Crossan's study of parables entitled *The Dark Interval: Towards a Theology of Story* (Niles, Ill.: Argus Communications, 1975).

low us to live in a dream world. We need to negotiate the tension between perfection and realism to live a balanced life. This kind of discovery and negotiation can challenge our rigid self-understanding and theology. For example, when we pigeonhole God as the Great Fixer, we pressure ourselves to become great fixers too — and we are doomed to fail.

If we as care givers model ourselves on certain biblical characters, we need to recognize that these characters show a complexity and a capability to change, and are often depicted with ambiguity. We are given just enough information to speculate about their motives but not enough to resolve our questions.[75] When we identify with characters in the Hebrew Bible, we must take care to notice if we have fixated on just one aspect of that character, and, in so doing, if we have concealed or revealed something about ourselves. Abraham, for example, seems the paragon of obedience and faith when he follows God without question to the land of Canaan from Haran (Gen. 12:1-9). But at the first sign of difficulty — famine — he heads for Egypt and hands over his wife, Sarah, to Pharaoh to avoid being killed (Gen. 12:9-20). David brings to Jerusalem the Ark of the Covenant (in which God is thought to be invisibly enthroned; 2 Sam. 6), but he commits adultery and murder (2 Sam. 11).

Images are suggestive rather than instructive, leaving us to tell our own stories in relation to them. Storytelling in conversation with the images reveals strands of both parable and myth. An image of God as Mother, for example, can be powerful and healing for some people, even as it strikes fear into the hearts of others. But we need to ask, What kind of mother is God? This question makes a difference, as does our reflection on it. If we don't ask such questions, we represent in our care giving the kind of unexamined mothering that we ourselves experienced. This can be said of any image we choose for God or for care. Leaders and care givers who undertake self-examination can grow in knowledge that fosters awareness of their limitations and strengths. This allows for an open and honest engagement with God images.

GROUP EXERCISE
Choose a biblical character from the Hebrew Bible with whom you identify as well as a character that challenges you.

---

75. Peter D. Miscall, "Introduction to Narrative Literature," in *New Interpreter's Bible*, vol. 2 (Nashville: Abingdon Press, 1998), p. 550. Miscall draws upon Robert Alter, *The Art of Biblical Narrative* (New York: Basic Books, 1981).

What have you revealed and/or concealed about yourself, your call, or your ministry by your choice of these characters?

What myth do you hold about yourself as care giver? What parable challenges that myth?

Group Exercise

Henri Nouwen developed the concept of the "wounded healer" as a challenge to the ministerial myth of perfection. A wounded healer recognizes and tends to his or her own wounds before ministering to others. Calvin Morris speaks of "the walking wounded," care givers who deny their wounds and receive care from their counselees in a role reversal.[76]

Designate one end of the room as "one" and the other end as "ten." On a scale of one to ten, place yourselves on a continuum, with one being "walking wounded" and ten being "wounded healer." After seeing how each of you places herself or himself, sit down and discuss how your position on the scale is shaped by your image of God and your image of yourself as care giver.

Constructing a Name and Not Reinforcing the Myths

Central to the process of identity development in the Hebrew Bible is the ability to name, for in naming, identity comes into being. "Not to possess a name is tantamount to nonexistence in the world view of the ancient Near East. Name-giving was thus associated with creation and domination, for the one who gives a name has power over the object named."[77] In Genesis 1, God names day and night, the sky, the earth, and the sea, thereby establishing divine sovereignty over them. The man/earth creature *(ha'adam)* in Genesis 2:20 names each of the living creatures God brings to him/it in search of an *'ezer kenegdo* (counterpart), thereby establishing dominion over them. In Genesis 2:23, this *ha'adam* does not name "woman" with the same formula of naming used for animals, so he does not claim power over her.[78] Hosea names

76. Edward Wimberly, *Recalling Our Own Stories: Spiritual Renewal for Religious Caregivers* (San Francisco: Jossey-Bass, 1997), p. 9.

77. The Rabbinical Assembly, *Etz Hayim: Torah and Commentary* (New York: Jewish Publication Society, 2001), p. 5: commentary on Genesis 1:5.

78. Trible, *God and the Rhetoric of Sexuality,* pp. 99-100. Trible argues that the formula

his children Lo-ruhamah, meaning "Not pitied," and Lo-ammi, meaning "not my people" (Hos. 1:6, 9) as signs concretizing God's punishment of an idolatrous Israel. Here we find the danger inherent in naming. Naming can be a powerful means of constructing the world, but also of shaming and controlling it. The images that we think we see of God and of ourselves can have significant influence on our ministerial practices, for good or for ill.

Denise and I suggest that pastoral identity be a creative process embracing the tensions inherent in the human and the divine. Just as Joseph in Egypt named his two sons Manasseh ("God has made me forget") and Ephraim ("God made me fertile") to embrace the paradox of his situation,[79] so we, too, must name God and self in ways that acknowledge the paradox in us both. Naming has a quality of "trying but never fully grasping" because the object of our naming is not really an object separate from us, but glimpses of total reality of which we are a part. When we attempt to name these glimpses, we often run the risk of objectifying them.

These glimpses of reality are, in fact, deeply and intimately interrelated. Process theology calls this the doctrine of "internal relations": "people and things actually enter into the experiences of another . . . we carry the influences of one another within ourselves."[80] For Christians, Jesus Christ is the embodied manifestation of God's Self. We struggle to name this reality: Jesus' identity is both fully God and fully human, inextricably linked and at the same time impossibly nameable. Yet in our struggle to name, we learn that our truest and deepest identity is connected to God's Self, and our identity is always in the process of reaching toward its fullest response in communion.

Naming ourselves in connection to our naming of God is perhaps

---

"call the name" (see also Gen. 4:17, 25, 26ab), which was used earlier to name the animals, is not used here: "This shall be called *'ishshah* [woman]."

79. Zornberg, *The Beginning of Desire*, pp. 284-90. With these names, Joseph acknowledges both the bitterness and the sweetness of his life. With Manasseh, Joseph celebrates the oblivion of his and his people's suffering. He is not haunted by memories of the past, so he can concentrate on survival in this moment ("that we may live and not die"; see Gen. 43:8; 47:19). The naming expresses his ambivalence and regret about dislocation. With Ephraim, he celebrates procreation in the face of impending famine, but he longs for ways to negotiate the deathly perils of life on alien soil.

80. Mary Elizabeth Moore, *Teaching from the Heart: Theology and Educational Method* (Minneapolis: Fortress Press, 1991), p. 40. See also Bonnie Miller-McLemore, "The Living Human Web," in Dykstra, *Images of Pastoral Care,* pp. 40-46.

best reflected in action verbs or phrases with multiple nouns and adjectives that honor the complex dynamics of our being and of God's. Such naming recognizes that identity is not a "thing" or a person, but rather a relational and active process. Examples include the following:

"He who cares with the compassion of Mother God."

"She who looks over the congregation with the watchful protection of Father God."

"He who plays with the abandon of the Trickster God."

"The Namer who helps God name."

"The one who breaks idolatrous images, for God's image is beyond our knowing."[81]

"The hospitable hostess who welcomes the sojourner."[82]

"One who hovers over the chaos waters like the Creator at creation."[83]

"A gold prospector who digs deep for value like God."[84]

"A blue-collar blood brother who models a God of connections."[85]

"A jazz musician who takes cognitive dissonance and turns it into music, like God, who works through whatever is there."[86]

"The artist who encourages interplay between Creator and created."

Our pastoral task is not to assert one dominant metaphorical view of God or care and deny the submerged or not-yet-realized images. Rather, we create space for people to hold traditional images in tension with those that are newly emerging. We can never fully anticipate all the questions, challenges, and problems that people bring with them. Nevertheless, as care givers we can observe how people relate to images, noticing what is particularly attractive or repulsive to them. Our job is to observe along with them and avoid forcing an interpretation or theological framework. Rather, we attend wholeheartedly, with both emotion and intellect, letting the image itself guide, trusting God's abiding presence and care.

81. Suggested by Michael Smith, an M.Div. graduate of Wesley Seminary.
82. From Sue Walters, a Wesley graduate.
83. From Duane Clinker, a D.Min. student at Wesley.
84. From Wesley student Candyce Loescher.
85. From Brand Eaton, a D.Min. student at Wesley.
86. From Joe Ranager, a D.Min. student at Wesley.

QUESTIONS FOR REFLECTION

- How comfortable are you with ambiguity, tension, and paradox? What explains your level of comfort?
- How does your degree of comfort or discomfort shape your images of God and of yourself as care giver?

TAKE-AWAY POINTS

1. Differentiate between asking and telling about God.
2. Contemplate how God experiences you.
3. Identify the biblical images that shape your God image.
4. Open yourself up to new images of God and care giver.
5. Be conscious of the positive and negative connections between your God image and your practice of ministry.
6. Embrace tensions in your images of God and care giver.
7. Play with naming yourself with multiple nouns and adjectives.
8. Practice reverencing and ir-reverencing biblical texts and images.
9. Unpack traditional images of God and care giver.
10. Welcome unconscious images.

CARE PRAYER

O God of Infinite Images,

We pray that we might come to embrace you, who comes to us in the myriad metaphors of biblical story, in our imaginations, and in our encounters with one another. Keep us from staking too narrowly our claim to the richness and mystery of your holy ground as we engage in ministries of care. May we minister in and beyond the imaginable in many ways, trusting that you meet us there. Amen.

Chapter 4

Life at Opposite Ends of the Spectrum: Youth and Old Age

Dad's Story

My [Denise's] worst fears had been realized. My 86-year-old father, who had steadfastly refused to accept a home health-care aide or move to an assisted living facility, had fallen in his bedroom. Unable to get up, he remained on the floor for two nights and a day, forgetting the medical alert button around his neck. My mother, struggling with Alzheimer's, was in a nursing home, and I lived in another state. He was all alone. Luckily, when Meals on Wheels came to his door and there was no answer, they called me. The chain of events that followed led to his hospitalization, a brief stay in a rehab facility, and re-admittance to the hospital for surgery.

He never left the hospital the second time. After a month of rapid decline, he died. The day before his death, I had consulted with the nursing staff and, using my father's health-care proxy, authorized the removal of his feeding tubes and antibiotics. My 26-year-old son, Brian, looked me in the eye after my conversation with the staff and asked, "Mom, are you trying to get rid of Grampy because it's convenient?" I answered, "No, I'm trying to allow him to die a natural death."

• •

My son's question took my breath away, challenging both of us that afternoon to articulate in a lengthy conversation our views of living, aging, and dying. Exhausted from trips to upstate New York to tend to my parents while dealing with my son struggling to find his way after college,[1] I made space for this hard conversation. Hard conversations need to become a more natural part of intergenerational exchange. These conversations need not be limited to the end of life or to dialogue within a specific age group. Physicians also need to do better when it comes to engaging in hard conversations. A recent study has shown that only 37 percent of doctors told patients with advanced cancer how long they had to live, even if the patient asked for the information.[2] Lack of communication about prognosis and treatment options often prevents patients from engaging in meaningful life review and preparation for death.

Whatever our age, we all need to contemplate that we will die someday. Death is not optional. Ministries of care can support and encourage hard conversations that need to take place along life's journey. Care givers can help us see how our stage in life shapes our attitude toward these conversations. While talking with my son that afternoon, I was acutely aware of the health-care proxy I had recently given to both him and my daughter. I wanted to impress upon my son how important it was that he follow my wishes for a natural death, given what I had been witnessing in my parents' struggle. I acknowledged that both my son and I were grieving my father's decline. I also stated firmly that I would withdraw the proxy if he did not accept my position. The situation called for clarity and firmness, and a naming of the emotional currents present.

How to Cultivate Space for Hard Conversations
1. Look at death as part of life.
2. Recognize the resistance, but don't give in to it completely.

1. Along with 20 million other Americans, I (Denise) am part of "the sandwich generation," struggling to raise children while caring for an aging loved one. See The Pew Research Center report of 2005: "Baby Boomers: From the Age of Aquarius to the Age of Responsibility" (pewresearch.org). Statistics show that 71 percent of boomers have at least one living parent. One of eight Americans between the ages of 40 and 60 are sandwiched; 7 to 10 million adults are caring for aging parents from a long distance. See also the segment commissioned by MSNBC for Take 3 by Julie Winokur and her husband, Ed Kashi, documenting their cross-country move with their children to care for her elderly father: cbsnews.com/stories/2006/05/08/eveningnews/main16000179.shtml.

2. Sarah Harrington and Thomas Smith, "The Role of Chemotherapy at the End of Life," *Journal of the American Medical Association* 299, no. 22 (11 June 2008): 2667-78.

3. Allow for messiness, fear, defensiveness, imperfection.
4. Deal with old baggage.
5. Start with a trusted other if you can't engage everyone.
6. Practice what you want to say with uninvolved others.
7. Collect facts, consider options, gather forms (e.g., health-care proxy forms).[3]
8. Speak honestly; don't sugarcoat things.
9. Be open to an unknown conclusion, which may not happen in one sitting.
10. Anticipate unexpected feelings.

Questions for Reflection

- What are your intentions for your care in older adulthood? Have you personally acted upon these intentions by preparing wills, living trusts, assignments of durable power of attorney, and funeral arrangements? If not, why not?
- How has your church or faith community helped you with thinking about care in older adulthood? How might your church better deal with this issue?

Making Connections

If life is a journey of faith, then what can the old and the young on opposite ends of the life span learn from one another about living and dying together in community? Studies of aging and adolescence are often conducted in isolation from one another. While the generations of which we are a part significantly shape who we are and script us, we need to remember that "youth" and "old age" are general categories that cannot contain the vast complexity of human development. While the categories themselves may give us a snapshot of a generation, they can also inhibit the surprises inherent in actual encounters with living beings and their stories. There is no such thing as a monolithic understanding of the aged or of youth. We must de-categorize — that is, let the story lead — to avoid distancing and denigrating stereotypes of either group. Even the AARP no longer explains its acronym as standing

---

3. Consult an elder-care attorney or go online, for example, to usa.gov. Click on "seniors" and follow the appropriate prompts.

for the American Association of Retired Persons. The letters stand without explanation so that the organization cannot be pigeonholed and its diversity can challenge stereotypes.

Recognizing life as a process invites us to appreciate the rhythm and patterning of relationships along the life span. Marjorie Suchocki sketches the contours of a process theology of creation in which we receive from others; integrate what we receive into ourselves; and give back of ourselves to others and, indeed, to the whole universe.[4] This complex rhythm describes physical as well as psychic reality and must not be distorted by oversimplification. We can get stuck in places along the way, but even when we do, receiving, integrating, and giving back occur whether or not we are conscious of it. We make connections more easily remembering that we affect others and others affect us. That is the way God has constituted the world.

Biblical texts can help young and old connect with one another. Intergenerational Bible study can evoke new insights, debunk stereotypes, and uncover similarities for each generation. The metaphors in Psalm 17, for example, prompt surprise and emotional honesty across generations. In the section on enemies in verses 8-12, I (Denise) often ask participants to particularize the metaphors with their own experience: "hide me in the shadow of your wings, from . . . my deadly enemies who surround me. They close their hearts to pity. . . . They track me down; now they surround me. . . . They are like a lion eager to tear, like a young lion lurking in ambush."

When I ask, "Who are these enemies for you?" elderly people name adult children who monitor their decline in order to ship them off to a nursing home. Teens name parents who ground them when they arrive fifteen minutes late for curfew or perform poorly on a test. In this process teens and the elderly discover common cause against adults who are "out to get them." Young and old also come to recognize adults as "the sandwich generation" who are also engaged in their own struggles with "enemies": bosses who pressure them for results, teens who challenge them at every turn, and fearful parents who accuse them of not caring. Engaging in hard conversations around the Bible study table with a range of generations can create a space of gifted possibility.

---

4. Marjorie Suchocki, *Divinity and Diversity: A Christian Affirmation of Religious Pluralism* (Nashville: Abingdon Press, 2003).

QUESTIONS FOR REFLECTION
- How would you characterize relationships you have with elderly people and young people in your life?
- How might you strengthen those relationships?

The Verbing of Care

Intergenerational Bible study undercuts EDD, or "empathy deficit disorder," the inability "to step outside [our]selves and tune in to what other people experience."[5] EDD can create conflict and fuel communication failure. Empathy is not simply a feeling but includes a learned set of skills.[6] An empathetic imagination requires a willingness to set aside our own preoccupations and empty ourselves "to be fully present to the other."[7] Job's friends did this for him when they mirrored his behavior and sat with him in silence for seven days and nights (2:11-13; see Chapter One in this volume). God models empathy by receiving our prayers of lament, filled with doubt, questioning, and complaint, without becoming defensive or refusing to hear. We see an example in Psalm 77:8-9: "Has [God's] steadfast love ceased forever? Are [God's] promises at an end for all time? Has God forgotten to be gracious?" When Moses is called to lead the Israelites out of Egypt, God's empathy for their plight is expressed in a sweeping list of active verbs: "I have *observed* the misery of my people who are in Egypt; I have *heard* their cry on account of their

5. Douglas LaBier, "Empathy: Could It Be What You're Missing?" *The Washington Post*, 25 December 2007, sec. H, p. 5. LaBier argues that "empathy is what you feel when you enter the internal world of another person." Without abandoning your own perspective, you experience the other's emotions, conflicts, or aspirations. Empathy is not sympathy, which is an understanding of another's situation viewed through your own lens. Research shows that our capacity to feel what another feels is hard-wired through our neurons.

6. Michael S. Koppel, "Self Psychology and End of Life Pastoral Care," *Pastoral Psychology* 53, no. 2 (November 2004): 139-51.

7. Deborah van Deusen Hunsinger, "Paying Attention: The Art of Listening," *Christian Century*, 22 August 2006, p. 24. Hunsinger is the author of *Pray without Ceasing: Revitalizing Pastoral Care* (Grand Rapids: Wm. B. Eerdmans, 2006). According to Heinz Kohut, who distinguishes between intuition and empathy, empathy is the learned and skilled capacity to relate to the internal world of another person, to see into the inner landscape of another person's experience and to imagine what it might be like to inhabit this world. See *The Analysis of Self* (Madison, Wis.: International Universities Press, 1971), pp. 300-307.

taskmasters. Indeed, I *know*[8] their sufferings, and I have *come down* to deliver them from the Egyptians, and to *bring them up* out of that land to a good and broad land" (Exod. 3:7-8). For Christians, the Incarnation stands as the supreme example of God's empathy for humankind.

In the Exodus text, God models empathy in active verbs. God's relational connection with Israel teaches us about the relational nature of empathy, the reciprocal process of giving and receiving so that the other's heart is drawn up into one's own heart. Empathy reaches beyond simple sentimentalism to bold action that is decidedly other-focused and not self-centered. In Bible study, as we tell and receive, we create space for empathy and strengthen our love for one another. We learn to embody this love through practice of necessary skills and honing of intentional action.

As we remain fully present to another, we monitor our personal reactions while practicing three essential skills: accurate paraphrase, productive questioning, and perception check.[9] Since 93 percent of interpersonal communication may consist of the interpretation of nonverbal cues,[10] we cannot attend only to words. We must also consider tone of voice, facial expression, posture, and gestures that provide clues to another's feelings. In this connection, Jewish pastoral care givers cite Genesis 21:17, in which God is described as "hearing the voice of Ishmael *ba'aher hu sham*, exactly where he is. . . . The text does not mention that Ishmael has either spoken or cried. This offers us a model . . . for understanding more than is actually stated."[11] As good listeners, Christians can "participate in Christ's attentiveness"[12] and contribute to a dismantling of stereotypes that demean and block connection-making.

GROUP EXERCISE

Designate one end of the room "ten" and the other end "one." Ask the group to arrange themselves on a continuum from one to ten based upon their responses to these questions:

---

8. Walter Brueggemann suggests that God's actions show that "Israel is the object of God's intense attentiveness." See "The Book of Exodus," in *New Interpreter's Bible,* vol. 1 (Nashville: Abingdon Press, 1994), p. 712.

9. Hunsinger, "Paying Attention," p. 25.

10. Hunsinger, "Paying Attention," p. 29.

11. Rabbi Dayle Friedman, "Introduction," in *Jewish Pastoral Care: A Practical Handbook,* 2d ed., ed. Dayle Friedman (Woodstock, Vt.: Jewish Lights Publishing, 2005), p. xv.

12. Hunsinger, "Paying Attention," p. 30.

When it comes to listening to older people, I am open and receptive (ten) or reluctant and impatient (one).

When it comes to listening to younger people, I am open and receptive (ten) or reluctant and impatient (one).

I am good at reading body language (ten) or clueless about body language (one).

I meet difficult emotional topics head on (ten) or shy away from them (one).

Questions for Reflection

- What non-verbal clues are you aware of exhibiting when you listen to someone? List them.
- Which of these clues might be off-putting to another person? Which of these might be welcoming?
- How does love get "verbed" (expressed) between generations in your family? In your church?
- Where or with whom have you experienced meaningful empathic connection?

Lynn's Story

I [Michael] received a disturbing phone call during class. My mother, who had been otherwise fit and healthy, had gone to the emergency room of the local hospital and was eventually admitted for tests for what appeared to be a TIA (minor stroke). While in the hospital, she received a phone call from my sister's mother-in-law, who was herself under hospice care, dying from breast cancer that had resisted more than twenty years of treatment. Lynn wanted to know how my mother was doing, and said, "I hope you're going to be alright because I want Dylan [my nephew] to have at least one grandma."

•　　•

Lynn's gesture reached beyond personal well-being to a deep regard and hope for the next generation. In her dying days, Lynn was seeing to it, with the little energy she had left, that Dylan would be known and loved by an older woman. Lynn's story challenges stereotypes about the elderly. Youth and old people share the burden of being caricatured or stereotyped by images that are culturally constructed. Both groups are often labeled as self-centered, narcissistic, or self-preoccupied.[13] Life for older people may be diminishing temporally, physically, spatially, vocationally, financially, and/or relationally in a "constrictive process."[14] Self-preoccupation can be a result of diminished energy or constriction of environment. This does not necessarily mean, however, that one loses hope or becomes unhealthily narcissistic. Lynn's story certainly affirms an expanded awareness of life and pushes back against stereotypes of older people as self-preoccupied. Her concern was not for herself but for generations that would follow. Both young and old can teach us something valuable about positive self-regard, which needs to be nurtured throughout our lifetimes. Positive self-regard should be distinguished from unhealthy narcissism or narcissistic personality disorder, which is exhibited in a pervasive pattern of grandiosity, a need for admiration, and a lack of empathy for others.[15]

As human beings, we look at, look out for, and look for one another. New parents often assume that babies like to look at things and trinkets — mobiles, rattles, stuffed animals. But babies are far more fascinated with the human face than with these brightly colored objects.[16] We are hardwired before birth and in the formative stages of life to see and be seen by others. Some people, unfortunately, are not "seen" in their formative years. They do not receive "good-enough" care.[17] Some have experienced severe narcissistic injury, resulting from primary per-

13. See Trudy Bush, "Good Old Days?" *Christian Century*, 19 September 2006, pp. 30-33. Bush reviews three books on aging. One of them, George Valliant's *Aging Well: Surprising Guideposts to a Happier Life from the Harvard Study of Adult Development* (London: Little, Brown, 2002), maintains that conventional thinking links wisdom and spirituality with age and experience. Valliant's research challenges this assumption. He claims that old people tend to be narcissistic, move away from religion as they age, and become less dogmatic, especially the "fortunate old": those with health, means, and family support. Individual lifestyle choices are most important for "happy" aging.

14. *Aging, Death, and the Quest for Immortality*, ed. C. Ben Mitchell, Robert D. Orr, and Susan A. Salladay, The Horizons in Bioethics Series (Grand Rapids: Wm. B. Eerdmans, 2004), pp. 4-5.

15. *Diagnostic and Statistical Manual of Mental Disorders*, 4th ed. (Washington, D.C.: American Psychiatric Association, 1994), p. 658.

16. See Tracy Hogg, *The Baby Whisperer Solves All Your Problems* (New York: Atria Books, 2005), p. 84. My (Michael's) sister uses this book as a help for parenting my nephews, Dylan and Ryan.

17. This term is based on D. W. Winnicott's concept of "good-enough mothering." See Michael St. Clair, *Object Relations and Self Psychology: An Introduction* (Monterey, Calif.: Brooks/Cole, 1986), pp. 70-71.

sons (parents) being unable to relate meaningfully to them, affirm their sense of being, and call forth their highest aspirations. Such injured people can experience great difficulty in either receiving or giving empathic care to another person. They are desperate for the care they missed. Pastors can create a safe environment in which "a vulnerable, wounded person can begin to feel trust and move to a new relationship with God and others."[18]

Thus, "seeing" is both a real experience and a metaphor for narcissism. Narcissism is the dynamic energy of the self that seeks others to look up to, others to look at the self, and special friends to claim. Narcissism is a necessary component of healthy development. When we have experienced "good enough" care in our early years, when we have been sufficiently "seen" by people who matter to us, we are able to "see" ourselves and what we might become. We know our place in the broader community of relationships. We exhibit healthy narcissism, which provides the foundation and energy for moving competently and confidently out into our future. Lately, much of the popularized literature on narcissism reflects a misuse and misunderstanding of the term. It is too often seen negatively as self-centeredness and self-absorption.[19] Pastoral leaders can help by not perpetuating stereotypes of youth, old people, or narcissism. We all, young and old alike, need to be seen, admired, and affirmed for who we are. We need people who will mirror our selves to us. This affirmation can help to sustain healthy life ambition and assertiveness. These "mirroring" people can model for us ideals and values we can embody.

QUESTIONS FOR REFLECTION

- Do you remember your formative years as a time of "good-enough care"? If not, why not?
- Consider a time in your life when you were self-absorbed. Did you experience the affirmation of another who drew you out of yourself? How did this happen?

18. Michael S. Koppel, *Open-Hearted Ministry: Play as Key to Pastoral Leadership* (Minneapolis: Fortress Press, 2008), p. 49.

19. Narcissistic personality disorder is a clinical diagnosis determined by an experienced professional using criteria outlined in psychiatric and psychological literature. See *Diagnostic and Statistical Manual of Mental Disorders*, pp. 658-61.

Old Age

Our culture either demonizes or romanticizes old age. We honor the old as wise models for living or, more often than not, dismiss them as worn out and no longer useful. There is little room in our cultural thinking for anything in between. In his analysis of the Harvard Study of Adult Development, for example, George Valliant speaks of the elderly as the "happy well" and the "sad sick."[20] Sociologist William Sadler argues that our culture identifies aging with "D" words: decline, disease, depression, and decrepitude, to which Sally Palmer Thomason adds denial.[21] Carroll Saussy charges that "the stereotype persists of the old as finished, without enough energy to do much more than vegetate."[22] Tongue-in-cheek sarcasm that grudgingly acknowledges changes in aging is not much better. One newspaper columnist wrote recently about the sociological revolution that has banished the word *senior* from our vocabulary and given rise to "a new American icon: the frisky geezer."[23] Old age has been "redefined as a scientific problem" that must be medicalized and scientifically managed.[24] Body parts can be repaired and replaced.[25] The goal is "aging well" and "staying young" as long as one can.

Yet the reality is this: 65 million people in the United States today are 65 or older, equal to 12.4 percent of the population, or twelve times the number alive in 1900. By the year 2030, older adults over 64 will con-

20. Valliant, *Aging Well,* p. 211.

21. Sadler, quoted in Sally Palmer Thomason, *The Living Spirit of the Crone: Turning Aging Inside Out* (Minneapolis: Augsburg Fortress Press, 2006), p. 7.

22. Carroll Saussy, *The Art of Growing Old: A Guide to Faithful Aging* (Minneapolis: Augsburg Press, 1998), p. 67.

23. Joel Achenbach, "Senior Moment: The Rise of the Alpha Geezer," *The Washington Post,* 9 September 2007, sec. B, p. 3. As far as "geezer sex" is concerned, Achenbach quotes a recent University of Chicago study that reported 53 percent of Americans between the ages of 65 and 74 remain sexually active, along with 26 percent between 75 and 85, "despite the fact that 100 percent of their kids and grandkids would rather not picture it." Ha-ha.

24. Thomason, *The Living Spirit of the Crone,* p. 37.

25. See Sandra Boodman and Brenna Maloney, "Replaceable You," in the special section titled "Fifty Plus: Boomers Put 'Old on Hold'" at washingtonpost.com/wp-dyn/content/custom/2007/09/17/CU2007091701278.html. Boodman and Maloney discuss recent advances in repairing worn body parts — shoulders, knees, toes, and eyes. They report that 80 percent of older Americans are currently living with at least one chronic condition, and 25 million Americans have some type of medical implant such as an artificial knee, a pacemaker, or an eye lens. "Old" is assumed to be something to be avoided. See also Valliant, *Aging Well,* who repeatedly speaks of "successful aging."

stitute more than 21 percent of the population, or 68 million people.[26] Since old age may now cover a span of more than thirty years, we might more helpfully speak of the young old, ages 60 to 75; the middle old, ages 75 to 85; and the oldest old, 85 and older.[27] Longer life spans can be viewed as a positive development. Millions of well-educated baby boomers are entering "encore careers" in the second half of their working lives, seeking both "money and meaning."[28]

These statistics force us to consider "the longevity paradox" — that is, we have focused our resources and energy on "living longer rather than living better."[29] "Slow medicine," however, challenges "death by intensive care" and urges physicians and the elderly to be less aggressive about care, tests, and hospitalizations at the end of life. It has been reported that nine out of ten people who live past eighty will wind up unable to take care of themselves, either because of frailty or dementia.[30] This has led to a surge in cases of elder abuse, neglect, and financial exploitation.[31] Given reduced birthrates, widespread divorce, remarriage, geographic separation, fragmented families, and single-parent childbearing, we are "poised to usher in an era of uncertain obligation and complicated grief. . . . We will be dying much more alone."[32]

26. Thomason, *The Living Spirit of the Crone,* p. 28. The fastest-growing age group are those 100 years old and older. This growth is spurred by the decrease in infant mortality and infectious diseases, advances in medical diagnosis and treatment, better nutrition, and lower birthrates.

27. Karen D. Scheib, *Challenging Invisibility: Practices of Care with Older Women* (St. Louis: Chalice Press, 2004), p. 4. Thomason also notes the continual "barrage of anti-aging messages" in our culture that present aging "as a kind of pathology," which shapes the view that older women have of themselves (p. vii).

28. See Marc Freedman, "No Country for Old People: One More Time, with Meaning," *The Washington Post,* 27 January 2008, sec. B, pp. 1, 5.

29. See Marie-Therese Connolly, "No Country for Old People? A Hidden Crime," *The Washington Post,* 27 January 2008, sec. B, pp. 1, 4.

30. See Jane Gross, "Opting for 'Slow Medicine' in the Twilight Years," *International Herald Tribune,* 6 May 2008, p. 2. She quotes Tom Rosenthal, chief medical officer at UCLA, who suggests that "aggressive treatment for the elderly at acute care hospitals can be 'inhumane'; the culture has a built-in bias that everything that can be done will be done."

31. Connolly, "No Country for Old People?" sec. B, p. 4. A government study in 2002 reported that more than half of the nation's nursing homes are understaffed at harmful levels. One and a half million elderly people live in nursing homes, and ten million receive care at home, where lack of oversight cannot monitor elder abuse.

32. See Elizabeth Marquardt, "No Country for Old People: The New Alone," *The Washington Post,* 27 January 2008, sec. B, pp. 1-4.

QUESTIONS FOR REFLECTION

- What frightens you about growing old? What do you look forward to in aging?
- What do you enjoy about being old? What challenges you about being old?

Aging in the Hebrew Bible

The Hebrew Bible is also steeped in this dualistic view of old age. On the positive side, God is called "the Ancient of Days" in the book of Daniel (7:9, 13, 22). This ancient God seems to be especially interested in the old, as we see, for example, in Isaiah 46:4, in which God assures the exiles that "even to your old age I am he, even when you turn gray I will carry you. I have made, and I will bear; I will carry and will save." On the human level, "the association of advanced age with wisdom is made in Ugarit, Mesopotamia, Egypt, and Israel."[33] Often, "length of days" signifies God's blessing, as it does in Proverbs 16:31: "Gray hair is a crown of glory; it is gained in a righteous life" (see also Prov. 20:29). In Genesis 15:15, God promises Abraham that he will "be buried in a good old age." In Psalm 91:16, God declares of those who love God, "With long life I will satisfy them, and show them my salvation." Deuteronomy 5:16 offers a motivation for keeping the commandment to honor parents: "so that your days may be long." Ben Sira 3:6 in the Apocrypha eloquently echoes this view: "Those who respect their father will have long life." In 25:5 he asserts, "How attractive is wisdom in the aged, and understanding and counsel in the venerable." Ben Sira also supports the guilt of generational debt when he admonishes, "Remember that it was of your parents you were born; how can you repay what they have given you?"

Another positive view of the elderly is expressed in Leviticus 19:32: "You shall rise before the aged, and defer to the old; and you shall fear your God: I am the LORD." This verse is found in a distinct collection of priestly tradition called the Holiness Code, Leviticus 17–26, which outlines behaviors for Israel that reflect the holiness of God. Such behavior concerns not only the purity of religious practices, but also the

---

33. James L. Crenshaw, "Youth and Old Age in Qoheleth," in *Urgent Advice and Probing Questions: Collected Writings on Old Testament Wisdom* (Macon, Ga.: Mercer University Press, 1995), p. 535.

quality of social relationships and communal life. This respect bordering on reverence for old persons echoes concerns elsewhere for the weak, orphans, widows, and the defenseless, as we see, for example, in Isaiah 16-17; Amos 8:4-10; Psalm 146:7-9; and Deuteronomy 10:18-19.[34]

Rabbi Dayle Friedman suggests that one way to take Leviticus 19:32 seriously is to recognize the three challenges of aging: finding meaning in the wake of the accumulation of losses and "little deaths," dealing with time in the absence of routine, and handling disconnection and disjunction prompted by the death of friends and partners and by physical incapacity.[35] He suggests the "Mitzvah Model," which recognizes how each Jew is born into family and covenant and thereby bound to the *mitzvot* (ritual and ethical commandments given in the Torah and its interpretation). Regardless of age, each person is obligated to do as much as he or she can to fulfill the commandments. For example, if an older person can't recite a part of the synagogue service standing up, he or she can recite it sitting down. The "sliding scale" of *mitzvah* (singular, meaning "commandment") allows for adaptation. This flexibility empowers the elderly to contribute and to remain connected to community.[36]

Retirement home chaplains Ann Davie and Ruth Kent suggest adaptations for those missing a funeral. These "absentee memorial services" for residents unable to travel are condensed, fifteen-minute versions of memorial services held elsewhere at the same time, if that can be coordinated. Without musicians or prepared remarks, the chaplains create space for remembrance. A CD player is available for music selections. Davie and Kent also suggest short liturgies or blessings (e.g., a room blessing) for transitions such as moving into the retirement home, moving from independent to assisted living, and moving into a nursing unit. They also suggest marking transitions in mobility, such

---

34. See Walter Brueggemann, "Holiness," in *Reverberations of Faith: A Theological Handbook of Old Testament Themes* (Louisville: Westminster John Knox Press, 2002), pp. 98-100.

35. Rabbi Dayle Friedman, "Letting Their Faces Shine: Accompanying Aging People and Their Families," in *Jewish Pastoral Care*, pp. 344-74. Friedman works with a more literal translation of Leviticus 19:32 from Danny Siegel: "You shall rise before [elders] and allow the beauty, glory, and majesty of their faces to emerge" (p. 344).

36. Friedman, "Letting Their Faces Shine," p. 348. Obligations are categorized: Torah, Avodah (worship/service of God), and *gemilut chasadim* (deeds of charity, loving-kindness) are likened to the pillars on which the world stands (*Pirke Avot*, 1.2); see p. 351.

as moving to the full-time use of a wheelchair, with a chair blessing. In addition, they suggest blessing at the time of removing life-support systems.[37]

A QUESTION FOR REFLECTION

- What other adaptations can you suggest for the elderly in your church or faith community?

Honorific views of the old in the Hebrew Bible are countered by other texts, such as 1 Kings 1:1, which describes the mighty King David as "old and advanced in years; and although they covered him with clothes, he could not get warm." His servants attempt to remedy the situation by bringing him the beautiful young virgin Abishag, "but the king did not know her sexually" (1 Kings 1:4). This intentionally pitiful picture contrasts with the virile young King David and his women: Abigail (1 Sam. 25:3) and Bathsheba (2 Sam. 11:2).[38] The contrast underscores David's physical and political impotence, and sets the stage for Solomon's bloody transition to power. Solomon's son, Rehoboam, rejects the advice of his father's older counselors in favor of the advice given by the young men who had grown up with him. This decision results in the revolt of the northern kingdom, Israel, against Rehoboam's rule (1 Kings 12:1-24). Old, blind Isaac is tricked by his son Jacob and his wife, Rebekah, into blessing Jacob instead of Esau (Gen. 27:1-40). This was clearly a case of elder abuse. The fear of being abandoned in old age is expressed in Psalm 71:9: "Do not cast me off in the time of old age; do not forsake me when my strength is spent" (see also v. 18).

Other Hebrew Bible texts challenge the inevitability of the connection between age and wisdom. Psalm 119:99-100 boldly declares to God,

---

37. Ann Davie and Ruth Kent are Master of Divinity graduates of Wesley Theological Seminary and chaplains at Ingleside Home of Rock Creek in Washington, D.C. See their article in the February 2008 Ingleside newsletter titled "Are You Missing a Funeral?"

38. Choon-Leong Sow, "The First and Second Books of Kings," in *New Interpreter's Bible,* vol. 3 (Nashville: Abingdon Press, 1999), p. 14. Sow notes that the list of David's wives and sons in 2 Samuel 3:2-5 echoes the narrator's comment in 2 Samuel 3:1: "David grew stronger and stronger, while the house of Saul became weaker and weaker." Note also 1 Kings 1:2 on Abishag: "and let her wait on the king, and let her be his attendant; let her lie in your bosom." This is a clear allusion to Nathan's parable of the ewe lamb in 2 Samuel 12:3 as a metaphor for Bathsheba: "she used to lie in his bosom."

"I have more understanding than all my teachers, for your decrees are my meditation. I understand more than the aged, for I keep your precepts." In Job 32:6, 9-10, the young Elihu reveals some tensions between youth and the aged: "I am young in years, and you are aged; therefore I was timid and afraid to declare my opinion to you. . . . It is not the old that are wise, nor the aged that understand what is right. Therefore I say, 'Listen to me; let me also declare my opinion.'" 2 Maccabees 4:40 argues that an old man is advanced in years and folly. Ben Sira, who acknowledges the ambiguities in life, venerates old age, but also observes, "O death, how welcome is your sentence to one who is needy and failing in strength, worn down by age and anxious about everything. Do not fear death's decree for you" (Sir. 41:2-3a).

Culture and Aging

American culture echoes the Hebrew Bible's ambivalence about growing old. Our dualistic attitude toward the old is especially true for old women. Remember in this connection Rush Limbaugh's widely quoted rhetorical question about Hillary Clinton as president: Do Americans want to watch a woman grow old in the White House before their eyes?[39] In 2001, women made up 58 percent of the population over 60 and 70 percent of the population over 85.[40] Karen Scheib argues that old women are invisible in our culture. We judge who is old by looking at the body, and the visual cues we recognize are evaluated by means of culturally shaped assumptions.[41] People in what I (Denise) call our "Botox culture" spend billions of dollars each year to fight the effects of aging with creams and surgery. Wrinkles betray our age and must be banished. If we cannot maintain the facade of youth, we turn the wise old woman into the little old lady — sweet, proper, non-confrontational, or into the grandmother — nurturing, sacrificial, self-denying. Her opposite is the shrew — complaining, bitter, and selfish. Other stereotypes are operative

---

39. See this Web site: www.rushlimbaugh.com/home/daily/site_122007/content/01125108.guest.html. December 20, 2007.

40. Thomason, *The Living Spirit of the Crone*, p. 28.

41. Scheib, *Challenging Invisibility*, p. 30. Thomason, in *The Living Spirit of the Crone*, speaks of "enculturated habits of word usage" that convey meanings of which we are not aware as we enter into a "consensus trance" in which we unconsciously accept and act on something as true. For example, old women may protest, "But I don't feel old" (p. 5).

for older black women. "The mammy" takes care of white children, and "Jezebel" expresses an aggressive sexuality.[42]

In the Hebrew Bible, women are defined by the men in their lives — brothers, fathers, and husbands. An identity crisis emerges when old women can no longer conceive or contribute to the household economy as they once did. In the book of Ruth, for example, a bitter Naomi loses her husband and two sons. She laments her fate and defines herself in terms of the relationships she no longer has: wife and mother: "Turn back, my daughters. . . . Do I still have sons in my womb that they may become your husbands? Turn back, . . . for I am too old to have a husband" (Ruth 1:11-12). When Naomi returns from her sojourn in Moab, the shocked women of Bethlehem exclaim, "Is this Naomi?" (Ruth 1:19). Apparently, appearance mattered then, just as it does for women today. Perhaps Naomi expresses her "disillusionment with a world that calls itself godly and then throws old women away"[43] when she responds, "Call me no longer Naomi ["pleasant"], call me Mara ["bitter"]" (1:20). Because widows occupy such a precarious position in the Bible, Israel is repeatedly urged to care for them, as in Deuteronomy 10:14-19, Jeremiah 49:11, and Psalm 68:5. Widows relied on public charity to survive.

In relation to cultural scripts for aging, we either play the part or play against it. Adopting a script shapes not only our actions but our reactions to the response of others to us. This observation became clear when our class engaged in a small-group exercise spurred by a question for reflection in Carroll Saussy's *The Art of Growing Old*.[44] Two separate groups of students responded to this question: "Think for a moment about an old person you have known personally or through the media who has been particularly inspiring to you. What adjectives would you use to describe this person?" Saussy had introduced this question to elicit positive images of aging. She hoped to counter a list of negative

---

42. Scheib, *Challenging Invisibility*, pp. 30-35. Thomason, in *The Living Spirit of the Crone*, p. vii, notes the derivation of *crone*. She was seen positively as an ancient holy one or pejoratively as a worn-out old horse.

43. Joan Chittister, *The Story of Ruth: Twelve Moments in Every Woman's Life* (Grand Rapids: Wm. B. Eerdmans, 2000), p. 32. Chittister argues that "without Naomi — her wisdom, her strength, her determination — Ruth was nothing but a possibility waiting to happen" (p. 31). I (Denise) don't agree with this assessment. It is Ruth who sets in motion the rescue of both of them by offering to glean. Chittister astutely observes that as we attempt to cover up the signs of aging, we suggest that "being a Barbie doll is a woman's goal in life, a stage that, once passed, must never be noted for fear the game [will] be up."

44. Saussy, *The Art of Growing Old*, p. 72.

cultural stereotypes of the old: finished, physically unattractive, burdensome, and ready for discarding. We argue that juxtaposing such starkly polar images leaves out the vast majority of old people who live somewhere in the middle. The negative is countered by a romanticized opposite, just as "the person with disabilities is either divinely blessed or damned: the defiled evildoer or the spiritual superhero."[45]

The two student groups differed in their responses. Group A listed these adjectives: feisty, wise, determined, hip, physically fit, compassionate, hard-working, authentic, matriarchal, rich in spirit, full of laughter, bawdy, affirming, earthy, interested in partying (a "party animal"), and able to make others relevant. Group B listed these adjectives: dignified, humble, quiet, engaged, able to reach out, honest, grounded, able to laugh, connected, positive, tough, alive, wise, and creative. The two groups conducted themselves differently. One was quiet, the other boisterous, reflecting not only the personalities of the group but of the old people who had shaped them. Perhaps these groups had projected themselves into the future by crafting in their own image views of the old person they had chosen. However, the space that both groups constructed for the living of old age was a constricted one. The "scripts" revealed by their lists of adjectives didn't allow for uninspiring moments in these older persons' lives. Clearly, these students had romanticized their elders and put them on a pedestal.

GROUP EXERCISE

Hold a hand mirror up to your face. What do you see? Describe it.
  Does your description point to a cultural "script" that you
  have consciously or unconsciously accepted?
How do you challenge the cultural scripts in your life?

The Koan of Life

Ecclesiastes 11:7–12:8

Light is sweet, and it is pleasant for the eyes to see the sun.
Even those who live many years should rejoice in them all;
  yet let them remember that the days of darkness will be many.

45. Nancy L. Eiesland, *The Disabled God: Toward a Liberatory Theology of Disability* (Nashville: Abingdon Press, 1994), p. 70.

All that comes is vanity.
Rejoice, young man, while you are young,
    and let your heart cheer you in the days of your youth.
Follow the inclination of your heart and the desire of your eyes,
    but know that for all these things
    God will bring you into judgment.
Banish anxiety from your mind, and put away pain from your body;
    for youth and the dawn of life are vanity.
Remember your creator in the days of your youth,
    before the days of trouble come,
    and the years draw near when you will say,
    "I have no pleasure in them";
    before the sun and the light and the moon and the stars are
      darkened
    and the clouds return with the rain.
In the day when the guards of the house tremble,
    and the strong men are bent,
    and the women who grind cease working because they are few,
    and those who look through the windows see dimly;
when the doors on the street are shut,
    and the sound of the grinding is low,
    and one rises up at the sound of a bird,
    and all the daughters of song are brought low;
when one is afraid of heights,
    and terrors are in the road;
    the almond tree blossoms,
    the grasshopper drags itself along and desire fails;
because all must go to their eternal home,
    and the mourners will go about the streets;
before the silver cord is snapped,
    and the golden bowl is broken,
    and the pitcher is broken at the fountain,
    and the wheel broken at the cistern,
    and the dust returns to the earth as it was,
    and the breath returns to God who gave it.
Vanity of vanities, says the Teacher; all is vanity.

In an improvisational moment in the class that we (Michael and I) taught together, we invited the class to read this text aloud in unison.

Since the Bible gives no stage directions for this kind of speaking, we were surprised by the results. Without being cued, we slowed down as we spoke together, and our mood became more somber. The intensity of our experience suggested a koan in Zen tradition. A koan is an eternal paradox, akin to a complex mental riddle that cannot be solved in one sitting, or with the rational mind alone — for example, What is the sound of one hand clapping? We might grapple with its meaning for years, or we might grasp its meaning in a flash. Both old and young alike can grasp — and be grasped by — the awareness that the koan evokes. A koan demands a "working on" and "working out" of a spiritual truth. In this case, we were unraveling the reality of aging and death. The class felt a solidarity in our speaking the text; an encounter with aging and death united us across the age spectrum. We learned in our communal speaking of this text that old age is not only a personal koan but also a communal or human koan. This communal koan serves as a powerful check on our tendencies to either elevate or denigrate old age — or youth, for that matter.

In our joint speaking, we embraced the stark reality of aging and its inevitability. We understood in this speaking that Ecclesiastes "clung to the realistic description of the aging process but let go of the conviction that the best years in life accompanied white hair."[46] The necessary context for understanding 12:1-8 comes in 11:7-10. "Rejoice, young man, while you are young, and let your heart cheer you in the days of your youth" (v. 9). The juxtaposition of youth and old age highlights the need to seize the day and makes the deterioration of old age more poignant and gripping. We are warned to get the message because "the days of darkness [literally, "badness"] will be many" (v. 8). Ecclesiastes characterizes old age negatively: lack of sexual activity ("desire fails"; 12:5); disturbed sleep ("one rises up at the sound of a bird"; 12:4); lost teeth ("the women who grind cease working because they are few"; 12:3); and failing eyesight ("those who look through the windows see dimly"; 12:3).[47]

While the opening poem of Ecclesiastes describes the unending cycles in the world of nature, the closing poem "describes the undoing and cessation of the individual life, which is the world to that per-

46. Crenshaw, "Youth and Old Age in Qoheleth," p. 538.

47. Crenshaw, in "Youth and Old Age in Qoheleth," argues that these images can be seen in terms of describing the activities on an estate, allegorically (grinding refers to teeth) or literally. However one approaches this text, "there is nothing pleasant about old age and death" (p. 543).

son."[48] The poem concludes (12:8) where the book began (1:2): "all is vanity." As Michael Fox argues, Ecclesiastes is not simply communicating information about aging and death. "*How* a poem means belongs to *what* it means. . . . He [Qohelet] makes us go through a challenging and uncertain process of reading, and that process will presumably have effects beyond the conveyance of information."[49] Our class learned this in our communal reading of the text. "We see our own death, and Qohelet will not let us turn away."[50]

SMALL-GROUP EXERCISE
- Read Ecclesiastes 11:7–12:8 out loud together (using the same Bible translation). Discuss your reactions to the experience.

CARE PRAYER
O Cycle of Life,

We bring to you all of what our aging is, and that we want our aging to be. We come filled with fear, denial, disconnects, and romantic visions. Help us to accept the complexities and confusing realities of growing old, so that we may create a space for authentic living and ministering in your name. May we live in the tension that permeates aging as we struggle for blessing. Amen.

Youth

Just as the old do not form a monolith, so too the young defy homogenizing labels. The young include children (six to twelve years old), early adolescents (twelve to fifteen), middle and late adolescents (fifteen to twenty), and young adults (those between the ages of twenty and thirty),[51] each group with different needs and perspectives. Cultural

---

48. Michael V. Fox, *A Time to Tear Down and A Time to Build Up: A Rereading of Ecclesiastes* (Grand Rapids: Wm. B. Eerdmans, 1999), p. 320. Contra Crenshaw, Fox understands the closing poem as descriptive of communal mourning on the day of a funeral. 12:1-7 is one long sentence kicked off by the imperative "remember" (v. 1a), followed by three complex temporal ("before") clauses describing the time limit of the "remembering." Fox speaks of three ways to read vv. 1-7: literally, symbolically, and allegorically (p. 333).

49. Fox, *A Time to Tear Down and A Time to Build Up*, p. 333.

50. Fox, *A Time to Tear Down and A Time to Build Up*, p. 349.

51. Sharon Daloz Parks, *Big Questions, Worthy Dreams: Mentoring Young Adults in Their*

confusion about when we become adults cautions against using only chronology as a boundary marker. Demarcations between life stages can vary. To complicate matters, "while all parts of America are aging, we are experiencing a selective 'younging' in this country" among racial and ethnic groups; children under five in these groups make up the majority of the under-five population in twelve states.[52]

Just as the elderly have been romanticized or demonized, so too have children, John Wall argues.[53] He outlines three different approaches to children in the Christian moral tradition. The "bottom-up" approach draws on Jesus' declaration in Mark 10:14-15: "Let the little children come to me. . . . Truly I tell you, whoever does not receive the kingdom of God as a little child will never enter it" (cf. Matt. 18:3; John 3:3-5). In this approach, children are "the purest and most immediate 'image of God' in the world, to which adults should aspire in their hope to become 'children of God.'"[54] Sentimentalized as pure and good, children in America are in effect marginalized from the corrupt public sphere. This allows "the wealthiest country in the world, the United States, to romanticize children in politics and mass media while denying them guaranteed health insurance (unlike in any other developed country)."[55]

The "top-down" Christian tradition toward children views them as embodiments of sin who require discipline, particularly because of the erosion of the social order. Basically, ". . . children must be socialized *into* morality because they lack an intrinsic moral sense of their own."[56]

Search for Meaning, Purpose, and Faith (San Francisco: Jossey-Bass, 2000). Parks argues that young adults fall in the seventeen to thirty-year-old range. Development theory usefully charts general patterns of psychological and biological progression in human life, but these patterns ought not to be confused with the experiences of actual persons or with rigid chronological segments.

52. William Frey, a demographer quoted in "Update," The Lewis Center for Church Leadership, Wesley Theological Seminary, 14 May 2008. See lewiscenter@wesleyseminary .edu.

53. John Wall, "Human Rights in Light of Children: A Christian Childist Perspective," *The Journal of Pastoral Theology* 17, no. 1 (Spring 2007): 54-67.

54. Wall, "Human Rights in Light of Children," p. 56.

55. Wall, "Human Rights in Light of Children," p. 57. This bottom-up view has been espoused by Origen, Tertullian, Gregory of Nyssa, Chrysostom, Rousseau, and Schleiermacher.

56. Wall, "Human Rights in Light of Children," p. 58. This view is embraced by Paul in the New Testament, and also by Plato, Augustine, Calvin, Luther, and Kant.

A third approach to children is dialectical or developmental. It honors children's inherent natural potential to become developed adults.[57] In this view, children are "owed" health care and education so that they may develop into good adult citizens.

A QUESTION FOR REFLECTION
- Which of the three approaches to children listed above do you embrace? Why?

Wisdom's Constriction of Children

The Wisdom tradition in the Ancient Near East embraces both the top-down tradition and the developmental tradition. Proverbs 6:20, 23-24 illustrates the former: "My child, keep your father's commandment, and do not forsake your mother's teaching. . . . For . . . the reproofs of discipline are the way of life, to preserve you . . . from the smooth tongue of the adulteress." Proverbs 22:6 expresses the latter: "Train children in the right way, and when old, they will not stray." The larger worldview of Wisdom thinking easily encompasses these two traditions. The Wisdom tradition is inherently conservative, optimistic, pragmatic, and traditional.[58] The sages, or wise men of the Wisdom tradition, searched for ways to ensure well-being for the individual, make sense of adversity, and transmit this knowledge to the next generation. Their goal to find and live in harmony with God-given order fueled their search. Propriety, therefore, took center stage in the Wisdom worldview — that is, the idea that there is "the right time and place for each deed or word."[59] So, for example, Proverbs 12:18 declares, "Rash words are like sword thrusts, but the tongue of the wise brings healing." The sages taught the young to embrace their parents' legacy of restraint so that their character would be formed in an orderly way. The older generation attempted to convince the next that rocking the boat was not allowed.

The proverb, a short, pithy saying that sums up how life works, served as one of the primary vehicles for the transmission of this leg-

---

57. Wall, "Human Rights in Light of Children," pp. 58-59. Aristotle, Aquinas, and Locke espouse this view.

58. James L. Crenshaw, *Old Testament Wisdom: An Introduction* (Louisville: Westminster John Knox Press, 1998), p. 3.

59. Crenshaw, *Old Testament Wisdom*, p. 11.

acy. Proverbs often embodied the Wisdom theme of the "Two Ways," also called the idea of act/consequence, or "You get what you deserve."[60] Proverbs 13:9, for example, expresses this theme: "The light of the righteous rejoices, but the lamp of the wicked goes out" (cf. Ps. 1:6). Wisdom thinking is generally optimistic. If one observes the way life unfolds, one can act in harmony with the God-given order in the world and thereby prosper. Righteousness is rewarded. Contrast this optimism with the pessimism and sarcasm of today's bumper stickers, such as "The one who dies with the most toys wins."

Wisdom's worldview has sometimes been co-opted by proof-texting in order to promote children's unquestioning obedience through corporal punishment. We can see this approach in *To Train Up a Child* by Michael and Debi Pearl.[61] The Pearls quote Proverbs 13:24 — "Those who spare the rod hate their children, but those who love them are diligent to discipline them" — and Proverbs 22:6 (see above) as the basis for what one critic terms "punitive Christian parenting" that "undermines the priority of God's grace."[62] Some blame American culture, particularly advertising, music, and the media, for fostering the growth of out-of-control children.[63] Others counter that these aspects of culture "have become easy scapegoats in a culture that does not want to

60. Denise Dombkowski Hopkins, *Journey through the Psalms*, rev. and exp. ed. (St. Louis: Chalice Press, 2002), chapter 4.

61. Michael and Debi Pearl, *To Train Up a Child* (Orange, Calif.: Gospel Truth Ministries, 1994). The Pearls note that training children is similar to what the Amish do when they train stubborn mules.

62. Beth Felker Jones, "Spanking Away Sin," *Christian Century*, 1 May 2007, pp. 8-9. Jones argues that "the pursuit of flawless children is a cruel sort of domestic idolatry. Children are a gift from God, not a battlefield" (p. 8).

63. See Lillian Daniel, "Kid Stuff: Raising Children in a Consumer Culture," *Christian Century*, 11 January 2005, pp. 22-27. Daniel reviews three books about children in American society. She summarizes Susan Linn's *Consuming Kids: The Hostile Takeover of Childhood* (New York: New Press, 2004). Linn argues, "It's not just that our kids are consuming. They are being consumed" (p. 22). Daniel also takes a look at Gary Cross's *The Cute and the Cool: Wondrous Innocence and Modern American Children's Culture* (Oxford: Oxford University Press, 2004). Cross describes "cute" children who are showered with material things by adults hoping to recover the consumer innocence they have lost. They become "cool" children who are jaded consumers. The third book that Daniel reviews is Karen Sternheimer's *It's Not the Media: The Truth about Pop Culture's Influence on Children* (Boulder, Colo.: Westview Press, 2004). Sternheimer argues that our cultural focus on children being manipulated by the media frees us from confronting the real problem of adults being manipulated by the media.

address more complicated issues."[64] One psychologist observes that instilling respect has become "a lost art" because "helicopter [read "hovering"] egalitarian parents" have produced "over-parented and under-disciplined children" who are overly praised and thin-skinned and don't help around the house.[65]

Wisdom thinking's traditionalism and focus on legacy can provide the sense of belonging, the sense of meaning, and the challenge to competence that young adults crave.[66] Yet this traditionalism can also suffocate the "recomposing"[67] that young adults must do to make this meaning their own. Young adults recompose by discovering the limits of inherited or socially received assumptions about how life works. This recomposing is best fostered by adult mentors and institutions that exhibit "hospitality, commitment, and courage."[68] Jacob begins his recomposing in Genesis 27 when he goes to the opening *(petach)* of the tent of his father, Isaac, to fool him into thinking he is Esau. Norman Cohen argues that in doing so, Jacob leaves the safety of his relationship with his mother and passes through a liminal space of change. "He figuratively leaves his mother's womb and enters the real world of engagement with others, which demands that he remove his protective 'skins' and confront who he is at his core."[69] Just like Jacob, young

---

64. See Sternheimer, *It's Not the Media,* quoted in Daniel, "Kid Stuff," p. 23.

65. Patricia Dalton, "A Lost Art: Instilling Respect," *The Washington Post,* 11 September 2007, sec. F, pp. 1, 5.

66. Carol E. Lytch, *Choosing Church* (Louisville: Westminster John Knox Press, 2004), p. 25. Social relationships, especially peer-group relationships, help to create a sense of belonging. Clergy leaders who were respected by youth were "more humble than arrogant, . . . vulnerable instead of perfect" (p. 31), not the wise parents dispensing instruction in the Wisdom tradition. Yet in Lytch's study teens were divided about open-ended Sunday school discussions; some desired more definitive guidance about complex issues (p. 39). Teens were attracted to high goals, standards of excellence, demands worthy of their attention, and rites of passage in church (p. 40). See also "A Portrait of 'Generation Next,'" Pew Center for the People and the Press, http://people-press.org/report/300/a-portrait-of-generation-next.

67. Parks, *Big Questions, Worthy Dreams,* pp. 5-8.

68. Parks, *Big Questions, Worthy Dreams,* p. 8. Parks worries that mentoring has been weakened in our society. See Diane Thielfoldt and Devon Scheef, "Generation X and the Millennials: What You Need to Know about Mentoring the New Generations," *Law Practice Today* (August 2004).

69. Norman Cohen, *Hineini in Our Lives: Learning How to Respond to Others through Fourteen Biblical Texts and Personal Stories* (Woodstock, Vt.: Jewish Lights Publishing, 2003), pp. 40-41. Jacob's entry into Isaac's tent "signals his achieving full personhood: . . . when

adults encounter the ups and downs of fear and trust when they engage in this kind of "struggled knowing."[70] When Jacob enters Isaac's tent and calls out, "My father," Isaac, like a good mentor, responds "Here I am" *(hineini)*. "Such is the risk of *hineini*," Cohen says. "When we are willing to be vulnerable by being open and responsive, we can never be sure what kind of response we will receive in return."[71]

GROUP EXERCISE

Develop a list of proverbs that sum up your thinking about children and youth today. Create a proverb wall out of your pooled lists.

The conflict generated by analyzing received traditions and assumptions in the recomposing process parallels that found in the clash between core testimony and countertestimony. The tension between the two "belongs to the character and substance of Old Testament faith, a tension that precludes and resists resolution."[72] This tension evaporates when the Two Ways of Wisdom thinking becomes a formula that denies experience, as the innocent Job argued against his accusing "friends" in Job 9:22: "It is all one, therefore I say, [God] destroys both the blameless and the wicked." Ecclesiastes picks up this theme when he comments about the wise and fools: "Yet I perceived that the same fate befalls all of them" (2:14). Much of Wisdom thinking expresses core testimony. Job and Ecclesiastes, however, challenge it with countertestimony based on their own experience.

As young adults recompose, they can offer hope for the future with their fresh perspectives, cultural awareness, energy, and creativity. Dwindling North American mainline churches especially need this hope. They have suffered "a serious and sustained decline" in the number of clergy under the age of thirty-five. In many denomina-

---

we engage with others in our lives, especially those with whom we are closest, we have the chance to discover ourselves" (p. 43).

70. Parks, *Big Questions, Worthy Dreams*, p. 20.

71. Cohen, *Hineini in Our Lives*, p. 38. Cohen argues that we must be "willing to pay this price for the possibility of establishing a meaningful relationship with another human being." This risk does not guarantee a good relationship. Sometimes we "simply cannot recognize those ostensibly closest to us because of how they have responded to us."

72. Brueggemann, *Theology of the Old Testament* (Minneapolis: Fortress Press, 1997), p. 400. One moves back and forth between these two faith postures.

tions, the percentage of younger clergy is less than 5 percent. Young clergy, ironically, seem "particularly well-suited to the task of church planting."[73]

President Barack Obama spoke during his campaign of the energizing influence of the "millennials"[74] (the generation born between 1981 and 2002) on the boomer generation (those born between 1946 and 1964). He likened the difference between the two groups to that of the "Moses generation" that led the children of Israel out of slavery and the "Joshua generation" that established the kingdom of Israel. The former were the idealists and the latter were the builders.[75] To understand better the generations of today in our churches, we would do well to review the formative events that shaped them differently and the characteristics that mark them. Pastoral leaders can facilitate this review in a multigenerational group by creating space for sharing what resonates and what irritates about each generation's description. In this way, people of all ages can get to know one another in the church.[76] Bible study can be offered around common interests rather than age groups or life stages.[77]

GROUP EXERCISE

Pair up with a partner of a different generation than you. Generate a list of adjectives to describe your generation, and a list of ad-

73. See "Clergy Age Trends in the United Methodist Church, 1985-2007," a Lewis Center for Church Leadership Report by Lovett Weems Jr. and Ann Michel, 2008, www.churchleadership.com/research/um_clergy_age_trends08.htm, p. 2.

74. See Neil Howe and William Strauss, *Millennials Rising: The Next Great Generation* (New York: Vintage Books, 2000). Howe and Strauss coined the term. Millennials comprise more than 81 million people in the United States. They have mastered technology and are socially conscious.

75. Morley Winograd and Michael Hais, "The Boomers Had Their Day. Make Way for the Millennials," *The Washington Post*, 3 February 2008, sec. B, p. 1. Millennials are consensus-builders who vote and want to strengthen the political system, much like the GI generation after World War II. Boomers were and are highly divided idealists unwilling to compromise.

76. Edward Hammett with James Pierce, *Reaching People under Forty While Keeping People over Sixty: Being Church for All Generations* (St. Louis: Chalice Press, 2007), p. 43. See chapter 3, "When Generations Collide," and their description of the Builders or the GI Generation (born 1920-1946), the Boomers (1946-1964), the Busters or Generation X (1965-1983), and the Millennials (1984-).

77. Hammett and Pierce, *Reaching People under Forty While Keeping People over Sixty*, p. 150.

jectives to describe your partner's generation. Then share your lists and note the similarities and differences in them. What surprised you?

Interruption

Whereas the Wisdom tradition seeks stability, an "interruption" approach intentionally rocks the boat. According to Dana Fewell, "interruption is a way of stopping and questioning the text" rather than accepting a smooth, unquestioned transmission of it.[78] Interruption rejects passivity in reading and demands that we question and imagine the story told differently, with the result that we live our lives differently. In this way, "interruption is a strategy for both reading and living."[79] Fewell reads with interruption on behalf of the children in the world who are victims of abuse and civil war, who confront violence daily, and who recognize it when they see it in the Bible. I (Denise) own a slogan button that sums up the intent of interruption: "If you're not enraged, you're not paying attention." Fewell's way of reading allows the subject of children "to reconfigure what is at stake in the biblical text."[80] She points, for example, to the story of Noah's Ark as a story that invites interruption. Though it is a favorite children's theme expressed in toys and nursery art (I — Denise — still display the ark print that hung in my children's nursery for years), we must ask about the "innocent victims washed away by the text's own rhetoric."[81] We must ask why Noah failed to argue with God on behalf of the innocent. In her study of children and poverty, Pamela Couture links the traditional care practices of presence and conversation with action on behalf of the most vulnerable.[82] We must aslso ask why Noah did not invite people to repent to avert the Flood.

---

78. Dana Fewell, *The Children of Israel: Reading the Bible for the Sake of Our Children* (Nashville: Abingdon Press, 2003), p. 33.

79. Fewell, *The Children of Israel,* p. 34.

80. Fewell, *The Children of Israel,* p. 24. Fewell argues that the text becomes the "living space" (Emmanuel Levinas) in which we encounter ourselves and others and come to see ourselves and others in a new way. Liminality (the experience of being in between) permeates this space, which is full of vulnerability and risk.

81. Fewell, *The Children of Israel,* p. 29.

82. Pamela Couture, *Seeing Children, Seeing God: A Practical Theology of Children and Poverty* (Nashville: Abingdon Press, 2000).

From the pastoral side, we can consider children as the "second center" who disrupt or de-center society and call for its reshaping. John Wall calls this a fourth approach to children: the "circular" or "transformative" approach. Children's rights derive from Genesis 1:26-27. Created in God's image, they incarnate God in the world. Children remind us of society's creativity by their "capabilities for play and pretend" and their "energetic imagination" that finds wonder in the surrounding world. "Children are not little adults [top-down], non-adults [bottom up], or merely developing adults [developmental] but socially generative human beings."[83] Pastoral leaders can build on the gifts and imagination of childhood by encouraging the whole church community to develop and practice an attitude and posture of creative play.[84]

Real Care

What Michael and I call real care neither idealizes nor denigrates young people, but respects them in their full dignity as persons. Consider the influences of stereotyping. Patricia Davis explores how the cultural stereotype of "niceness" harms adolescent girls by limiting adults' experience of their genuine spirituality and personhood. "Nice" is a label that constricts genuine relationship as it interferes with being able to listen carefully to the complex lived experience of girls.[85] A study of the spiritual development of adolescent boys from the ages of eleven to fourteen shows how the negative stereotypes of boys as losers, loners, and rebels can adversely affect their spirituality in later life.[86]

Listening to our own stories of youth and adolescence can be instructive for ministry with others. Honoring the push and pull — that is, what impelled us and called us as youth, however positive or negative we may now view it — serves a vital function in ministry with young

83. Wall, "Human Rights in Light of Children," pp. 62, 64.

84. See Koppel, *Open-Hearted Ministry*.

85. Patricia Davis, *Beyond Nice: The Spiritual Wisdom of Adolescent Girls* (Minneapolis: Fortress Press, 2001). Davis reports on interviews with more than a hundred girls about the meaning of God, their churches, sexuality and embodiment, and violence. See also Kristen Leslie, *When Violence Is No Stranger: Pastoral Counseling with Survivors of Acquaintance Rape* (Minneapolis: Fortress Press, 2003).

86. Robert C. Dykstra, Allan Hugh Cole Jr., and Donald Capps, *Losers, Loners, and Rebels: The Spiritual Struggles of Boys* (Louisville: Westminster John Knox Press, 2007).

adults. Many youth tend to separate the positive aspects of their experience from the negative, telling them as distinct stories.[87] Communities of care can build trust so that the different strands of the youth narrative can be held together as youth gather up and carry forth a sense of their God-given and God-called selves.

Questions for Reflection

- How can we make space in our families, our churches, and our communities for children to shape the world around them and discover its wonder? What do we do that erodes this space?
- What other biblical texts can you think of that need to be read with interruption for the sake of children?

Group Exercises[88]

Think of the stories of Moses, Daniel, Joseph, Deborah, and Esther. What kinds of interruptions did they experience in their lives? How did these interruptions shape them as well as the people and the world around them?

Read Ezra 9:1-4 and 10:1-15, 44 about the Jews returning from Babylonian Exile in the sixth century B.C.E. and divorcing their foreign wives and children. What would this text sound like if you read it from the viewpoint of the children being sent away?

Resisting Categorization

Differentiating age groups within the youth category keeps us from objectifying the experience of youth. As important as generational studies are, we must exercise care for persons, not categories. The process of categorization can put unhelpful distance between people. However, Kenda Dean rightly argues that adolescence is particularly characterized by passion. This passion does not confine or stereotype adolescents. Rather, it links all people. As Dean puts it, "Young people have always served as barometers of the human condition, indicators of

---

87. Davis, *Beyond Nice,* p. 12. Davis also emphasizes an ability more prominent in later adulthood than in the adolescent years: holding different strands of a narrative together.

88. These exercises are prompted by Dana Fewell's discussions in chapters 2 and 5 of her book *The Children of Israel.*

rising and falling pressures on the psyche."[89] Consequently, we need what Robert Dykstra speaks of as "eschatological patience"[90] as we make space for the young to negotiate those pressures and grow into what God intends for them. Dykstra names this the "eschatological self": "a theological way of expressing the self's experience of newness, surprise, and hope, the sense that one's self is determined not solely by past childhood events, nor is it exclusively the product of one's own careful planning or prediction. One becomes oneself or better, comes to oneself, from the future as well as the past, from the self that is penultimately lodged, in part, in others, ultimately in Christ, a self actually delivered from some future beyond one's power to control."[91]

Denise and I argue that God intends and takes delight in the increasing complexity of our being. God does not intend that we follow any specific trajectory of our becoming, only that we continue to grow toward expressive creativity in community. Developmental theory teaches pastors and clinicians what is known and predictable about human growth and development. Eschatological theology teaches pastors to delight in and celebrate with others the surprising, the unexpected, and the unpredictable.[92] Pastors need both kinds of pastoral theological knowledge.

TAKE-AWAY POINTS

When dealing with youth and the elderly, we need to do the following:

1. Begin taking steps toward hard conversations.
2. Create space for intergenerational connections around biblical texts.
3. Disentangle the stereotypes that limit God-given personhood.
4. Pay attention to verbs in biblical texts and personal stories.
5. Reframe healthy narcissism as a vital part of youth and old age.
6. Catch ourselves when we fall into the dualism trap.
7. Adapt practices so that people of every life stage can give and receive as they are able.
8. Wake up to the insights and live with the tensions of paradoxical stories and biblical texts.

89. Kenda Creasy Dean, *Practicing Passion: Youth and the Quest for a Passionate Church* (Grand Rapids: Wm. B. Eerdmans, 2004), p. 10.

90. Robert C. Dykstra, *Counseling Troubled Youth* (Louisville: Westminster John Knox Press, 1997), p. 124.

91. Dykstra, *Counseling Troubled Youth*, p. 18.

92. Dykstra, *Counseling Troubled Youth,* p. 88.

9. Foster mentoring relationships that help youth to recompose their stories.
10. Revalue old age and youth.
11. Recognize the tensions for the elderly in leaving a legacy. Recognize the tensions for youth in inheriting a legacy.
12. Interrupt texts and spaces to make room for marginalized experiences.

CARE PRAYER

O Youthful One, O Ancient of Days,

We walk through these years with both excitement and fear. We sometimes feel unsure of who we are and unclear about where we are going. We sometimes cannot contain the exhilaration as we glimpse your vision for us and the world. Walk with us so that we might know your presence and respond with bold initiative. Hold us dearly in the place where we stand now and love us forth to the fullness you intend. Amen.

Chapter 5

Pain, Grief, and Lament

Andrew's Story

My father died suddenly when I was sixteen years old, and more recently, my daughter was stillborn. Through both of these unexpected losses, I experienced a profound sense of alone-ness. My psychological withdrawal was matched by a physical withdrawal as my senses grew dull. My hearing and sense of touch, taste, and smell disappeared. As a person of faith, I believe that I was not actually alone, but such beliefs mean little to a person in "the Pit." At the time, I didn't merely feel alone; I was alone. My own isolation was so great, at first, as to exclude the very God Who Abides. How are we to minister to those in such deep isolation? What are we to do? More importantly, what are we not to do?

•   •

Andrew's story has been and will be told by many, many people grieving their losses. The names and circumstances may change, but the experience of alone-ness runs like a thread through these stories. In Andrew's case, the pain newly experienced (his daughter's being stillborn) connected with pain remembered (his father's death) to increase his sense of isolation. Previous losses may exacerbate our current experience of loss. This was certainly true for Andrew, and for me (Denise) as well, when my father died last year. While cleaning out the house he had shared with my mother in order to ready it for sale, I was forced to cull through a lifetime of family photos and mementos. In so doing, I was thrust back into grieving my brother's drowning death thirty years ago. Not only is the past dredged up again, but the future is newly negated. Andrew experienced the loss of an imagined future with his daughter. As I watch my children grow into adulthood, I grieve the relationship they do not and will not have with the uncle they never knew, as well as the seeming incongruity between past and present.[1] For those grieving the progression of a chronic illness, the pain of past, present, and future becomes a constant companion. As my mother marches relentlessly into third-stage Alzheimer's disease, I experience little deaths daily. Fittingly, Alzheimer's has been described as "the funeral that never ends."[2]

Grief comes when people miss one another, and many types of missing occur in care giving ministry. Grief is an emotional recognition that something is missing. To acknowledge rather than dismiss this missing is a sacred act of reverencing absence. We can miss what has been — a person, a thing, a relationship, or a commitment that no longer exists. We can also miss what has never been. "Missing" embraces two distinct yet interrelated notions. To miss each other can mean to walk past, to talk past one another, to fail to connect. This kind of missing means we are not meeting one another at the level of our deepest humanness. In another sense, to miss is also to remember what may have been, to remember with fondness and appreciation. The latter suggests that we are far away from where we used to be, and the former suggests that we are never going to be where we hope to be. Both evoke a sense of alone-ness.

Life in "the Pit"

Psalm 88 expresses Andrew's sense of aloneness, isolation, loss, and thwarted future in vivid metaphors. It is the only psalm of lament that does not anticipate deliverance and a hopeful future. It ends, literally

---

1. See Jane F. Maynard, *Transforming Loss: Julian of Norwich as a Guide for Survivors of Traumatic Grief* (Cleveland: Pilgrim Press, 2006), pp. 35-36. Maynard cites the work of K. W. Sewell and A. M. Williams with trauma survivors. They use a process called "metaconstruction" to integrate past and future self-conceptions and overcome this incongruity. Linking allows a sense of future events and relations.

2. Sam Sligar, "A Funeral That Never Ends: Alzheimer's Disease and Pastoral Care," *Journal of Pastoral Care* 41 (December 1987): 344.

and figuratively, in darkness: "You [God] have caused friend and neighbor to shun me; my companions are in darkness" (v. 18). For the psalmist, who has been crying night (v. 1) and day (v. 9) to God for help without any divine response, life is experienced in "the Pit" — "the regions dark and deep" (v. 6). In the Hebrew Bible, "Pit" (bor) literally means "cistern" and appears as a metaphor for death and a synonym for Sheol, the place deep in the bowels of the earth where the dead go to exist as shades of their former selves. In Psalm 88, the psalmist feels as good as dead: "I am *counted* among those who go down to the Pit; I am *like* those who have no help, *like* those forsaken among the dead, *like* the slain that lie in the grave . . ." (Ps. 88:4-5, emphasis ours). One can hear in the language of Psalm 88 the isolation of being trapped in an "iron cage of despair," the psalmist unable or unwilling to hear the good news of God's presence.[3]

"The Pit" bars our exit. An inescapable void of despair, an unreachable space in which we feel completely immobilized, "the Pit" functions as more than simply a metaphor. A psychological, spiritual, emotional reality like no other, it swallows us up. Walter Brueggemann declares that Psalm 88 "is an embarrassment to conventional faith" because it honestly portrays the terror of a God who does not answer.[4] Because Psalm 88 bristles with countertestimony about God's hiddenness, I (Denise) used it in a memorial service for a young woman who had taken her own life. Her parents wanted people to begin to feel how deeply isolated and afraid their daughter had been so that they could begin to understand what she did. I juxtaposed Psalm 88 with Genesis 32 (Jacob wrestling at the Jabbok River with God), and Romans 8 ("Nothing can separate us from the love of God in Christ Jesus").[5]

These three texts embrace the tensions inherent in death and loss, divine absence and presence. Such tension also emerges in juxtaposed psalms. The countertestimony in Psalm 88 about God's hiddenness stands in tension with the core testimony in Psalm 139 about God's

3. Wayne Oates, *The Presence of God in Pastoral Counseling* (Waco, Tex.: Word Books, 1986), pp. 105-6.

4. Walter Brueggemann, *The Message of the Psalms* (Minneapolis: Augsburg Publishing House, 1984), p. 78.

5. For information on suicide prevention, support, consultation services, training and educational programs, see the Organization for Attempters and Survivors of Suicide in Interfaith Services (OASSIS) at http://www.oassis.org. The founder and contact is James T. Clemons, Ph.D.

presence: "Where can I go from your spirit? Or where can I flee from your presence? If I ascend to heaven, you are there; if I make my bed in Sheol, you are there" (vv. 7-8). These two psalms offer two very different approaches to the experience of "the Pit." One is not more "right" than the other. Too often, however, care givers hold up Psalm 139 as the faithful model for dealing with pain and loss. By doing so, they add to the pain of the one they are trying to help.

Living Ourselves Out of the Pit

We cannot easily hoist ourselves out of this pit with only sheer determination. Nor can we neatly plot our departure according to a set timetable. Rather, we *live ourselves out of* the Pit, somehow, step by step. Kim's story illustrates this:

> *2001 was a nightmare year. On May 1, my husband was admitted to the hospital with the first identifiable symptom of inoperable stage-four brain cancer. By the end of May, he was home with hospice care in place. On Friday, July 13, our youngest son hung himself in our basement. In September, I had to have my son's dog put to sleep. On October 23, my husband died.*

Kim could not simply will herself out of this nightmare. The hospice chaplain carried her through by continuing to give her permission to express all of her feelings, however raw. The chaplain offered a hospitable space in which Kim could tell and retell the nightmare. Two members of the church whom she did not know very well made a covenant with her to provide tangible help — cooking, cleaning, errand-running — throughout the year. The fatigue of grief doesn't end with the funeral. Two friends asked questions to help her claim good memories of her son. Getting through meant simply taking one small step at a time toward living and accepting help, putting one foot in front of the other. Like a child learning new words and skills, connecting the dots of the world, one who experiences the loss of a loved one must rearrange the pieces of life and learn how to function anew. How long it takes depends on the individual. There is no template or set schedule for this kind of work. Care givers, however, are called to notice when someone becomes "stuck" in grief and unhealthy behaviors; at that point they refer the individual to the appropriate professionals.

Kim also experienced unhelpful care during her "nightmare year," care that worked against her living herself out of the Pit. Several people suggested that she was somehow at fault for her son's suicide by asking "Didn't you know something was wrong?" That question made her angry. Of course she knew something was wrong. Her son had been hospitalized for depression, something about which the questioners had little clue. One woman who had come to help after her husband's death asked how she was doing. When Kim answered honestly and talked about her pain, the woman instructed her not to lose faith over this. Kim described herself as "dumbfounded" by the woman's comment, since it dismissed the reality of the "nightmare year" she was experiencing. Perhaps the worst response came from pastoral colleagues who looked at her with pity, saying nothing or turning away. "Their avoidance felt like rejection and condemnation," she recalled. Kim dreaded attending denominational events because she knew she would encounter silent stares.

Another way to live oneself out of the Pit is to pay attention to images from the unconscious. During the summer of my second year in seminary, I (Michael) experienced a dream that would release a sense of guilt that I had carried for more than two years. My college friend, Bill, took his own life by hanging himself two weeks before I left for seminary. The image of my friend hanging from the light fixture in the room he had rented in a house shared with friends was often too much to take. Though I had never actually set foot in that room, I went there in my mind many times. I walked through the grieving process of this tremendous loss, carrying a sense of guilt-filled responsibility. I knew on a conscious level that Bill's death was not my fault, but as is the case with many people grieving the loss of someone to suicide, I still felt responsible (or, more appropriately, irresponsible) in some way. Questions plagued me. What could I have done to change the course of events? What could I have done to stop him? Then one night I had a dream: I trudged up a long and winding pathway to a hut at the top of a mountain, walked inside, and heard a voice say, "You are not responsible." After rising the following morning, I recounted this dream to many friends and described the relief I felt. Initially I attributed the voice to my friend, since I didn't know who else it could be. But I came to realize that it was God speaking to me in that hut.

- Think about a time when you found yourself in the Pit. What were you feeling during that time?
- What and who helped you the most during that time? What did you find least helpful?
- How did you live yourself out of the Pit?

Private and Public Grief

Both Andrew and Kim are ordained pastors. How do pastors carry on in the face of their own devastating losses? As we saw in Kim's story, her own pastoral colleagues didn't feel comfortable dealing with her grief, which added to Kim's pain. Often, too, congregations put their pastors up on pedestals and expect them to be present and functioning, no matter what. This leaves little room for the pastor's own vulnerability and grief, which she or he often attempts to hide from the congregation. One pastor we know lost his grown son to suicide. Pastor Dan's congregation relied on associate pastors and lay leadership for many months during his initial grieving. However, after about a year, resentment started to build among the congregation. They wanted *their* hurts tended to and were weary of tending to their pastor's hurts and listening to his stories of pain.

The story of King David and his son Absalom (2 Samuel 13–18) showcases the tension between private grief and public roles, not unlike the tension this bereaved pastor faced. When Absalom rebelled against his father and took control of Jerusalem, David's general, Joab, killed Absalom. The news prompted a chilling lament from David: "O my son Absalom, my son, my son Absalom! Would I had died instead of you, O Absalom, my son, my son!" (18:33). Instead of celebrating a victory, the troops had to mourn (19:2). Joab chastised David, telling him not to forget his people and to resume the role of king (19:1-8), which he did. "The troops were all told, 'See, the king is sitting in the gate'" (19:8).

Lewis Parks and Bruce Birch suggest several points that pastoral leaders would do well to embrace in this story: recognize and tend to your own vulnerability; balance public and private responsibilities; model good behavior, since public and private lives cannot be separated; and be attentive to ongoing public responsibility in the midst of grief.[6] "Our vulnerability is not a private matter alone but is to some degree a sharing of public vulnerability as well. . . . The effort to be leaders while our pain is visible forges new bonds of community."[7] Michael and I question whether or not such balance is achievable or even desirable. Grief unbalances us and interrupts regular, expected rhythms. "Ongoing responsibility in the midst of grief" may need to be suspended for a time. The congregation may need to pick up the slack, giving their leader emotional space and time to grieve. "New bonds of community" may be forged in visible pain, but as we have seen, so may congregational resentments and impatience. Such a situation may require shifts in emotional expectations for both pastor and congregation.

A QUESTION FOR REFLECTION

- Have you experienced the tensions that emerge when private grief clashes with your public role? What problems emerged? How did you handle them?

The Positive Value of Suffering?

To answer Andrew's question above, what we are *not* to do in the face of pain-filled isolation is rush people through their pain, skip over the hard parts of their stories, or assert our core testimony about a God who is always present. To do so is to negate their pain and their experience. To short-cut the grieving process is dishonest. We need to be vigilant that as care givers, our concern for hope and the positive value of suffering doesn't trump the care receiver's situation. We cannot insist that we *know* that something good *will* come out of suffering. To do so is to glorify suffering. Job's "friend" Eliphaz does just that in his response to Job's suffering: "How happy is the one whom God reproves" (Job 5:17). He basically insists that suffering is good for you. That's easy for him to say; he's not sitting on the dung heap! Such insistence may make us feel better, but it may push the one grieving further into despair. I (Denise) have been told many times that my work with psalms of lament is the good that has come out of my brother's death. He

6. Lewis Parks and Bruce Birch, *Ducking Spears, Dancing Madly: A Biblical Model of Church Leadership* (Nashville: Abingdon Press, 2004), pp. 138-42.

7. Parks and Birch, *Ducking Spears, Dancing Madly*, p. 142.

drowned at age twenty-three when I was twenty-seven. I feel that none of my work fills the gaping hole of his absence in my life. Good has come out of his death, but it does not negate, justify, or lessen the pain of losing him.

Most of us would like to wrench some positive value out of suffering so that it does not seem senseless or arbitrary. Harold Kushner, for example, wrote the best-selling book *When Bad Things Happen to Good People*[8] to redeem his son's death at age fourteen from progeria, a rapid-aging disease. He argues that God is not finished creating. There are pockets of chaos to overcome that cause the innocent to suffer. Job's friends also attempted to provide reasons for his suffering, ostensibly for Job's sake. In reality, they wanted to protect themselves against the terror of his unjustified suffering. They argued the traditional worldview of Wisdom literature: Job had done something to deserve his suffering.

So, too, ancient Israel sought to make sense of its suffering in Babylonian exile through the words of the prophets. Pre-exilic prophets such as Isaiah of Jerusalem, Jeremiah, and Ezekiel warned the people that their idolatry and social injustice violated their covenant with God. Consequently, God would punish them. The Babylonian exile and the destruction of Jerusalem and the Temple in 587 B.C.E. confirmed their message, rescued God from arbitrariness, and allowed the exiles to hear new prophetic messages of hope.

The Deuteronomistic History (DH) was edited in exile to help Jews understand how the Exile had come about. Beginning with Deuteronomy, with Israel poised to enter the Promised Land, DH traced Israel's history through the period of settlement in Joshua and Judges, to the rise of the monarchy in First and Second Samuel, to the division into two kingdoms, Israel and Judah, in First and Second Kings. Second Kings ends with exiled King Jehoiachin of Judah eating at the table of the Babylonian king and receiving a daily allowance from him. DH, with its southern-kingdom bias, suggested that the split in the kingdom led to the Exile. It left open the hope that if the people repented, their covenant relationship with God would be reaffirmed.

Second Isaiah, prophet of the exiles, went beyond the idea of suffering as a payment for past sins. Israel's suffering involved more than

---

8. Harold Kushner, *When Bad Things Happen to Good People* (New York: Schocken Books, 1981).

retributive justice. The servant songs make the point that Israel suffered for the benefit of others: "I will give you as a light to the nations, that my salvation may reach to the end of the earth" (Isa. 49:6). Israel's suffering was a sign to the nations that it had accepted a difficult mission. Similarly, Jeremiah, whose book in its final form addresses the exiles, proclaims that if Israel repents (*shûb,* to turn around), "nations shall be blessed" by the Lord (4:2). A repentant Israel as God's instrument transforms the nations. This urge to seek the positive in the midst of tragedy can be seen in people with chronic or terminal illnesses who volunteer for experimental therapy or protocols, hoping that their suffering can benefit someone else. This approach to suffering can be dangerous if we glorify suffering as bringing us closer to God. By doing so, we run the risk of accepting suffering as normal, or worse, as desirable, or as a test of our faith.

As Job's friends remind us, it is cruel to value suffering when you do so from a position of comfort. Liberation theologian Gustavo Gutiérrez argues that Job's suffering gives him solidarity with the poor and oppressed that his friends do not have. In his suffering, Job learns "a way of talking about God on the basis of his experience." He learns a way "to go out of himself and help other sufferers (without waiting until his own problems are first resolved)" and "to find a way to God."[9] Job's solidarity with the poor gives weight to his question about theodicy (God's justice).

Questions for Small-Group Discussion
- Think back to a time of illness or loss that you or someone close to you has experienced. Did you see then the positive value of suffering? Why or why not?
- Do you see the positive value today? Why or why not?

The Care Giver's Dilemma

The care giver's dilemma for ministry with people experiencing intense soul suffering involves differentiating self while receiving undifferentiated language from the sufferer. This metaphorical language is raw, un-

---

9. Gustavo Gutiérrez, *On Job: God-Talk and the Suffering of the Innocent* (Maryknoll, N.Y.: Orbis Books, 1987), p. 48.

reflective, searing, and emotional. What does it mean to differentiate self in this situation? The concept of self-differentiation comes from family systems theory. Systems theory describes the family as an emotional, interdependent unit. A change in one person's functioning prompts changes in the functioning of others in the unit. This can contribute to cooperation or a heightening of tension and anxiety, thereby straining emotional connectedness within the family. This theory has been extended to units other than biological families, including congregations.[10] Whatever the unit, self-differentiation allows the care giver to remain close to the situation and relate with the people involved without internalizing their anxiety and tension. "Differentiation means the capacity to be an 'I' while remaining connected," explains Edwin Friedman.[11] Care givers want to be helpful, but sometimes in the rush to help, they get tangled in the web of family systems anxiety; self-differentiation can help them clarify their role and responsibility. Ministers with people in pain and grief can benefit from this clarification. This arduous work of self-differentiation avoids moralizing, patronizing, minimizing, distancing, or explaining away, and it can yield comforting care for people in pain.

Care givers as "first responders" to soul pain listen and receive; they do not dissect and dispute. This is what it means to maintain compassionate composure in the face of undifferentiated language. Job's friends were unable to do this over the long haul. After their initial silence, they could not see that Job's questions about why he was suffering "were not a theological question at all, but a cry of pain."[12] The depth of his cries required an exclamation point rather than a question mark. Questions of "Why?" and "How long?" in psalms of lament (Pss. 6:3; 13:1-2; 22:1; 42:9; 44:24; 74:1, 10, 19; 77:9; 79:5) and in the book of Job are rhetorical questions. They express the pain and urgency of the situation for the one suffering. They are not invitations to theo-

---

10. Psychiatrist Murray Bowen originated this theory and its eight linked concepts. See "Bowen Theory" at http://www.thebowencenter.org/pages/theory/html; The Bowen Center for the Study of the Family, Georgetown Family Center. For a discussion of differentiation in congregations, see Ronald W. Richardson, *Creating a Healthier Church: Family Systems Theory, Leadership, and Congregational Life* (Minneapolis: Fortress Press, 1996).

11. Edwin H. Friedman, *Generation to Generation: Family Process in Church and Synagogue* (New York: Guilford Press, 1985), p. 27.

12. Kushner, *When Bad Things Happen to Good People*, p. 88.

logical debate. Such debate can distance us and distract us from those in pain. Care givers first meet those in care on the "survival level" of suffering where we mediate God's presence through our presence. The "intellectual level" of suffering comes later,[13] when those in pain are more ready to contemplate reasons for suffering.

Competent and compassionate care, though, does not end with being present to persons in pain. The community must also be present to the one suffering in its acts of recognition, remembrance, and prayer. Reverend Tom, a pastor of a large congregation, illustrates this kind of communal presence in his account of his mother's struggle with Alzheimer's disease. When she could no longer recognize friends or family, he felt disconnected and alone. One visit to the nursing home offered a moment of connection. Going to feed his mother at lunch, Tom noticed that the menu included a piece of wheat bread and grape juice. He was inspired to share a communion service with his mother right there in the dining room, using the "elements" at her table. In his words, this "accidental" and "impromptu" service made manifest "the presence of God even when we feel forsaken and alone." In the prayerful words of consecration of the Eucharist, Tom and his mother joined with others in the body of Christ. This healing, communal ritual in the middle of a nursing-home dining room allowed Tom to recognize both his mother as she was now and himself as he was now. He recalled memories of her and of their relationship. The paradox of care is this: When we as care givers learn to differentiate ourselves and our stories from those of other people, we are increasingly able to stay connected to those in pain and their stories.

The Many Faces of Grief

Grief is defined as "the normal but bewildering cluster of ordinary human emotions arising in response to a significant loss, intensified and complicated by the relationship to the person or the object lost."[14] Losses can be of several different kinds.[15] They can include the material

13. Daniel Simundson, *Faith under Fire: Biblical Interpretations of Suffering* (Minneapolis: Augsburg Press, 1980), p. 97.

14. Kenneth R. Mitchell and Herbert Anderson, *All Our Losses, All Our Griefs: Resources for Pastoral Care* (Louisville: Westminster John Knox Press, 1983), p. 54.

15. Mitchell and Anderson, *All Our Losses, All Our Griefs*, pp. 36-46.

loss of a physical object or of familiar surroundings. Ancient Israel mourned the loss of Jerusalem during the Babylonian exile, as we read in Psalm 137:1: "By the rivers of Babylon — there we sat down and there we wept when we remembered Zion." There is also relationship loss, the ending of opportunities to relate to, share experiences with, and be in the presence of a cherished other. In Psalm 10:1, the psalmist agonizes, "Why, O LORD, do you stand far off? Why do you hide yourself in times of trouble?" In 2 Samuel 18:33, King David mourns the loss of his son Absalom. People can also suffer the intrapsychic loss of an emotionally important image of themselves, of a dream or future plans. "Jacob was left alone" (Gen. 32:24) and "was very afraid" (Gen. 32:7) at the Jabbok River, where he was poised between his brother Esau and God the wrestler. People can also experience the functional loss of physical vigor or of mental agility. The psalmist moans, "I am poured out like water, and all my bones are out of joint" (Ps. 22:14). There is also role loss, the loss of a social role or accustomed place in a social network. In Genesis 37, we read that Joseph's father and his older brothers resented him for his suggesting, because of his dream, that he would one day reign over them. Jacob rebuked him: "Shall we indeed come, . . . and bow to the ground before you?" (v. 10). Finally, systemic loss can be experienced within a familial, social, or institutional context because of change: "Jerusalem sinned grievously, so she has become a mockery" (Lam. 1:8).

QUESTIONS FOR REFLECTION
- Think back over your life and categorize the kinds of losses that you have experienced. Which were the most painful, and why?
- Think about characters in the Hebrew Bible who struggle with loss. How do they react to their loss? Is their reaction a model for you? Why or why not?

Undercurrent and Undertow

Grief work involves knowing and working with what we call the undercurrent and undertow of ministry, the emotional and spiritual movement that cannot be seen from the surface. Working with grief engendered by loss through committed and ongoing practice keeps the undercurrent and undertow from becoming deadly. Such work requires that we recognize the common elements of grief: numbness; emptiness, loneliness, and isolation; fear and anxiety; guilt and shame; anger; sadness and despair; and somatization (physical expressions of emotional pain).[16]

Care givers swallow grief by dismissing its presence, dampening their expression of feelings out of their need for self-control, or by refusing the reality of deaths in whatever form they take. Swallowing grief represents an undercurrent that can, as James Dittes suggests, eventually sap care givers' spiritual and emotional vitality.[17] He believes that ministry can be strengthened as pastors become acquainted with grief[18] and work through grief.[19] In fact, ministry itself is grief work:

> To be a minister is to know the most searing grief and abandonment, daily and profoundly. To be a minister is to take as partners in solemn covenant those who are sure to renege. . . . To be a minister, then, as God knows, is to be forsaken regularly and utterly, by those on whose partnership one most relies for identity, meaning, and selfhood, as these are lodged in the vocational commitment.[20]

We engage in pastoral grief work when we name the ways in which ministry may not have unfolded as we expected.

A QUESTION FOR REFLECTION
- Name the griefs you have encountered in ministry. What hasn't turned out as you expected?

The prophet Jeremiah engaged in this kind of grief work in his series of laments in chapters 11-20 of the book that bears his name. Keeping in mind that Jeremiah is a literary figure given to us by later editors rather than a historical personality,[21] we can see that these laments are both a record of his inner life and an expression of the grief of the community he addressed. Jeremiah remembered the early joy of his prophetic calling: "Your words were found, and I ate them, and your

---

16. Herbert Anderson and Edward Foley, *Mighty Stories, Dangerous Rituals: Weaving Together the Human and the Divine* (San Francisco: Jossey-Bass, 1998), pp. 62-85.

17. James Dittes, *Re-Calling Ministry* (St. Louis: Chalice Press, 1999), pp. 20-21.

18. Dittes, *Re-Calling Ministry*, pp. 17-19.

19. Dittes, *Re-Calling Ministry*, pp. 22-27.

20. Dittes, *Re-Calling Ministry*, p. 15.

21. Jorge Pixley, *Jeremiah* (St. Louis: Chalice Press, 2004), p. 43.

words became to me a joy and the delight of my heart" (Jer. 15:16). But the prophetic word of judgment he preached in the early sixth century was not heeded, and his pain became "unceasing, [his] wound incurable, refusing to be healed" (15:18). He sat alone (15:17). His life in turmoil, Jeremiah expressed his frustration and loneliness in vivid metaphors that accused God of duping him (11:19a; 20:7) and of allowing enemies to prevail over him (12:1-2; 15:15; 17:18; 20:10). Jeremiah's laments mark the loss of his prophetic sympathetic identification with the people.[22] Jeremiah experienced role loss and relationship loss (see above), which was worsened by God's command in 14:11: "Do not pray for the welfare of this people." Jeremiah could not do the very thing he was called to do (see also 7:16; 11:14; 15:1; 16:5-9). Jeremiah recognized his estrangement from both the God who called him and the people he was called to serve.

Fighting the Fear

We often care at the edge of our intellectual and emotional knowledge, fearing that we don't know enough (see Jeremiah's protest in 1:6: "Ah, Lord GOD! Truly I do not know how to speak, for I am only a boy") or that we can't be sufficiently present to meet care-giving demands. Perhaps such fear fueled the inability of Kim's pastoral colleagues to minister to her grief. On another level, the fear of pain and grief itself can be as problematic for care givers as their over-identification with those in pain. Neither running away from pain nor running toward pain is helpful. In our effort to assert our sympathy and get close to the sufferer, we may insist, "I know just how you feel," when in fact we do not, we cannot know. Each of our experiences of loss and pain is unique. My (Denise's) mother had always resisted participating in bereavement support groups for parents who had lost a child. Her stock response was, "No one can know how I feel." The challenge for me was to honor her unique experience and memory of my brother, while not enabling her to isolate herself in despair. I regret to say that I was never able to meet that challenge.

Rather than over-identify with pain, we as care givers may distance

22. Mark Smith, *The Laments of Jeremiah and Their Contexts: Jeremiah 11–20* (Atlanta: Scholars Press, 1990), p. 65.

ourselves from pain because it triggers our own. We distance ourselves by preferring to "look on the bright side" of things. In doing so, we fail to realize that we are actually embracing a false optimism that tends toward the trivial, rather than a hope that recognizes the reality of pain without succumbing to its power. We may also fear that another's pain may weaken us or that it might be "catching." Psalm 41 captures this feeling with its metaphors of spatial and psychological distancing from disease: "They think that a deadly thing has fastened on me, that I will not rise again from where I lie" (v. 8).[23] As personified and dynamic powers, death and disease are hostile to human beings. It's no surprise that we don't want to get too close to a hospitalized patient. When we ourselves are patients, we know that visitors leave to "whisper together" (v. 7) about our condition. While I (Denise) was hospitalized for a severe case of pneumonia that almost killed me, visitors would insist that I looked great, when in fact I knew that my ribs were protruding (my weight had dipped to 85 pounds), and my own teenage son was afraid to visit, fearing that I would die right before his eyes. I literally looked like death warmed over; I couldn't even bear to look at myself in the mirror.

Not being afraid of someone else's feelings is a gift for both care giver and care receiver. Working with pain, we who are care givers come face to face with a paradox: As we are willing to tolerate the presence of pain, we become more available to the other person. This never becomes easy. One of our students, Drew, is doing his field education in a hospital. He shared his frustration about an encounter he had with a patient in ICU who could barely speak. Try as he might, he could not understand what the patient was trying to tell him. Consequently, Drew left the ICU feeling frustrated, helpless, and discouraged. "I couldn't do anything; I couldn't fix anything," he said. "I wanted to leave the man in a state of peace, but I failed." We discussed both the family, marital, and ministerial myths (see Chapter Two) and his pastoral image (see Chapter Three) and how they might have shaped his need to fix and rescue. We also discussed strategies for "good enough" pastoral care in this situation, including the offering of light touch and calm speech. The care giver can say, "I know that you want to tell me something important, but I'm having trouble understanding you. I'll try hard to understand. I'm going to try a few things, and you can let

---

23. For a more detailed discussion, see Denise Dombkowski Hopkins, *Journey through the Psalms* (St. Louis: Chalice Press, 2002), p. 125.

me know if they're helpful or not. Now I'm going to pray, read Scripture, sing a hymn, hold your hand [choose one]." If the care giver announces what he or she is about to do, it can be calming for the patient.

I (Denise) had wanted the same "peace" for my mother in her struggle with Alzheimer's. After months of agonizing over her agitation, I realized that a lifetime of her repressed anger and disappointment was now finally being released in tearful, angry tirades. I came to understand that my gift to her was to receive those angry tears without censure or redirection. My gift to her was holding her hand in that place of chaos. The spiritual and pastoral challenge for care givers can be summarized in a question: Can we stay faithfully present with people in grief, pain, and lament? Can we create a space for the grief work that must be done?

The frustration that Drew felt is not reserved for students. Seasoned pastors also struggle with their inability to alleviate pain and suffering, as Linda's story illustrates:

> I am a hospice chaplain who has been racking my brain to bring healing and comfort to a woman with ALS (Lou Gehrig's disease). She has had a difficult life and few positive relationship experiences, except with her own mother, who died several years ago. The patient is emotionally and physically distraught. My usual care style is to get my patients to talk and express their feelings, but she has trouble speaking because of a mechanical device inserted in her larynx. When she cries, fluids pool in her throat, making speech nearly impossible. So I read to her, mostly from psalms, trying to capture rage, loneliness, and hope, while trying to avoid triggering depression. I try not to stimulate too much emotion because I don't want to make her cry. Visits with her are emotionally challenging for me.

Linda decided to turn her own feelings of helplessness toward helpful care for her patient. She focused on one part of the patient's personhood that was still intact: her sense of humor. Linda's intuitive sense surfaced in the midst of her frustration as she considered what, specifically, could be helpful to *this* patient at *this* time. She realized the unique aspects of this pastoral conversation. Linda settled on reading Bible jokes as a way to nurture her patient's humor. Linda knew that she had touched the living core as a twinkle of gladness appeared in her patient's eyes. Linda modeled how both clergy and laity can take existing rituals (reading the Bible) and "make them into something personal and meaningful."[24]

Linda's approach is a simple one. Its power evokes a scene from the Pulitzer prize-winning play *Wit* by Margaret Edson. The play was made into a movie starring Emma Thompson. The protagonist, Vivian Bearing, is a professor of English literature known for her keen intellect. While battling ovarian cancer, Vivian confronts her own mortality and realizes that there is no time for her usual detailed, scholarly analysis. Speaking to the audience after a conversation with Susie, the night nurse, who has just split a Popsicle with her while discussing her "no code" and DNR choices, Vivian says, "Now is a time for simplicity. Now is a time for, dare I say it, kindness."[25]

Susie bears witness to Vivian's suffering so that she does not suffer alone. Redemption is rooted in the shared Popsicle and the expressed yearning for simplicity, for the bare bones of accompaniment.

QUESTIONS FOR REFLECTION

- When were you afraid of someone's suffering? Why? How did you express this fear?
- When did you over-identify with someone's pain? Why? How did you express this over-identification?

GROUP EXERCISE

Begin by reading the following poem, "The Guest House" by Rumi:

> This being human is a guest house.
> Every morning a new arrival.
>
> A joy, a depression, a meanness,
> Some momentary awareness comes
> As an unexpected visitor.
> Welcome and entertain them all!
> Even if they're a crowd of sorrows

---

24. Megory Anderson, *Sacred Dying: Creating Rituals for Embracing the End of Life,* rev. and exp. ed. (New York: Marlowe & Co., 2003), p. 61. For other helpful practices for ministering in the presence of suffering, see Kenneth C. Haugk, *"Don't Sing Songs to a Heavy Heart": How to Relate to Those Who Are Suffering* (St. Louis: Stephen Ministries, 2004), and Jeffry R. Zurheide, *When Faith Is Tested: Pastoral Responses to Suffering and Tragic Death* (Minneapolis: Fortress Press, 1997).

25. Margaret Edson, *Wit* (New York: Faber & Faber, 1999), p. 69.

Who violently sweep your house
Empty of its furniture,
Still, treat each guest honorably.
He may be clearing you out
For some new delight.[26]

How does your life feel like a "guest house"?
Share your reactions to this poem.

The Psalms of Lament

The psalms of lament in the Hebrew Bible remind us that grieving is a *process* that cannot be rushed to get to the happy thoughts and self-satisfaction that our culture promotes. As a nation, we do not like to dwell on defeat or pain; we take pride in our can-do attitude of overcoming adversity. Our commercials suggest that a pill can alleviate the pain of what ails us ("Just ask your doctor"), and our sitcoms imply that problems can be wrapped up in a thirty-minute format. But life is not like that for most of us. Just one short month after 9/11, commentators were telling us that we were "moving on" when, in fact, most of us were still in shock. The psalms of lament can help us give voice to our lived experience and the reality of pain. Laments comprise nearly one-third of the 150 psalms in the Psalter. Only six of those can be called penitential laments that confess sin as the cause for the psalmist's suffering (Pss. 32, 38, 51, 102, 130, and 143).[27] The others are angry laments that declare the suffering undeserved and complain about it to God, who is expected to deliver the psalmist from the present distress.

As I (Denise) have argued elsewhere,[28] despite the frequency of la-

---

26. Jalal al-Din Rumi, *The Essential Rumi*, trans. Coleman Barks (San Francisco: HarperOne, 1997), p. 109. Rumi was a thirteenth-century Persian Muslim poet, Islamic jurist, and theologian in what is now Afghanistan.

27. Traditionally, the church has spoken of seven penitential laments. I (Denise) have deleted Psalm 6 from the list because there is no overt linkage made between suffering and the psalmist's sin. Act/consequence *may* be implied by verse 1 ("O LORD, do not rebuke me in your anger, or discipline me in your wrath"), but the real problem seems to be the psalmist's terror in verses 2 and 3, probably caused by the enemies mentioned in verses 7, 8, and 10. See Kristin Swenson, *Living through Pain: Psalms and the Search for Wholeness* (Waco, Tex.: Baylor University Press, 2005).

28. Hopkins, *Journey through the Psalms*, pp. 77-133.

ments in the Hebrew Bible, they are seldom used in worship. If we do use responsive lament readings in the back of our hymnals, we cut out the angry parts. Many believe that it is "unChristian" to complain to God, but we (Michael and I) argue that "lament" and "faith" are not a contradiction in terms. Laments can be called legitimate complaints in faith to God when we experience God as absent. Laments allow us to be honest before God in public and in private prayer.

The structure of the lament offers us a guide to the process of grieving losses, as it moves in six stages (not always in this order) from complaint to anticipated praise of God.[29]

The first stage is *address* — it identifies the one to whom the psalmist prays. It is short and packed with emotion.

The second stage is *complaint*, which is made in vivid, metaphorical language. The complaint can focus on the psalmist's suffering ("I/we"), the psalmist's enemies ("they"), and the psalmist's accusations that God is not caring or doing something ("You").

The third stage is *petition*. The psalmist asks God to save him, deliver him, rescue him, hear him.

The fourth stage involves suggested *motivations* for God to deliver the psalmist — confession of sin, protestation of innocence, and "public relations value."

The fifth stage involves the psalmist's confession of trust, usually introduced by "but" in anticipation of deliverance.

The sixth stage is a vow of praise, offered in anticipation of deliverance that hasn't yet happened.

The psalms of lament can help us tell our stories of suffering, loss, and pain. Unfortunately, these stories are often muted by theologies that consider doubts, laments, and questions to be unfaithful; liturgies that are committed to the upbeat, no matter what; modern medicine that limits our stories to the medical chart; Western culture, which enshrines power and success; and "scripts" that shape our attitude toward illness. Arthur Frank argues that "sooner or later, everyone is a wounded storyteller"[30] and that we need to pay more attention to the way in which we deal with illness and tell our stories about it.

Frank suggests that when we are ill, we operate out of one of five

---

29. Hopkins, *Journey through the Psalms,* pp. 81-82.

30. Arthur W. Frank, *The Wounded Storyteller: Body, Illness, and Ethics* (Chicago: University of Chicago Press, 1995), p. xiii.

ideal "bodies" that represent different choices that we make as we deal with our illness. These bodies serve as scripts for acting out our illness.[31] The *disciplined body* considers the crisis to be a loss of control and attempts to reassert predictability through therapeutic regimens. The *mirroring body* attempts to recreate the body in the image of other healthy bodies. The *dominating body* displaces its rage against the contingency of disease by directing it against other people. The *communicative body* is the ideal body that accepts contingency as normative and as a reflection of the suffering of other bodies. The *chaos body* is the "other" against which the first three define themselves. The chaos body does not attempt to reassert control, recreate itself, or accept what has happened to it. It wallows in its brokenness and sees no other possibilities, no future.

These different "bodies" tell different stories. The disciplined, mirroring, and dominating bodies embrace the *restitution narrative*. This culturally preferred story insists upon a cure, believing that we can be as good as new. The goal becomes renewed life after treatment. This story is told, for example, in cancer-center brochures that show people after treatment, but not in treatment. The *communicative body* adopts the quest narrative, which meets suffering and tries to gain something from it. Quest stories are filled with the heroic and inspirational. They testify – "I did it, and you can, too" – and run the risk of "romanticizing illness."[32] Nancy Eiesland speaks in this vein of the misuse of stories of "overcomers,"[33] disabled individuals who conquer disability and achieve success. Simplistic misuse of their stories can feed their own denial and the demand for heroic suffering or miraculous healing, negating the possibility of an "ordinary" life.

In Frank's topology, the *chaos narrative* may be the most difficult for care givers and receivers to accept. The chaos narrative feels only the immediacy of illness and doesn't anticipate getting better. Told by the chaotic body, this story generates fear and anxiety in others. Frank cautions that the usual immediate response of most "would-be helpers" is "first to drag the teller out of this story . . . that dragging called some version of 'therapy.'"[34] We either try to rush patients through their

31. For what follows, see Frank, *The Wounded Storyteller*, pp. 40-49, 97-114.

32. Frank, *The Wounded Storyteller*, p. 135.

33. Nancy Eiesland, *The Disabled God: Toward a Liberatory Theology of Disability* (Nashville: Abingdon Press, 1994), p. 31.

34. Frank, *The Wounded Storyteller*, p. 110.

story or document it as depression. We try to shield ourselves from the story's raw, unsettling force by censuring, judging, or rejecting it, which in turn diminishes the teller. Thus the biggest challenge for care givers is to receive the chaos narrative while recognizing how uncomfortable it makes us.

QUESTIONS FOR REFLECTION

- Think about a time in your life when you or a loved one was seriously ill. What kind of "body" and "script" did s/he or you live out of?
- Why did you or your loved one choose one body/script and not another?

The Challenge of Laments

Building on Frank's call to honor chaos stories, Michael and I suggest that psalms of lament can powerfully express our chaos. They do so while keeping us connected to God, even in our anger and our experience of God's absence. Laments keep us talking with God at a time when we need God most. As part of our canon, psalms of lament offer us ready-made vehicles for the expression of chaos. Psalms of lament embrace the full spectrum of human loss: death, illness, divorce, job loss, child or spouse abuse, rape, foreclosure, Wall Street meltdowns, global warming. Anything that challenges our sense of a world well-ordered can plunge us into the chaotic Pit. The lament structure[35] names all of these kinds of chaos with metaphorical language, but doesn't give chaos the last word.

The complaint describing the distress embraces "evocative and provocative" metaphorical language meant to get God's attention and communicate the urgency of the situation. Enemies like wild animals surround the psalmist (Pss. 7:2; 10:9; 17:12; 35:17; 58:3-6; 59:6). The waters of chaos threaten to annihilate her (Pss. 18:16; 69:1-2, 14-15; 144:7). He complains that he is worn out from weeping and petitioning God (Pss. 6:6-7; 22:14-15). She wonders "How long?" until God rescues (Pss. 13:1-2; 35:17; 44:24; 77:7-9). As care givers, we are called to receive this language

---

35. See Hopkins, *Journey through the Psalms*, pp. 83-114, for what follows on psalm structure.

and not dismiss it as "over the top," too dramatic, or grossly exaggerated. "You don't really feel like that," we're inclined to insist. But "Pit language" is not measured, calm, or rational. It is raw, wild, and terror-filled: "My bones are shaking with terror *[bahal]*," cries the psalmist in 6:2. Because we particularize these metaphors with our own experience, they can speak for many different sufferers at different times experiencing different kinds of pain.

As uncomfortable as complaints about suffering and the enemies may be in the psalms of lament, care givers might have the most difficulty receiving complaints about God not caring or doing. Psalm 44 rails against the slumbering God: "Rouse yourself! Why do you sleep, O Lord? . . . Why do you hide your face? Why do you forget our affliction and oppression?" (vv. 23-24). Psalm 77 wonders if God forgets: "Has God forgotten to be gracious?" (v. 9). Some people consider such complaints about God to be blasphemous. Our core testimony asserts that God never forgets or sleeps. But psalms of lament offer counter-testimony about life in the Pit. In hindsight, sufferers may come to realize God's presence in their Pit experience, but when they are *in* the Pit, they experience only God's absence. Care givers are called to recognize and name the tension between core testimony and counter-testimony. By so doing, we allow sufferers to express what it's like to live in that tension. The ability of sufferers to lament embodies not weak but strong faith, embedded in their visceral declaration of God's presence in the midst of God's perceived absence. The level of their anger toward God may match the level of their dependence upon God and desire for intimacy with God.

Another source of discomfort in the use of psalms of lament as vehicles for our chaos stories is the motivation that the psalmist offers to convince God to act (if the vivid complaints haven't done so already). Years of teaching laments has taught me (Denise) that people seem most comfortable with motivations expressing confession of sin and pleas for forgiveness, as in Psalm 51:1-2 (my translation): "Grace me, O God, according to your covenant loyalty *[chesed]*. . . . Wash me thoroughly from my offense." Many of us approve the psalmist's taking the blame for her suffering. However, when it comes to motivations that protest innocence — "Vindicate me, O LORD, for I have walked in my integrity. . . . I wash my hands in innocence" (Ps. 26:1, 6) — we dismiss such protests as acts of self-righteousness. Bible study groups often laugh sheepishly or squirm when introduced to these verses.

As care givers, we are called to evaluate our own reactions to such protests, lest we censure sufferers who express them. Perhaps we need to uncover our own hidden admiration of stoicism that equates faithfulness with not complaining. Perhaps we need to acknowledge that we embrace a theodicy (an explanation of God's justice in the face of evil and suffering) that lets God off the hook at human expense.[36] Perhaps we need to re-evaluate our tradition's view of God and how that view engenders consolation or pain in the experience of people who suffer.[37] Perhaps we need to re-examine our understanding of covenant. As a mutually responsible pledge to be in relationship, covenant allows both God and us to call one another to account. This understanding gives rise to the *chutzpah* tradition in the Hebrew Bible — that is, boldness in petitioning or challenging God for the sake of justice and community. Jacob's wrestling with God at the Jabbok River shows *chutzpah* (Gen. 32), as does Abraham's arguing over the fate of a few righteous in Sodom (Gen. 18:16-33), as do the psalmists in the laments.

A third motivation, the "public relations value" of the psalmist,[38] reminds God of the psalmist's value as one who praises God: "In death there is no remembrance of you; in Sheol who can give you praise?" (Ps. 6:5; see also Ps. 88:10; Isa. 38:18). These rhetorical questions imply that we matter to God as people who praise. This implication raises flags for many. How dare we suggest that God needs us to protect and enhance God's reputation! Yet other passages affirm this empowering message. Genesis 1:27 dares to insist that we are created in God's image and likeness. Psalm 8:5 declares us to be "a little lower than God."

---

36. See James L. Crenshaw, "Introduction: The Shift from Theodicy to Anthropodicy," in *Theodicy in the Old Testament,* ed. James L. Crenshaw (Philadelphia: Fortress Press, 1983). Crenshaw defines theodicy as "the attempt to pronounce a verdict of 'Not Guilty' over God for whatever seems to destroy the order of society and the universe" (p. 1). The notion of reward and punishment in the Hebrew Bible "presented a ready defense of God" and the tension "between divine and human culpability was nearly always eased by stressing the latter's sinfulness. In short, defense of God occurred at human expense" (p. 5). In this way, anthropodicy — that is, a justification of humans to themselves — replaced theodicy, a justification of God to humans.

37. Leonard M. Hummel, *Clothed in Nothingness: Consolation for Suffering* (Minneapolis: Fortress Press, 2003). This study examines Lutheran theology in relation to lived suffering in a series of interviews with Lutherans.

38. Hopkins, *Journey through the Psalms,* p. 103.

QUESTIONS FOR REFLECTION
- Think of a time when you were in the Pit. What kind of prayers did you pray to God?
- Did you pray angry psalm laments? Why or why not?
- Could you pray psalm laments today? Why or why not?

The Process of Grief

Care givers are called to honor the process of grieving. There can be no shortcuts. As the structure of the angry lament shows, we cannot leap over the complaint to get to the happy ending of praise and vows of trust. The confession of trust and the vow of praise in the laments surprise us. Something happens as we move across the dotted line of the lament structure to this part. Instead of complaint, the psalmist offers up praise in anticipation of deliverance that has not yet taken place: "I *will* sing to the LORD, because [the Lord] has dealt bountifully with me" (Ps. 13:6, emphasis ours). Dismissed as acts of bargaining, these parts of the lament actually grow out of the core belief undergirding the whole lament process: that God will come through for us. Often, we must rely upon the congregation to hold up this belief for us because we simply cannot do it while in the depths of the Pit.

The congregation can hold up that place of hope for us, like a light shining at the end of a tunnel. This place-holding cannot be confined to hospital visits or the church coffee hour. It must be built also into our liturgies and acts of worship. Qualities that define the essential elements of worship include a sense of awe, delight, truth, and hope.[39] Using the laments in worship helps to cultivate the sense of truth — that is, the gap between what is and what ought to be — between core testimony and countertestimony, between a God present and a God absent. Laments also contribute to our sense of awe, which is not confined to nature and beauty. Awe also recognizes human frailty and the power of God in the midst of crisis. Awe can reinvigorate "domesticated" worship that is nothing more than pleasant and friendly.[40] If liturgy is "a work performed by the people for the benefit of others,"[41]

39. Don E. Saliers, *Worship Comes to Its Senses* (Nashville: Abingdon Press, 1996).
40. Saliers, *Worship Comes to Its Senses*, p. 20.
41. James White, *Introduction to Christian Worship*, 3rd ed. (Nashville: Abingdon Press, 2000), p. 26.

then laments belong in worship as a vehicle for honoring pain and grief. When we use laments in worship, we create a "liturgical 'truth'" that is "an engaged, embodied, and particular truth, a truth that cannot only be talked about, but must be done."[42]

A lament does not give up on God but rather keeps us talking to God even when we are angry at God, our enemies, and our situation. Laments can take care givers to the depths with the sufferer, whom we can "hear into speech"[43] and out of silent isolation. This journey, however, requires us to be willing to put our hands into the wounds of others, as Thomas did with Jesus. Writing about his son's death, Nicholas Wolterstorff declares, ". . . as I rise up, I bear the wounds of his death. My rising does not remove them. They mark me. If you want to know who I am, put your hand in."[44]

David's mourning over the loss of the child produced by his rape of Bathsheba offers us another model for the grieving process (2 Sam. 12:5-23). When the child becomes ill, David pleads for the child, fasts, and lies on the ground all night. The elders urge him to get up and eat (v. 17). When the child dies on the seventh day, the servants fear telling him, believing that "he may do himself some harm" (v. 18). Instead, reversing the usual mourning customs, David gets up, washes, anoints himself, changes clothes, worships, and eats (v. 20). His response is "an appropriate acknowledgment of the reality and power of death in our human existence. It is an expression of our vulnerability and a recognition that we are not in control"[45] and that death does not have the last word.

The power of lamentation is not confined to personal crises. Laments can speak to ethnic and national crises as well. This was made clear in faculty conversations with human rights activists Annie Namala, from the dominant caste in India, and N. Paul Divakar, a *dalit* (untouchable) from India. They described the plight of 200 million *dalits* or "broken people" in India and their efforts to emancipate them by educating, organizing, and agitating for justice. Christian *dalits* are being killed and their churches destroyed. Namala and Divakar argued that no theology

---

42. Marjorie Procter-Smith, *In Her Own Rite: Constructing Feminist Liturgical Tradition* (Nashville: Abingdon Press, 1990), p. 13.

43. Nelle Morton, *The Journey Is Home* (Boston: Beacon Press, 1985), pp. 127-28.

44. Nicholas Wolterstorff, *Lament for a Son* (Grand Rapids: Wm. B. Eerdmans, 1987), pp. 92-93.

45. Bruce Birch, "The First and Second Books of Samuel," in *New Interpreter's Bible*, vol. 2 (Nashville: Abingdon Press, 1998), p. 1299.

existed in the church in India to help *dalits* grapple with their situation. Forgiveness as traditionally understood does not help *dalits* work through their rage and internalized prejudices. "How do we digest the anger and desire for revenge?" they wanted to know. They noted a complete absence of laments in their worship services and agreed that laments could be a vehicle for expressing simmering *dalit* anger.

QUESTIONS FOR REFLECTION

- Do the liturgies of your worship service make room for chaos stories that reflect real experience?
- Does your church or faith community use laments in its worship? Why or why not?
- Do you think that lamenting belongs in worship? Why or why not?

Tears and Ministry

What should a care giver do when encountering tears of loss and grief? Care receivers might initially feel inhibited or self-conscious about shedding tears or talking about their tears. Nevertheless, tears that well up from the depths signal the undeniable: the heart is speaking. We should listen for the heart speaking in the tears and curiously and gently ask, "What are these tears saying?"[46] Judith Kay Nelson has developed a comprehensive theory of crying and suggests practical approaches for clinical care and counseling. Nelson argues that "crying is above all a relationship behavior, a way to help us get close and not simply a vehicle for emotional expression or release. We do not cry because we need to get rid of pain, but because we need connection with our care givers — literal, internal, fantasized, or symbolic — in order to accept and heal from our pain and grief."[47]

Certainly the psalmists understood this concept. The laments are saturated with the tears of those who long for connection with God: "Every night I flood my bed with tears; I drench my couch with my

46. See Jeffrey Kottler, *The Language of Tears* (San Francisco: Jossey-Bass, 1996).

47. Judith Kay Nelson, *Seeing through Tears* (New York: Routledge, 2005), p. 6. Nelson builds on the attachment theory of John Bowlby, who describes attachment as a "lasting psychological connectedness between human beings," formed in early infancy and in childhood experiences of care givers and significant others. See Bowlby, *Attachment*, Attachment and Loss Series, vol. 1 (New York: Basic Books, 1969), p. 194.

weeping. My eyes waste away because of grief" (Ps. 6:6); "Hear my prayer, O LORD . . . do not hold your peace at my tears" (Ps. 39:12); "My tears have been my food day and night, while people say to me continually, 'Where is your God?'" (Ps. 42:3); "You have kept count of my tossings; put my tears in your bottle" (Ps. 56:8). Job complains that his "face is red with weeping" (16:16) and that his eye "has grown dim from grief" (17:7). Many call Jeremiah "the weeping prophet."

The book of Lamentations has been called a "house for sorrow" and "a safe place for tears."[48] Probably produced by survivors of the Babylonian destruction of Jerusalem in 587 B.C.E., it juxtaposes hope and despair without resolving the tension between them. Personified daughter Zion/Jerusalem "weeps bitterly in the night, with tears on her cheeks" (Lam. 1:2; cf. 1:16, 18; 3:49). The "poetry of truth-telling" in Lamentations constitutes "an act of survival" because it "affirms the humanity of victims, gives them agency,"[49] and gives the numbed a voice. Traditionally, interpreters have devalued the laments in the book by focusing exclusively upon chapter 3:21-24: "But this I call to mind, and therefore I have hope: The steadfast love of the LORD never ceases, his mercies never come to an end; they are new every morning; great is your faithfulness."[50] The Common Lectionary and the hymn "Great Is Thy Faithfulness" by Thomas Chisholm (music by William Runyan, 1923) both draw upon these verses.

The ignored laments surround and challenge this core testimony in the book of Lamentations. The majority of the book proffers another strategy, calling the reader to face pain squarely by embracing the tears of chapters 1 and 2. Lamentations does not sustain the hope of chapter 3. It cannot. "To do so would be to lie, to cover over, to deny the reality of the survivor's longing for God's missing voice," says Kathleen O'Connor.[51] The book refuses to place hope at the end. Instead, we find petitions for God to at least show up in the relationship: "Restore us to yourself, O LORD, . . . unless you have utterly rejected us, and are angry with us beyond measure" (5:21-22). Lamentations does not neatly package Israel's grief.

48. Kathleen O'Connor, *Lamentations and the Tears of the World* (Maryknoll, N.Y.: Orbis Books, 2002), p. xiv.

49. O'Connor, *Lamentations and the Tears of the World*, p. 6.

50. As argued by Tod Linafelt, *Surviving Lamentations: Catastrophe, Lament, and Protest in the Afterlife of a Biblical Book* (Chicago: University of Chicago Press, 2000), pp. 2-3.

51. O'Connor, *Lamentations and the Tears of the World*, p. 79.

GROUP EXERCISE

Choose a vessel with a wide enough mouth to represent the bottle that God uses to collect our tears in Psalm 56. Using cut-out tear shapes or simply small pieces of paper, write down the loss you are grieving, the connection you are yearning for, the hope you are releasing, or the pain you are experiencing. With appropriate music playing in the background, drop your "tears" into God's "bottle." When everyone has had the opportunity to "weep," join in this prayer based on Psalm 56:

> O God of our tears,
>   You have kept count of our tossings.
> Put our tears in your bottle.
> Are they not in your record?
>   In God, whose word we praise,
>   In the Lord, whose word we praise,
> In God we trust. We are not afraid. Amen.

God's Tears

God also weeps. Some are reluctant to attribute grief to God because their core testimony affirms a God of strength. Tears signal divine weakness and vulnerability. A KINGAFAP God does not cry. Disagreements over the translation of Jeremiah 9:10 express this reluctance. The NRSV, following some versions, translates the verse as God's command to the people: "Take up weeping and wailing for the mountains . . ." The NIV, following the Hebrew text, translates with God as the subject: "I will take up weeping and wailing. . . ." God calls for professional female mourners in Jeremiah 9:17 (cf. Amos 5:16-17), using the first-person plural: "Let them quickly raise a dirge over *us*, so that *our* eyes may run down with tears" (9:18, emphasis ours). God is both mourner and mourned for. Terence Fretheim argues that "the godward side of anger is grief, not satisfaction."[52] God grieves *with* the people over their destruction. God grieves *because* the people have broken their covenant relationship with God. God's memory of a good relationship with Israel causes God's anger and hurt in Jeremiah 2:1–3:5 and erupts into a

---

52. Terence Fretheim, *Jeremiah* (Macon, Ga.: Smyth & Helwys), p. 155.

divine lament over the lack of connection. God's tears express God's authenticity in relationship with us.

Although interpreters usually assign the tears in Jeremiah 8:18 9:2 to Jeremiah, Kathleen O'Connor assigns them to God. The divine sorrow leads to two wishes: (1) to weep forever ("O that my head were a spring of water, and my eyes a fountain of tears, so that I might weep day and night for the slain of my poor people!"; 9:1/8:23), and (2) to escape ("O that I had in the desert a traveler's lodging place, that I might leave my people and go away from them!"; 9:2/9:1). The people's betrayal of God leads not to anger, violence, and vengeance but to divine empathy and sorrow. For O'Connor, the tears of God "are part of the imaginative literary enterprise that ruptures [traditional] theological language."[53] We could say that they give countertestimony about God. The divine tears counter the other two images of God in chapters 2–9: that of enraged divine husband (2:1–4:2), and that of destructive military general (4:5–6:30).

Pastoral ministers who care with people at critical times benefit from learning about tears and anticipating a helpful response. We as care givers need to ask questions about our own relationship to tears. Do we feel emotionally secure in the midst of weeping? Do we avoid situations of emotion? Do we feel ambivalent — that is, physically present and yet emotionally absent? Do we believe that God weeps? Do we believe that pastors and care givers are allowed to weep? Do we use the phrase "breaking down" as a negative euphemism for weeping?

GROUP EXERCISE

Designate one end of the room as ten (always) and the opposite end as one (never). Ask people to position themselves along a continuum from one to ten in response to each of the following statements:

---

53. Kathleen O'Connor, "The Tears of God and Divine Character in Jeremiah 2–9," in *Troubling Jeremiah,* ed. A. R. Pete Diamond, Kathleen O'Connor, and Louis Stulman, JSOT Supplement Series 260 (Sheffield: Sheffield Academic Press, 1999), p. 401. O'Connor argues that "the character of God in the book of Jeremiah is multiple and unstable. Images and metaphors about the deity tumble over and contradict each other . . ." (p. 387). This is contra Fretheim, who argues that God's anger and tears go together (*Jeremiah,* p. 165). My (Denise's) students suggest that God's weeping comes out of God's blaming Godself — "Did I do enough?" — or out of God's worry that God will not be able to save God's people because they will not repent.

- Tears make me uncomfortable.
- Tears are a sign of weakness.
- Tears are a sign of strength.
- God weeps.
- I weep in care situations.

Discuss your observations about placements you observed on the continuum. What surprised you?

The reference points of "always," "never," and "sometimes" can frame reflections on our own tears. Crying with people can sometimes be a spiritually and emotionally connective experience and a vital pastoral practice. In fact, the absence of crying, or at least tearing up, may indicate the care giver's avoidance or emotional caution. "Sometimes" becomes the helpful pastoral watchword for our own tears. It's fine to cry sometimes in our caring ministries. But if we always feel ready to cry in any situation of care related to pain and grief, then we might seek out professional help for ourselves in order to negotiate this psychological terrain. Conversely, if we never feel like crying or having an emotional response to care receivers in situations of grief, there isn't necessarily cause for alarm. Some people process grief cognitively by thinking it through, with relatively little expression of emotion. However, if we never experience feelings of emotion *and* we frequently hear from others that we seem distant and disconnected, this may be a sign that we need to seek guidance from other professionals or colleagues.

Language about Death

The capacity for care givers to speak directly about matters of life and death can be valuable in religious and cultural contexts in which people usually avoid difficult subjects. When the situation warrants, we can engage in meaningful care as we listen to others and talk about death in a forthright and non-euphemistic way. Anthropologists caution that when it comes to death language, "it pays to treat everyone as though he or she were from a different culture," as a way to overcome our own presuppositions about death and to understand people on their own terms. There is no single ideal way to name death or to grieve.[54]

54. Donald P. Irish et al., *Ethnic Variations in Dying, Death, and Grief: Diversity and Universality* (Philadelphia: Taylor & Francis Publishers, 1993), p. 18.

My (Michael's) own experience in clinical education is filled with examples of talking about death indirectly. At UCLA Medical Center, for example, people who die in the emergency room are called "M-5s," a reference to the form number completed at the time of death. At several other major hospitals in which I worked, a patient death was referred to as an "expiration." An operator calling a chaplain during the night would simply say, "There's been an expiration in Room 1211."

Euphemistic language serves as a buffer against emotionally laden experiences of attending to dead bodies, grieving families, and anxious staff. We need to examine this language because it also reflects deep-seated beliefs about grief and death. Pastoral theologian Roslyn Karaban[55] has developed an exercise to identify foundational attitudes about grief and death; we offer it below, with some modification.

INDIVIDUAL OR GROUP EXERCISE

Read the following list of words and place a plus sign (+) next to the ones that you deem positive, and a negative sign (-) next to the ones that you deem negative. Leave a blank space for the terms that appear neutral. Then repeat the exercise by relating the words to an actual person: for example, "My father is *dead*."

Dead	Abandoned
Dying	Suicide
AIDS	Cancer
Loss	Passed away
Passed over	Buried
Cremated	Gone
Murdered	Kicked the bucket
Went away	Absent
Lost	Expired
Bought the farm	Went to sleep

Discuss your insights with another person or share together in a small group. What feelings accompanied the use of different words?

Generate a list of euphemisms and phrases from your own experience that have not been identified in the list above.

---

55. Roslyn Karaban, *Complicated Losses, Difficult Deaths: A Practical Guide for Ministering to Grievers* (San Jose, Calif.: Resource Publications, 2000), pp. 105-6.

Stewards of Soul Language

Pastoral care givers serve as stewards of soul language. We help people sit with, make sense of, and eventually narrate their pain. As care givers, we exercise a dual function when dealing with people in the Pit of pain and grief: we attend to emotion, and we help them to reconstruct meaning in response to a loss.[56] The Bible can serve as a companion in both functions by validating and modeling feelings and emotions and by helping persons and communities to develop or deepen a sense of purpose and identity in the midst of, and following, an experience of loss. These functions often operate simultaneously in actual practices of care. Also, putting the second before the first can slow down the healing process or block it entirely. Aware of personal, familial, and cultural influences, care givers need to attend to emotion-expressing and to meaning-making. Grieving and expressing pain can be emotionally complex and potentially meaning-rich experiences. We must come to respect these experiences in order to be able to wrest meaning out of them.

TAKE-AWAY POINTS

Unhelpful Practices for Care Givers

1. Building a wall around our own pain ("His pain cannot touch me").
2. Categorizing loss according to a hierarchy ("She experienced more pain than he").
3. Minimizing the pain of another (victimizing).
4. Inflating the experience of another (idealizing, hero-izing).
5. Imposing a timeline for the grieving process ("You should be moving on").
6. Sharing stories of greatly disproportionate magnitude ("My mother died"; "My dog died").
7. Reframing toward the positive ("Look on the bright side").
8. Refusing to receive chaos stories ("You shouldn't talk like that").
9. Over-identifying with someone's pain ("I know exactly how you feel").

56. Robert A. Niemeyer, *Meaning, Reconstruction, and the Experience of Loss* (Washington, D.C.: American Psychological Association, 2001), p. 4.

Helpful Practices for Care Givers
1. Tending to stories and places of pain in our own lives.
2. Establishing and maintaining soul restoratives such as self-care and spiritual practices.
3. Trusting memories of grief, pain, and lament.
4. Becoming more comfortable with long silences and feelings of helplessness and inadequacy.
5. Staying present with intense emotions while practicing self-differentiation.
6. Meeting every situation with the expectation of cultural variance.
7. Refraining from critical theological judgments and responses to cries of pain.
8. Creating safe spaces for honest sharing of raw pain.
9. Recognizing that God weeps.
10. Allowing grief processes to unfold in their own time.

CARE PRAYER
Compassionate God,

Deep in the iron pit of despair, pain, and grief, we grope and scream our way with clenched fists through lament, fearing that there is no way out. When we feel abandoned in this place where our bodies shiver with emotion and our minds reel with images of destruction, you cry with us and accept us where we are. You reach into our deepest agony and suffering through a warm, friendly hug, a healing dream, a nourishing meal, or a community of care. As questioning anger, searing pain, and writhing grief gradually subside, we open ourselves to shoulders of strength to lean on as we move forward, one laborious step after the other, supported and loved. Amen.

Chapter 6

Contested Narratives, Conflicted Forgiveness

Denise's Story

In the early nineties I taught a large Introduction to the Hebrew Bible class at Wesley Seminary. Two male M.Div. students who had recently fled the civil war in Liberia offered up their interpretation of Rahab in Joshua 2. These two young men had been force-marched from their village and had watched helplessly as people in the line ahead of them were gunned down by members of rebel Charles Taylor's drugged children's army. With angry tears they denounced Rahab as a traitor to her people in Jericho. Rahab with her crimson cord (Josh. 2:15, 18) was no better than the prostitutes with whom Charles Taylor had made a deal: nail red cloth to your door as a sign of safe haven for my men, and you will be spared as we march toward the capital city of Monrovia.

Most of the students in the class sat in stunned silence as the pair told their story. I daresay that no one in that class had ever heard such an interpretation. After all, the New Testament lists Rahab as one of only five women in Matthew's genealogy of Jesus; Hebrews 11:31 includes her in the roll call of the faithful; and James 2:25 praises her as justified by works, not faith alone. How jarring to consider Rahab as a traitor in the context of the Liberian civil war that killed an estimated 300,000 people and uprooted hundreds of thousands from their homes. It seems fitting that Charles Taylor is to go on trial in The Hague for allegedly backing rebels and their atrocities in neighboring Sierra Leone.

•   •

I continue to tell my Liberian students' story when introductory classes study Joshua 2. Why? To illustrate the complex ambiguities and tensions in the story of Rahab on the theological, economic, psychological, and political levels — not only for Rahab, but also for her interpreters. These tensions challenge a passive or hegemonic interpretation of the text that refuses to see other interpretations from diverse contexts. Traditional readings of Joshua 2 favor a co-opted Rahab who serves the purposes of the colonizing Israelites claiming God on their side. Too many of us come to Joshua 2 identifying with the Israelites in order to affirm our superior self-understanding and to invoke divine approval for our politics. Encountering the radical "other" Rahab can be a practice of community-building and a spiritual/pastoral practice of growth in individual and national awareness. Can we let Rahab be "other" and a person, not simply "the prostitute," without domesticating her for our individual and national purposes?

Intercultural Bible Study and Care

The approach that we (Michael and I) advocate for communal and contextual Bible study in local congregations and communities is postmodern and postcolonial.[1] This kind of inquiry takes everyone's voice seriously and exercises care so as not to privilege one voice above others. Wanting to be reflective of God, who is radically inclusive, we begin with the faithful practice of listening to the many voices in the room and within the text. Pastoral theology as a discipline recognizes that knowing is "provisional," and values "the fact of multiple perspectives and irreducible differences in human experience."[2] Here we wish to demonstrate through a reading of a particular text — Joshua 2 — how challenging this multiplicity can be. We will examine tensions in the text and tensions within our present construction of reality in order to investigate the challenges to reading, listening, and knowing together. It is helpful to remember at the outset of our study that, in some respect, we all have access to various aspects of truth. We all bring impor-

1. These concerns surface in recent works on theory and practice within the field of pastoral theology and care. See Nancy J. Ramsay, *Pastoral Care and Counseling: Redefining the Paradigms* (Nashville: Abingdon Press, 2004), and Carrie Doehring, *The Practice of Pastoral Care: A Postmodern Approach* (Louisville: Westminster John Knox Press, 2006).

2. Ramsay, *Pastoral Care and Counseling,* p. 158.

tant knowledge to the discussion, shaped by our different experiences. Some of us, by virtue of our relative privilege and access to power, need to learn the value of making concessions and of acknowledging value in another's perspective or life experience. This concession-making involves yielding the space for another's truth or story to be expressed. It reflects the intentional Christian practice of hospitality. We physically create spaces of welcome for others to tell their stories in detail without judgment or condemnation.

The practice of listening in intercultural Bible study and care is a faithful exercise grounded in yearning to grow in knowledge of God, our sisters and brothers, and ourselves. We practice listening together in community because we don't know everything. Our vantage points in life are partial and biased by our position and social location. We know what we know; and others know what they know. We must risk stepping over the chasms that often divide us. As we risk meeting and listening to especially the disregarded or socially disgraced other, we come to know more intimately the face of reality. Assumptions and stereotypes may be turned inside out and upside down. Most of us do not take kindly to such shape-shifting of our mental scaffolding. We grow accustomed to ordering the world in a way that suits us. But such ordering can be odious and hostile to those who do not stand to benefit from it.

Rahab's Story

Rahab's story is plurivocal: it offers multiple voices that can be read from multiple contexts. For example, postcolonial feminist Musa Dube argues that Rahab represents "a land to be colonized. . . . Rahab is the only land [the spies] enter. . . ."[3] Robert Coote suggests that Rahab's prostitution is a result of her family's poverty. Her story is at base a folk narrative about the poor pitted against kingly power, meant to appeal to debtor families under King Josiah's reign who would sympathize with her.[4] Of course, debt slavery and debt prostitution still exist in our

3. Musa Dube, *Postcolonial Feminist Interpretation of the Bible* (St. Louis: Chalice Press, 2000), p. 77.

4. Robert Coote, "The Book of Joshua," in *New Interpreter's Bible*, vol. 2 (Nashville: Abingdon Press, 1998), pp. 592-96. The Deuteronomist co-opted the populist story of Rahab to appeal to Canaanite clients of Josiah's landed-elite opponents who might de-

world today.[5] Carmen Nanko-Fernandez, speaking of contemporary Latino/a (im)migrants, issues a warning that we might heed when romanticizing Rahab in Joshua 2: "Naive interpretations of border-crossings as passion/resurrection experiences downplay the ongoing uncertainty and risk of life in the 'promised land.'"[6] Robert Warrior of the Osage Nation insists that God the deliverer has become God the conqueror in the Joshua narratives. Consequently, Native Americans must identify with the Canaanites who already lived in the promised land but whose story has been silenced.[7] Trent Butler sees Rahab's story as Israelite ironic humor in a spy story with folkloric elements.[8]

These multiple interpretations born of diverse social locations may cause those of us in comfortable, homogenous mainline churches to become defensive and dismissive. As we argued in Chapters Two and Three, group biblical interpretation, whether in classroom or church, inevitably engages us in the caring of one another. Our identity emerges in our relationships with the biblical text and its characters, with others past and present studying the text, and with God. These relationships, however, can challenge who we are and what we think a text means, and create confusion about boundaries long held between "us" and "them." Like us, Rahab is a person of contradictions, necessarily so in order to navigate life in community. Yet we assume that to be faithful people, we need to be conflict-free and contradiction-free. Though we may want to romanticize her and put her on a pedestal, Rahab refuses to allow us to escape her contradictions or our own.

How we conduct Bible study matters in terms of our pastoral caring of one another. In the case of Rahab's story, to start off by saying "You/We are the colonizers" would be to shut down dialogue, listening, and discovery for those in positions of power. On the other hand, a

---

cide to submit to Josiah's sovereignty. Coote argues that Joshua essentially gave Rahab a green card, treatment that can model our approach to sweatshops and migrant workers.

5. Siroj Sorajjakool, *Child Prostitution in Thailand: Listening to Rahab* (New York: Haworth Press, 2003).

6. Carmen Nanko-Fernandez, *Perspectivas: Hispanic Theological Initiative,* Occasional Paper Series 3, no. 10 (Fall 2006), p. 58.

7. Robert Warrior, "A Native American Perspective: Canaanites, Cowboys, and Indians," in *Voices from the Margin: Interpreting the Bible in the Third World,* ed. R. S. Sugirtharajah, new ed. (Maryknoll, N.Y.: Orbis Books, 1995), pp. 277-85.

8. Trent C. Butler, *Joshua,* Word Biblical Commentary, vol. 7 (Waco, Tex.: Word Books, 1983).

dominant or traditional reading of Rahab as faithful heroine can block contributions from colonized peoples, such as the Liberian students discussed earlier. Marginalized people are often too polite. Out of concern for their safety, they hesitate to share what Gerald West calls the "hidden transcript" of their story.[9] What matters is honoring the social location of each of the readers of a text. As A. Samuels points out, "Pastoral theology and care cannot be separated from the social, political, and cultural context."[10] Neither can Bible study.

The field of pastoral psychology can provide language to help navigate multiple voices in our inner world as that world encounters multiple voices of the inner worlds of others in a biblical text like Joshua 2. Self-knowledge is key to all forms of relational knowing. If we don't know ourselves, or are unwilling to know ourselves, then all of our relationships suffer. Yet we live in a time of information overload that outpaces our ability to know, so knowing who we are has become more difficult. It takes focused work for us to recognize shadow and light, perfections and flaws, warts and beauty, all that gives us joy and makes us fearful.

Our inner landscape is no more terrain to be "conquered" and "colonized" than the actual land that Rahab inhabited. Sometimes, however, this is exactly the way we approach our knowledge of self and others. A student in a pastoral-care course once commented that we must "bust our self-deceiving idols in the service of Christ." This well-intentioned student unwittingly conveyed a sensibility that many of us harbor: change takes place by aggressive means of control. Unfortunately, this pattern of conquering and colonizing, learned from our outer experience and taught to us through history, media, politics, and the Bible (i.e., Holy War, war waged in God's name), is imported to our inner world at great cost. We cede trust-filled, ease-filled, relational patterns to patterns of violence and unhealthy aggression. This becomes dangerously detrimental when we are frightened into a corner. There we are more likely to pull inward even further, narrowing our ability to engage with others. We might also lash out with hostility as we attack and seek to annihilate the potential threat.[11]

---

9. Gerald West, *Reading Other-Wise: Socially Engaged Biblical Scholars Reading with Their Local Communities* (Atlanta: Society of Biblical Literature, 2007), p. 17.

10. A. Samuels, *The Political Psyche* (London: Routledge Press, 1993), p. 340.

11. See Walter Wink, *Engaging the Powers: Discernment and Resistance in a World of Domination* (Minneapolis: Fortress Press, 1992). Wink speaks of the "myth of redemptive vio-

GROUP EXERCISE

Designate one end of the room a "ten" and the other end a "one."

Ask each member of the group to position himself/herself along a continuum from one to ten in response to these questions:

1. When I encounter difference, I tend to retreat into a corner (one) or lash out with hostility (ten).
2. I consider myself privileged (one) or marginalized (ten).
3. When I encounter something new, it takes me a while to come to terms with it (one), or I jump onboard right away (ten).

Have the group discuss their responses.

Biblical Text as Contact Zone

We can begin to create a space for interpretive encounter by looking at Joshua 2 as a "contact zone" — that is, "the space of colonial encounters" where separated people come into contact with one another.[12] This text is a contact zone between Israelites and Canaanites, specifically on the border between them in Jericho, near fords of the Jordan River. This text also provides a contact zone for us as readers to make multiple contacts with Rahab, the Israelites, the people of Jericho, God, ourselves, other readers, our group/nation, and our myths. Joshua 2 creates a space (borrowing from postcolonial theory) that is "hybrid," porous, and unfixed. This means that boundaries shift, and we are pushed to confront what we think we know about others and about ourselves. It is a liminal or threshold space[13] for Rahab, but also for us as readers. Just as Rahab shifts her tone from confession to negotiation in verse 12, as signaled by the words "Now then . . ." — so we

---

lence" that can be traced back to the thirteenth-century B.C.E. Babylonian creation myth called *Enuma Elish*. This myth undergirds American popular culture, civil religion, nationalism, and foreign policy. Wink argues that Holy War is based on this myth. Its theology proclaims God's victory over chaos by violence. With this thinking, "there can be no compromise with an absolute evil"; it must be "totally annihilated or totally converted" (p. 19). This leaves no room for the "other" and precludes negotiation and dialogue.

12. Mary Louise Pratt, *Imperial Eyes: Travel Writing and Transculturation* (London: Routledge Press, 2007), pp. 6-7.

13. In *Playing and Reality* (New York: Basic Books, 1971), D. W. Winnicott calls this space the "intermediate area, or the third area of experience" (p. 14).

readers turn from confessional certainties about identity to negotiated understandings of one another and the text. The contact zone provided by Joshua 2 makes space for this to happen.

How we make contact will depend upon our own contexts and the skill of the facilitator. Out of his context in South Africa, Gerald West urges us to create interpretive space for "ordinary readers" (i.e., non-scholars) to "bring their life experiences and perspectives to the text and to articulate the meaning they find in the text in their own words."[14] As Nancy Ramsay cautions, it is naive for instructors (and, we would add, for pastors leading Bible study) to imagine that they can create a completely safe space.[15] We can, however, model a readiness to work through painful experiences without allowing anyone to be shamed. Ramsay insists that we must know our students, rejecting stereotypical knowledge of them, and recognize the three concerns held by those who are not Euro-American like their instructors: alienation, isolation, and vulnerability of self-esteem.[16] As noted above, we must also know ourselves as instructors, becoming self-aware of our own cultural identity and asymmetries of difference, and how our racial privilege might distort self-understanding.

Taking a cue from Daniel Smith-Christopher, we suggest that we must also become "good coyotes" or border runners.[17] Smith-Christopher builds on the work of Bob Ekblad and his work with (im)migrant workers in Washington state.[18] Ekblad challenges the negative image of border runners between the United States and Mexico, especially the *polleros,* or coyotes, who help people from Central and South America cross over. Many (im)migrants call them "good coyotes" and heroes. For Smith-Christopher, Jonah, Jesus, and Harriet Tubman were "good coyotes," and Christians are called to violate borders that become excuses for conflict, bigotry, and war. It takes a strong conscience to be a good coyote. In metaphorical language, if the self is

14. West, *Reading Other-Wise,* p. 72.

15. Nancy Ramsay, "Teaching Effectively in Racially and Culturally Diverse Classrooms," *Teaching Theology and Religion* 8 (2005): 20.

16. Ramsay, "Teaching Effectively in Racially and Culturally Diverse Classrooms," p. 19.

17. Daniel Smith-Christopher, *Jonah, Jesus, and Other Good Coyotes: Speaking Peace to Power in the Bible* (Nashville: Abingdon Press, 2007).

18. Bob Ekblad, *Reading the Bible with the Damned* (Louisville: Westminster John Knox Press, 2005).

the vehicle — say, the ship — then the superego/conscience is the rudder and compass. A moral compass is necessary for navigating the inner and outer worlds and crossing borders. The compass of our conscience gives focus and direction to life.

Our moral compass, however, needs sufficient flexibility not only to keep us on course, but also to alter direction, sometimes slightly and at other times radically. The conscience (superego) is developed through meaningful interaction with significant others: first parents and primary care givers, then teachers and mentors in educational and church communities. What happens when the lessons and ideals we learn need to change, as they might when we cross the border with Rahab? Who decides what changes need to be made and why? A "weak" superego (conscience) can leave people subject to driving impulses (e.g., lashing out at the prostitute with hatred, superiority, or judgment), but are these impulses necessarily negative for oppressed peoples? A "weak" superego can also lead to the exercise of a powerful and tyrannical external authority (e.g., killing the Canaanites in a Holy War), but these impulses are often endorsed by the dominant culture. A "strong" superego (conscience) allows for honest exploration of self, community, and other. Our individual and communal moral compass is culturally conditioned. We must be on the lookout for ways in which our superego navigates harm or healing.

QUESTIONS FOR REFLECTION

- What is your initial response to Rahab? In your opinion, what kind of woman is she? Generate a list of adjectives to describe her.
- When in your life were you a "coyote" — that is, when did you cross a boundary and who/what did you meet on the other side? What was your reaction?
- How likely are you to cross a boundary again?
- How is your moral compass culturally conditioned?

Cultivating Conscience in Bible Study

A number of practices can help to cultivate a healthy conscience in Bible study. A healthy conscience allows one to develop the ability to differentiate between right and wrong as well as to reflect on what blurs the distinctions between the two and how context shapes those distinctions. Cultivating conscience can lead to a healthy sense of ethical and moral responsibility that is not injurious to self or neighbor. Bible study leaders, particularly within dominant culture groups, need to encourage and model three different levels of listening:[19]

> *Consonant listening:* Consonant listening recognizes places of agreement and commonalities. This kind of listening is relatively easy for group participants and builds a sense of *simpatico,* not sympathy.[20] Consonant listening emerges when we identify with and can relate to aspects of the narrative being studied and the experiences of our fellow readers. The caution here is that we can easily see in the text only what we want to see, what makes us comfortable. From the viewpoint of the dominant culture, Rahab would represent a model of faith who risks everything for Israel's God.
>
> *Dissonant listening:* Dissonant listening recognizes places of discomfort, disagreement, and conflict and perceives commonalities between texts, narratives, and readers, and among readers themselves. The experience of dissonance can prompt an internal shutting-down or closing off so that the listener actually stops listening, even while perhaps pretending to do so. This dissonance would emerge in those who would be shocked by the description of Rahab as a traitor to her people.
>
> *Harmonious listening:* This kind of listening recognizes the emotionally, spiritually, and intellectually arduous posture of listening to and through commonalities as well as differences in stories, while intentionally staying open and attentive to self and others in the process. As in music, harmony in listening blends these

19. Emmanuel Lartey, *In Living Color: An Intercultural Approach to Pastoral Care and Counseling,* 2d ed. (New York: Jessica Kingsley Publishers, 2003), p. 34, citing Kluckholn and Murray, *Personality in Nature, Society, and Culture* (New York: Alfred Knopf, 1948). Lartey argues that every human person is (1) like all others (universal), (2) like some others (cultural), and (3) like no other (personal).

20. David W. Augsburger, *Pastoral Counseling across Cultures* (Philadelphia: Westminster Press, 1986), pp. 27-32. Augsburger distinguishes among concepts of sympathy (a projective, spontaneous identification with another's feelings that assumes some commonality); empathy (an intentional sharing of another's feelings that assumes some difference); and interpathy (an intentional envisioning and experiencing of another's worldview that assumes vast differences).

commonalities and differences for pleasing effect in terms of our relationships with one another. Such listening builds on David Augsburger's idea of "interpathy" (see the previous footnote). Harmonious or interpathic listening is a border-crossing practice which builds on the assumption that people on both sides of the divide are "equally human."[21] Herein lies the challenge, as Rahab's story shows. To assume that a foreign prostitute operates with a moral compass that generates concern for herself and for her family's survival is beyond the comprehension of many.

Pastoral care practices in Bible study can foster personal edification and growth, as well as develop and strengthen moral conscience for the betterment of community. Growth in consciousness (the ability to see and know the environment) needs to coincide with growth in conscience (the ability to engage morally in a decidedly ambiguous world). Concretely, this means that Bible study ought to recognize the power in ambiguity.[22]

Suggestions for Recognizing the Power in Ambiguity
1. Challenge the ease of constructing narratives that always make us look and feel good.
2. Honor the text/story enough to push back.
3. Risk "real" relationship, not one based on either idealization or pity/patronage.
4. Examine language, double standards, rules, and policies for their colonizing effects.
5. Pay attention to the interrelated dynamics of power and its influences.
6. Try to see differently.

21. Lartey, *In Living Color,* p. 94. See also Kathleen Greider, "From Multiculturalism to Interculturality: Demilitarizing the Border," *Journal of Supervision and Training in Ministry* 22 (2002): 40-58. Greider argues that movement toward interculturality requires development of the spiritual capacity and the gift of receptivity. See also Emma Justes, *Hearing Beyond the Words: How to Become a Listening Pastor* (Nashville: Abingdon Press, 2006). Justes suggests that caring relationships emerge through humility, thoughtful availability, vulnerability, and reciprocity.

22. Rev. Dr. David J. O'Malley remembers that Professor Letty Russell often referenced the phrase "There is power in ambiguity."

7. Learn to negotiate ambivalence; make it a life skill.
8. Accept ambivalence as a source of knowing, seeing, and healing.

GROUP EXERCISE: RAHAB AND THE ROAD MAP

To understand better the interpersonal and intercultural dynamics of Joshua 2, speak the story. Assign speaking parts for the story's characters: the narrator, Joshua, Rahab, the informants in verse 2 (which will require several speakers), the king, the spies (also requiring several persons speaking in unison). Read through the story once; then read it a second time.

Note any speed bumps in the story that slow you down or push your emotional buttons. Who has the largest speaking part in the story? Is this surprising? If so, why? These questions emerge from step two of the Road Map for biblical interpretation (see Chapter One).

Next, consider step one of the Road Map. How has your personal context or your community's social location pointed you to these speed bumps? Reflect intentionally on what may be unconscious or partially conscious in your reaction to these speed bumps.

For step three of the Road Map, look for repeated phrases in the story. Is there an envelope that brackets the story? What is it? Where is the turning point in the story? What details are significant in the story? Why?

For step four, consider the place of Joshua 2 in the larger book of Joshua and in the context of Holy War. Read about Holy War in a good Bible dictionary. Investigate the status of prostitutes in ancient Israel, and the structure of city walls (v. 15).

Finally, tackle step five of the Road Map. What message(s) do you take away from this story? Can you affirm this message? Why or why not?

Border Crossings

What borders must those in the dominant culture cross to reach Rahab? What borders must she have crossed to be described as having "lived in Israel ever since" in Joshua 6:25? What borders must readers cross to hear one another from their different contexts? How do we cross those borders?

To reach Rahab, those of us in the dominant culture must recognize that Joshua 2 is a "contested narrative." Interpathy suggests crossing borders with the intended purpose of reaching out to others, while simultaneously reaching in to one's own sense of self.[23] The problem from a biblical standpoint is that Rahab's world, thoughts, and feelings are not unmediated but communicated through Israelite eyes. The Israelites are telling this story from the vantage point of having taken the land from the Canaanites. Thus, the reader is faced with a double challenge that parallels Rahab's own. A contemporary illustration of this "double consciousness" (a term coined by W. E. B. Du Bois) emerged in Barack Obama's campaign for President of the United States. Amina Luqman called it "Obama's tightrope."[24] That is, the media buzz over whether Obama was "black enough" was really a question of whether white America trusted that Obama was not "too black." Luqman asserts that black Americans walk this tightrope every day.

If part of a marginalized group, we must struggle to recover Rahab's voice when reading Joshua 2. If part of the dominant culture, we must struggle to uncover what we don't want to hear or see. "Not seeing" takes effort. Paradoxically, however, it is a recognition of seeing and not wanting or being willing to work with the challenges of what is seen. The class's shocked, silent response to the story told by the Liberian students offers a case in point. The Liberians' emotional interpretation of Rahab challenged the class's self-validation. The class had been predisposed to view Rahab positively as a paragon of faith who recognized the inclusive nature of Israel's God — and thus of our Christian God.

Tikva Frymer-Kensky illustrates this approach by arguing that Rahab's words "I know" (v. 9) are a conversion formula for foreigners acknowledging Israel's God (Exod. 18:11; 2 Kings 5:15) in a kind of "proto-conversion" (a kind of rough, initial model for later, more formalized conversion).[25] To strengthen the case for a positive view of Rahab, she

23. Reaching in and reaching out is informed by theories of depth psychology and theories of human personhood. Even these theories, however, are culturally conditioned. Therefore, care must be exercised so as not to universalize the tools and methods of Western psychology.

24. Amina Luqman, "Obama's Tightrope," *The Washington Post*, 6 July, 2007, sec. A, p. 15.

25. Tikva Frymer-Kensky, *Studies in the Bible and Feminist Criticism* (Philadelphia: Jew-

notes extensive parallels between the Exodus stories and Rahab's story.[26] "Once again, the saved are to stay inside the house marked in red; Rahab's family is to be rescued from Jericho, as the Israelites were from Egypt."[27] Rahab is a "new Israel." This interpretation evidences consonant listening for the dominant culture. It is a comfortable reading that obliterates the Canaanites.

Rahab's World

How are we to enter Rahab's world? More importantly, what world does she inhabit? The text of Joshua 2 offers several clues, but each can be interpreted in different ways depending upon the reader's context. In 2:1, Rahab is called a prostitute — in Hebrew, *zonah*. The NIV offers a footnote that suggests this term can be translated as "innkeeper." This translation suggests Miss Kitty from the TV show *Gunsmoke* or the glamorous and shrewd businesswoman played by Dolly Parton in the movie *The Best Little Whorehouse in Texas*. However, this is not an option in the semantic range of the word in Hebrew. Prostitutes formed part of the underclass in ancient Israel. The book of Leviticus forbids priests to marry prostitutes (21:7) and forbids fathers to force their daughters into prostitution, perhaps as a way out of the family's poverty (19:29). Prophets like Hosea, Jeremiah, Ezekiel, and Isaiah used prostitution as a metaphor for Israel's unfaithfulness to God (see Chapter Three).

---

ish Publication Society, 2006), pp. 213-14. Frymer-Kensky supports this claim by pointing to Rahab's asking for *chesed* from the spies in exchange for her demonstration of loyalty. She negotiates a formal Deuteronomic covenant with them, which includes preamble and prologue (vv. 9-11); Rahab's stipulations — salvation for family and a sign of assurance (vv. 12-13); the spies' stipulations — keeping silent and obeying the command to stay in the house (vv. 18-20); an oath (vv. 14, 17); and a sign — the scarlet cord (vv. 18-21).

26. In Exodus 2:2-3, Moses' mother saves him by hiding him. Hiding Moses begins the events in Exodus, while hiding the spies begins the process of conquest in Joshua. Like the midwives who defy Pharaoh in Exodus 1, Rahab lies to the king of Jericho about the spies. In Joshua 2:18, Rahab lets the spies down from her window with a crimson cord, which recalls the slaying of the firstborn of Egypt in Exodus 2. One of my (Denise's) students, embracing the dominant interpretation, called this Rahab's "umbilical cord to a new life." We can also look ahead to the New Testament and the "cup of blood" in 1 Corinthians 11. Rahab uses the language of Holy War in the words *eima* ("dread") and *namog* ("melt"), which echo Exodus 15:15-16.

27. Frymer-Kensky, *Studies in the Bible and Feminist Criticism*, p. 213.

A man's having sex with a woman outside of the family or household, such as a prostitute, threatened the very definition of the family and its economic stability because the act endangered inheritance. Consequently, sexual relations are closely regulated in Deuteronomy. Rahab is also a foreign woman, a Canaanite. In the Hebrew Bible, foreign women are blamed for enticing Israelite men into apostasy. Even King Solomon "turned away his heart after other gods" because of his foreign wives (1 Kings 11:4). Crossing this prostitution boundary, or what we call "the forbidden zone," means that we must examine prostitution in the ancient world and our own attitudes toward prostitutes. Think of the many versions of the word *prostitute* in our culture that expose our ambivalence: *whore, lady of the night, harlot, slut, hooker, madame, escort*. The wildly popular movie *Pretty Woman* starring Julia Roberts and Richard Gere romanticizes prostitution. Hookers have a heart of gold and can "clean up real good" and be "rescued" by powerful men.

Some readers will take a hard line and reject prostitutes (and liars) as morally depraved. This makes it easy to lump the "bad" (from a moral standpoint) Rahab in with her fellow "bad" (from a religious standpoint) Canaanites. Frymer-Kensky, for example, notes that Rahab's name means "wide, broad" and that she is "the 'broad of Jericho' — the wide-open woman who is the wide-open door to Canaan and maybe the open door to apostasy."[28]

Other readers will resonate with Musa Dube, who argues that Rahab's story is "loaded with colonizing ideologies."[29] As a prostitute, she is wild and must be saved by superior, moral conquerors. Because the spies in verse 24 repeat Rahab's words in verse 9, Dube insists that Rahab's voice has become one with that of the colonizer. She is the "mouthpiece of their agendas" and their "textual fantasy"[30] who proclaims the colonizer's superiority, pledges loyalty, and surrenders rights. Dube's observation about this text is echoed in an editorial piece by Uzodinma Iweala from Nigeria, who warns us in the West to "stop trying to 'save' Africa." She reacts to the West's celebrity-led campaign (e.g., by Bono, Angelina Jolie) to stop genocide in Darfur. Iweala observes that stereotypical reports about Africa as a "black hole of disease and death," with tribal conflicts, child laborers, corruption, and abused women, are

---

28. Frymer-Kensky, *Studies in the Bible and Feminist Criticism*, p. 217.
29. Dube, *Postcolonial Feminist Interpretation of the Bible*, p. 77.
30. Dube, *Postcolonial Feminist Interpretation of the Bible*, p. 78.

reminiscent of reports from "the heyday of European colonialism." Africans who are working to address these problems are ignored. They are "used as props in the West's fantasy of itself."[31]

GROUP EXERCISE

Share your reactions to interpreting Rahab in non-traditional ways. What energizes and/or troubles you about these different interpretations? Why?

The Wild One Within

Animal energy, the unconscious, the id, the untamed and unknown, is in a sense our inner Rahab: the image of the unwanted/unknown/radical "other" inside of us and also within our community. We must recognize and name this image; otherwise, we will remain consonant, comfortable listeners. We may venture into this area with absolute terror that can possibly lead to our undoing, unless we are bolstered by the strength of self/community that allows for this stepping out in faith. Acknowledging our inner Rahab relates, in part, to our development of trust, which is foundational to all other life stages. We can call this a practice of spiritual hybridity, taking our cue from Rasiah Sugirtharajah, who declares that "the postcolonial notion of hybridity is not about the dissolution of differences but about renegotiating the structure of power built on differences. . . . Hybridity is a two-way process in which both parties are interactive so that something new is created."[32] Practicing spiritual hybridity can be challenging.

For example, dominant-culture readers and feminists (how ironically complex!) connect with Rahab by arguing that she is the wealthiest member of her family and therefore negotiates for them ("my father and mother, my brothers and sisters, and all who belong to them" — Joshua 2:13, 18; 6:23). She subverts the patriarchal household. Yet she is still identified as "Rahab the prostitute" in Joshua 6:25. Musa Dube warns that imperialism in Rahab's story undercuts any

---

31. Uzodinma Iweala, "Stop Trying to 'Save' Africa," *The Washington Post*, 15 July 2007, sec. B, p. 7.

32. Rasiah Sugirtharajah, *Postcolonial Criticism and Biblical Interpretation* (Oxford: Oxford University Press, 2002), p. 191.

use we can make of her for feminist ideals.[33] Because Rahab hid the spies in the stalks of flax on her roof (2:6), some argue that she had wealth, since flax was made into linen, a luxury fabric (Isa. 3:23). But flax was also made into sails, nets, and twine — the stuff of everyday life of the period. Rahab spread the flax on her roof not only to dry it but first to have it moistened by the dew, which produced a coarser product compared to soaking it in water.[34] The coarser product would have been used in the making of everyday goods, not luxury items. Robert Coote reminds us that "poverty was by far the most common cause of prostitution in the ancient world" and that the poverty of Rahab's father's house (in Hebrew, *bet 'ab*) was what forced her into prostitution in the first place. He argues that people in churches who are not poor might not recognize how this text resonates with the experience of the poor.[35] Prostitution as a way out of poverty continues to be practiced today.

Another comfortable, consonant reading pities and romanticizes "poor" Rahab. Some have pointed to Rahab's physical habitation in Jericho as a symbol of her underclass status: she was living "on the outer side of the city wall and she resided within the wall itself" (2:15). Archeological excavations of Canaanite city walls reveal casemate walls that surrounded cities. Casemate walls consisted of two parallel walls separated by about five or six feet of space with crosswalls at regular intervals separating off rooms or rectangular compartments within the wall.[36] Sometimes these spaces were filled with rubble to strengthen the wall; sometimes they were used for storage or incorporated into the back wall of a house. Perhaps Rahab's "house" was in one of these rooms. She lived a marginalized life on the boundary of Jericho society, hanging on by her fingertips. Perhaps she even "serviced" the king, who was watching what went on (2:2). This can help readers from the dominant culture to understand what was at stake in her decision to lie to the king about the spies' location and send his men on a wild goose

---

33. Dube, *Postcolonial Feminist Interpretation of the Bible,* pp. 70-75.

34. Suzanne Richard, "Linen," in *Harper's Dictionary of the Bible,* revised and updated (San Francisco: HarperCollins, 1996), pp. 608-9. Also, see Philip King and Lawrence Stager, *Life in Biblical Israel* (Louisville: Westminster John Knox Press, 2001), p. 150: "Flax had many uses, depending upon the quality of the flax plants." Flax could be used for everything from thread and fine linen to lampwicks.

35. Coote, "The Book of Joshua," p. 592.

36. King and Stager, *Life in Biblical Israel,* pp. 32, 232.

chase (vv. 4-5). By protecting the Israelite spies, Rahab, "the woman on the edge," hoped for possibilities and a different future for her life.

However inspirational that may seem, as a foreign woman, Rahab found herself in a precarious position. At the mercy of the approaching Israelite army waging Holy War, she was threatened by the ban *(cherem)* of total destruction (Deut. 20:16; Josh. 6:21). Women have been and remain spoils of war. They have been raped and then often killed. Systematic rape has been used as one of the weapons of the international war in the Congo that has been raging since 1996. Human rights groups estimate that hundreds of thousands of women have been raped by militias from Uganda, Burundi, and Rwanda.[37] Rahab focused on survival for herself and her family. Who among us would not do the same?

As we reach inward in self-examination, we can learn that shadow and light dwell within us as well as in "the other."[38] Rather than being a selfish or navel-gazing practice, this spiritual looking and reaching has, paradoxically, profound implications. It connects us to — rather than disconnects us from — our neighbors and even to the alien "other." For if we look inward and acknowledge what we see, even when we don't like it, we move closer toward compassion. Compassion is the courage to come close to "the other," even if it challenges our own self-identity. This looking, it is hoped, is also non-violent. It can challenge the link between violence in our own personal interactions and the violence between nations and groups in the world. A pastoral care practice of non-violent listening in Bible study groups would mean acknowledging histories of violence in families, institutions, economic systems, and nations. Reading Rahab with interpathy means that we acknowledge her position between a rock and a hard place in her own city of Jericho and in relation to the Israelites.

---

37. Kathleen Kern, "Victims as Pariahs," *Christian Century,* 24 January 2006, p. 9. Raped women are considered "contaminated" and are driven with their children from the village. Children of rape often become pariahs too — street children in the cities. Rape as a military weapon has also led to an increase in sexual assaults among civilians.

38. Pamela Cooper-White, *Many Voices: Pastoral Psychotherapy in Relational and Theological Perspective* (Minneapolis: Fortress Press, 2007). White urges us to embrace chaos, silence, and therapeutic love.

Caught in the Center

As Letty Russell argues, there are three choices for those marginalized by gender, ethnicity, and economics: (1) choose the center and copy the oppressors to be accepted by the dominant group; (2) choose not to choose and internalize oppression in resignation and loss of self-esteem; and (3) choose the margin — work in solidarity with others to move toward the center through resistance that can lead to transformation.[39] Choosing the center is saturated with ambiguity. Dominant culture values Rahab's choosing positively. However, the Liberian students discussed earlier deem Rahab's choice of the center a "sellout": she betrayed her own people. Musa Dube would agree with the students. Israel uses Rahab as an example of a preserved artifact to retain power in Canaan. Native culture and people survive as suppressed entities. Yes, Rahab and the Gideonites live in Israel (Josh. 6:25; 9:1-27), but as a way for the colonizer to maintain power. The insider/outsider distinction "is never meant to be absolute."[40] Former identities can never be completely erased; they linger. Rahab is still called "the prostitute" in Joshua 6:25, even though she saved the spies and began living among the Israelites. One wonders what kind of life she lived among them with these layers of identity. Recognizing the tension in otherwise rigid categories can help guard against the self-delusion of thinking that we are working at the margins when we are actually caught in the center. This is duplicitous and warrants continual "checks" with others who can call us on it.

In Joshua 2:11, Rahab mimics the Israelites with her declaration ("The LORD your God is indeed God in heaven above and on earth below"). We can view this mimicry in two ways: as a genuine confession, or as a subversion of patriarchy, because Rahab knows that this is what the Israelites want to hear. As a genuine confession, Rahab's declaration corresponds to or imitates what the Israelites themselves testify to about their God. Her words may also constitute the first step to surrender and her "perfectly colonized mind" (Dube). She buys hook, line, and sinker the story of Israel's liberating God, and appears to be an ex-

---

39. Letty Russell, *Church in the Round: Feminist Interpretation of the Church* (Louisville: Westminster John Knox Press, 1993), pp. 192-93.

40. Similarly, the palimpsest (written-over space) left by Queen Vashti's ejection leaves a space that remains when Esther takes her place. See Timothy Beal, *The Book of Hiding: Gender, Ethnicity, Annihilation, and Esther* (New York: Routledge, 1997).

ceptional "outsider" who becomes an "insider." This serves to reinforce the colonizers' identity as divinely sanctioned conquerers of the indigenous Canaanites. Rahab's words also give the green light to Israel to cross over the Jordan into the Promised Land in Joshua 3.[41]

In a subversion of patriarchy, Rahab presents herself as a traitor. By siding with the Israelites, she abandons her own people. The Israelites have succeeded in isolating her belief from that of her community, thereby fragmenting solidarity with her people in good colonial fashion. Rahab is damned either way. A woman caught in mutiple worlds, she is not free to be who she really is, her authentic self. Here is another "text of terror" that can be added to Phyllis Trible's list.[42] I'd never looked at Rahab that way before because I (Denise) wasn't ready to. How do we ready readers to see differently?

We can see differently by identifying the national myths that shape our beliefs, our relationships with others, and our roles in life. In addition to considering the personal, marital, family, and ministry myths articulated by Edward Wimberly,[43] we (Michael and I) suggest considering how national myths shape our life's meaning and purpose. We are called to evaluate the positive and negative elements of all of these myths. When we discover aspects of our national myths that block human community, we can "re-author" and "re-story" them by bringing new perspectives to past experiences.[44] We recognize that such re-authoring constitutes a border-crossing into unknown territory. Re-authoring begins with an identification of themes that make up the myth.

One such theme is American expansionism. Ryan LaMothe suggests that this theme is "deeply rooted in the American psyche." It has

41. Frymer-Kensky, *Studies in the Bible and Feminist Criticism*, p. 217. The mention of Shittim in verse 1 links Rahab with Numbers 25, in which Israel angered God by associating with women from Moab. Phineas is rewarded for his zeal in killing an Israelite man and the Midianite princess he had brought into camp. But even Rahab as the exceptional outsider can create problems for Israel. Frymer-Kensky argues that saving Rahab as an act of reciprocal *chesed* (covenant loyalty based on the agreement with the spies) violates *cherem* (the Holy War's ban on cities that results in their total destruction) as the first act of apostasy after Israel enters the land. This act contains the first seed of Israel's destruction.

42. Phyllis Trible, *Texts of Terror: Literary-Feminist Readings of Biblical Narratives* (Philadelphia: Fortress Press, 1984).

43. Edward P. Wimberly, *Recalling Our Own Stories: Spiritual Renewal for Religious Caregivers* (San Francisco: Jossey-Bass, 1997), pp. 1-72.

44. Wimberly, *Recalling Our Own Stories*, pp. 73-88.

been supported by religious-mythic narratives that proclaim the United States' divinely sanctioned role in history. He calls this the "empire psyche" and outlines four themes that mark it: (1) the illusion of American altruism, (2) a sense of entitlement, (3) simplification into "us" and "them," and (4) pride and arrogance. These themes elevate the war dead to hero status and diminish the humanity of "the other." LaMothe urges prophetic pastoral care to confront this empire psyche.[45] Perhaps we could ask how faithful Christians and Jews today are "breaking the Second Commandment by too closely identifying the purposes of God with the purposes of the nation."[46]

Group Exercise

Make a list of bumper stickers that express the "empire psyche." Develop a counter-list of bumper stickers that challenge this psyche.

Intercultural Bible Study

Intercultural Bible study creates a safe enough zone in which people can meet, express themselves, and listen together in order to chart new steps in faith. Pastoral and lay care givers serve as the stewards and guardians of such space, helping to ensure respect among all people. Structured guidelines must be implemented to ensure that the space does not inadvertently become a hostile and threatening zone for marginalized people. Studying, sharing stories, and learning together can be border-crossing work. To make the effort to know and truly be known requires courage and strength of heart and mind because we often do not have equal footing. Some of us have to stand down so that others may be able to stand up. Though sensitive and resilient beings, we are also scared, bruised, and co-opted by systems and patterns of economic disparity, social injustice, and national hypocrisy. Sign-

45. Ryan LaMothe, "Render unto Caesar: Pastoral Care and the American Empire," *Pastoral Psychology* 55 (2007): 339-51. A similar approach is taken by Laurel Dykstra in *Set Them Free: The Other Side of Exodus* (Maryknoll, N.Y.: Orbis Books, 2002). She challenges the dominant culture in North America to read the Exodus narratives from the viewpoint of the Egyptian empire rather than from the perspective of the enslaved Israelites.

46. Nancy Duff, "Locating God in All the Wrong Places: The Second Commandment and American Politics," *Interpretation* 60, no. 2 (April 2006): 182-93.

posts of border crossings may include tempers flaring, tears flowing, a knot in the pit of the stomach or a tightness in the throat. Leaders and care givers need to pay attention to these signs and teach others to do so as well. Aware of these signs, participants may choose to share or withhold information based on levels of trust and empathy within a group. Study leaders must exercise care and caution in the sharing and investigating of stories, since borders and boundaries are rarely clear.

Border crossing sometimes leaves people feeling confused, questioning, perplexed, or angry. It is "edgy" work whose internal and interpersonal stirrings reflect a blurring of the boundaries between "us" and "them." The marginalized may move from refusing to have their identity assigned or co-opted by others to constructing their own reality. Stories of pain and anger may be the only means available to voice the frustration that underlies being pushed aside or marginalized. As people both within and outside the center share and listen to stories, everyone experiences the de-stabilization, either consciously or unconsciously. In this way, the ground of participants' souls is being tilled. Hopefully, few can read texts and hear stories without being changed. Realignment of perspective for those in the dominant culture can result when people begin to feel their own pain and recall their own experiences of being marginalized. Subtly and maybe even unwittingly, people begin to see the "other" in themselves.

Intercultural Bible study and care, based in principle and process on postcolonial theory, models realignment so that together we might know something more profound about the God who refuses stereotypes and realigns all relationships.

TAKE-AWAY POINTS FOR BIBLE STUDY IN THE CONTACT ZONE
1. Begin with the spiritual practice of adopting a "not-knowing" perspective.
2. Unravel the stereotypes based in large part upon misconceptions, prior learning, comfort, and ignorance.
3. Use "I" statements for one's own experience and avoid general, universalizing declarations.
4. Challenge those in the group who don't use "I" statements.
5. Look for the love and respect what others cherish.
6. Assume that everyone has some kind of pain.
7. Build up courage to cross borders and think differently.

8. Ask permission at the border or crossing to delve more deeply. Ask open-ended questions.

9. Identify and critique the national myths that shape our intercultural approach to texts.

10. Welcome "the wild one" within.

Bibliodrama

Peter Pitzele describes Bibliodrama as "a form of role-playing in which the roles played are taken from biblical texts. . . . [It is] a form of interpretive play."[47] Through Bibliodrama (see Chapter 2), readers from the dominant culture can better understand Rahab's conflicted position. To speak in the first person as Rahab can help us become aware of the tensions that her story generates. For the purposes of warm-up, a spectrogram for this text is presented below.[48] These pairs of opposites are meant to bring to the surface the tensions in Rahab's story.

Spectrogram

1. Biblical authority: The Word of God has power over my life (one) or no power over my life (ten).

2. I crave validation (one) or don't give a hoot (ten).

3. I'm very good (one) or not at all good (ten) at seeing what I don't want to see.

4. I thrive on (one) or run away from (ten) ambiguity.

5. My people are the colonizers (one) or the colonized (ten).

47. Peter Pitzele, *Scripture Windows: Towards a Practice of Bibliodrama* (Philadelphia: Alef Design Group, 1997), p. 11. The roles can be those of characters in the Bible or those we can infer from our imaginative reading of the text, whether animate or inanimate — for example, Noah's wife or the reed basket in which Moses was placed. Pitzele notes that Jewish tradition speaks of the Bible being composed in black and white fire. Black fire is the printed word on the page, and the white fire is the space between and around the black. Black fire is fixed, but white fire is always kindled anew. "Bibliodrama takes place in the open spaces of the text for which the black fire, the black letters, are the boundaries," says Pitzele (p. 24).

48. We have prepared this specific spectrogram in accordance with the "Bibliodrama Guidelines" prepared by Arlene Kiely, an MTS graduate of Wesley Seminary who was a guest lecturer in our class. She offers Bibliodrama workshops and retreats for churches and other groups; she can be contacted at arlkiely@comcast.net.

Set up chairs in a circle for the role playing. Let everyone know that not all have to play; one can simply listen. One person can speak multiple times, as long as he or she speaks in the first person, using "I."

Have participants work through the spectrogram first. Then have them switch gears and let themselves imagine that they are Rahab the prostitute in Jericho. They have just let the spies down a crimson cord out of their window and struck a deal with Joshua's spies: their safety and their family's safety in exchange for the spies' escape. What are their thoughts now, as the Israelites prepare to conquer Jericho?

Next, have participants de-role. Have them shake off their role as Rahab and return to the here and now.

QUESTIONS FOR SILENT REFLECTION

- When in your life have you felt like an outsider or experienced an in-between situation? What did people say or do to make you feel that way?
- Think back to a time when you surprised yourself by acting to protect someone you loved. What gave you the courage to act as you did?
- Have you ever found help from unexpected sources? Did your opinion of those helping you change? Why or why not?
- In what ways are you an insider or an outsider in your church? In your community?
- What compromises do you make in the way you live your life when it comes to your national identity?
- What would you pledge your life for today?
- What would it look like to work in solidarity with those on the margins of your community toward transformation of the center?

Conflicted Forgiveness

Perhaps the picture in Genesis 33 of a weeping Esau throwing his arms around Jacob's neck brings tears to our eyes. Before grabbing for the tissues, however, we would do well to recognize how we can too quickly romanticize the idea of forgiveness. We may think that it's easy, warm-and-fuzzy work, when in reality it can be among the most difficult of emotional and spiritual tasks. The story does not tell us how Esau came to forgive Jacob. There is no description of Esau's night wrestling with God. We can chalk up Esau's shift to God's mysterious activity, but this activity takes place in a human being who probably bears terrible emotional scars. After all, Jacob had stolen Esau's blessing and his birthright, and had humiliated him by dressing up in animal skins to suggest Esau's hairiness. The last we heard of Esau, he wanted to kill Jacob (Gen. 27:41). Twenty years later, he meets his brother. What went through Esau's mind during the intervening years? How did he deal with the betrayals of both his brother and his mother (who had planned Jacob's deception of the dying Isaac)?

At the same time that we romanticize forgiveness, we often blow out of proportion the crisis or conflict that precipitated the need for it. We assume that both the problem and its resolution need to be properly or better "managed."[49] Many assume that the pastor must take primary responsibility for this management in a congregation. Conflict management is far too technical a term to describe the ongoing responsibility of each person and of the community as a whole to practice forgiveness. The opposite danger is, of course, that we practice forgiving in a naive way.

We (Michael and I) suggest reflection on the theme of "conflicted forgiveness" in order to navigate these two extremes. Conflicted forgiveness accentuates the patterns of forgiveness and "unforgiveness" underlying tension, disagreement, and conflict within congregations and between people. The relational trio of self-forgiveness, other-forgiveness, and God-forgiveness informs our discussion and analysis. Within these broad relational categories complex dynamics complicate forgiveness. Forgiveness of self can be easy for some and tremendously difficult for others. Forgiveness of others can be blocked by an offending person's inability or unwillingness to ask for or receive forgiveness. Forgiveness of God can be difficult for people whose theological views conflict with the idea of God needing either forgiveness or protection from our criticism.

---

49. Solomon Schimmel, *Wounds Not Healed by Time: The Power of Repentance and Forgiveness* (New York: Oxford University Press, 2002), pp. 91-97. Drawing upon Robert Enright's work, Schimmel identifies at least twenty intricate steps related to forgiveness. He writes that counselors and therapists need to have a philosophical and theological framework for understanding forgiveness. While we (Denise and I) agree that such a framework is necessary, we question how user-friendly these steps are. One cannot dictate a template for forgiveness for another person. Not everyone will or can follow the same process for forgiveness.

Getting in Touch with Assumptions

Forgiveness is a somewhat difficult topic for me (Michael) to explore because I have not known any "large" experiences of forgiveness in my life. Culturally, we tend to focus on sensational events and national tragedies when dealing with the notion of forgiveness, as recent documentaries demonstrate — e.g., *The Power of Forgiveness* about 9/11 (see page 196 in this chapter). When Denise and I screen such documentaries in our classes, students react in emotionally stunned silence, overwhelmed by the immensity of what is depicted. It's difficult to tear our voyeuristic selves away from this immensity to focus on forgiveness in our own lives from day to day. We need models for the more mundane aspects of forgiveness that express the complexity of our journey towards it. For example, I (Michael) can remember the pain I experienced as a young campus minister when I was not hired for a job in which I had been serving as an intern for a year. Relationships were tangled because I had worked collegially with people who had also been my ministers in college. Untangling the hurt in this relational matrix became my work of forgiveness. This untangling occurred in a process rather than a one-time event.

Part of what makes forgiveness so difficult is the set of assumptions about it that many of us bring to the table. Michael and I identify some of these assumptions below:

- It has to happen for everyone.
- There is a predetermined timetable for it.
- We are not good Christians/Jews/people if we are unable to forgive.
- It should be easy or automatic.
- It means forgetting what happened.
- After forgiving, we return to square one.
- The hurt is too serious to warrant forgiveness.
- It is a place we get to rather than a process.
- It won't do any good; what's done is done.
- Justice doesn't allow forgiveness.
- We can't be forgiven unless we deserve to be forgiven.
- We must forgive because God forgives.

QUESTIONS FOR REFLECTION
- What assumptions do you make about forgiveness?
- Why do you think Esau forgave Jacob? Could you have forgiven Jacob? Why or why not?

When we asked our students in class to share their definitions of forgiveness, they found it much easier to tell us what forgiveness was *not*, rather than to define it positively. For them, forgiveness was not going back to square one, absolving, sugar-coating, saying everything was OK, claiming it didn't matter, avoiding anger, forgiving the family of the perpetrator, responding to an apology, or necessarily about reconciliation. By beginning with what forgiveness was not, our students were then able to attempt a definition of what it was, albeit with continuing difficulty: letting go of the trauma's or the perpetrator's power over me; speaking truthfully about the harm done, and choosing life anyway; knowing that both I and the offender would stand before God as equals; releasing the offender from the responsibility of who I am today and tomorrow; the ability to see a person who has wronged me not as an ememy, but as a person who made a mistake, is liable to make mistakes, and is broken; letting go of revenge; and remembering without debilitating pain.

These definitions veered from focus on the self to focus on the other; some of our students recognized the trio of self, other, and God, while others left God out of the equation altogether. Detached from the lived experiences that shaped these definitions, we groped our way toward some corporate understanding and realized that there was none. Forgiveness is situational, which means that one definition can hardly encompass the variety of human experience. Recognizing this, caring communities need to avoid imposing a template for forgiveness upon themselves or individuals within the community. Michael and I offer this definition of forgiveness: for peace, either from one asking for it or one struggling to grant it, forgiveness is an open-ended prayer that is not necessarily answered in ways that we expect or even desire.

As much as we may idealize forgiveness as our preferred goal, ample biblical warrant exists for "unforgiveness."[50] The lament psalmists complain about "enemies" who are vicious; metaphorically they are likened

---

50. For what follows, see Denise Dombkowski Hopkins, *Journey through the Psalms* (St. Louis: Chalice Press, 2002), pp. 87-94.

to mad dogs, bulls, or lions. The modern equivalent may be a pit bull. Psalm 17:10-12 describes the enemies this way: "They close their hearts to pity. . . . They track me down. . . . They are like a lion eager to tear." Most of us can concretize the enemies in Psalm 17 from our own experience, be they parents who don't trust their teenagers, adult children who watch their elderly parents for the first signs of senility, doctors who treat their patients simply as bodies and not whole persons, or church committees critical of their pastor. Especially problematic for some is the revenge language that peppers the lament psalms, which we see, for example, in Psalm 58:6-8: "O God, tear out the fangs of the young lions. . . . Let them vanish like water that runs away; like grass let them be trodden down and wither." This petition seems to conflict with Jesus' admonition to "love your enemies" and "turn the other cheek" (Luke 6:27-31; Matt. 5:43-46). Perhaps the angry psalm language "recognizes the difficulty of commanded love and speaks to the process of loving. Can we love someone before we acknowledge our hatred of him or her? Can such an acknowledgment of hatred be cathartic and defuse a hateful action, especially if it is offered up in the context of worship within the community of faith?"[51] The violence of enemy language offers a needed corrective to an overemphasis on God setting things right in the next life, after death. Psalms of lament insist upon justice in this life. Without justice, forgiveness can become nothing more than "cheap grace."

Reconciliation

Forgiveness sometimes may eventuate in reconciliation. When it does, forgiveness can be viewed as a relational process that requires *an awareness and a reckoning* on both sides: an awareness of being hurt or hurting others, as well as a reckoning experienced within confrontation with self, others, and God in order to move on. This relational process requires another subject, even if that subject is simply an aspect of oneself. We have already seen, for example, how Arthur Waskow suggests that Jacob was wrestling with himself by the Jabbok River, even as he wrestled with God and with Esau. (See Chapter Two.) Some people argue that the apology they offer for wrongdoing, even if not accepted, honors their self-wrestling and frees them of their burden of guilt. In

---

51. Hopkins, *Journey through the Psalms*, p. 91.

this situation, awareness and reckoning happen on one side and can open the possibility of the other side's response of forgiveness, but the situation doesn't demand it.

The reconciliation of Joseph and his brothers takes place in Genesis 42–45. Both he and his brothers experience an awareness and a reckoning. In these chapters we learn that Jacob sends his sons down to Egypt to buy food because of the famine in Canaan and orders them to return a second time when the food from the first trip runs out. The first time in Egypt, the brothers "bowed themselves before him [Joseph] with their faces to the ground" (Gen. 42:6). They do not recognize Joseph, but he recognizes them; still, "he treated them like strangers and spoke harshly to them" (Gen. 42:7). He peppers them with a series of hostile questions and accuses them of being spies (Gen. 42:7-17). Joseph acts out the alienation and pain that he had experienced at their hands. They had plotted to kill him but sold him into slavery instead, ignoring his cries from the cistern into which they had thrown him.

Aviva Zornberg argues that Joseph instills a "radical anxiety" in his brothers with his harsh questioning.[52] They experience the terror that Joseph himself experienced because of their cruelty many years before. At this moment, they, like Joseph then, are no longer in charge of their own story. "This is no simple act of revenge," Zornberg says, "but an invitation to them to live through that fragmentation of a given reality that has been his own experience. . . . Before he can be at one with his brothers, it seems, it is essential that they too know that fragmentation."[53] Here we can say that Joseph re-experiences his own hurt and forces his brothers to re-experience their hurting of him. Memories come flooding back for Joseph (in his dreams; 42:9), for his brothers (in

52. Aviva Gottlieb Zornberg, *The Beginning of Desire: Reflections on Genesis* (New York: Image Books, 1995), p. 263.

53. Zornberg, *The Beginning of Desire,* p. 266. Zornberg discusses in this connection the symbolism of Joseph's coat that his brothers had dipped in goat's blood to show their father, Jacob. They had literally "stripped" (Gen. 37:33) that coat from Joseph, a verb used for skinning animals for sacrifice. The coat symbolized the quality in Joseph that was "both grace and irritant" that they envied and hated (p. 267). Like a burnt offering, Joseph was consumed utterly, so that nothing remained of him. After checking the pit into which he and his brothers had thrown Joseph, Reuben reported, "The boy is gone" — literally, "He is not" *(einenu)* (Gen. 37:30). The brothers had distanced themselves from Joseph by conspiring to kill him when they saw him at a distance: "They saw him from afar, and before he came close to them, they conspired to kill him" (Gen. 37:18-19).

their guilt over Joseph; 42:21-22), and for their father, Jacob (42:36). The narrative makes it clear that God has made this possible: "So it was not you who sent me here, but God" (Gen. 45:8a).

Perhaps Joseph had used "unconscious defenses" all these years to repress his feelings about his severe childhood trauma of betrayal, separation from his beloved father and home, and imprisonment in a foreign country. Using "psychological numbing" in order to survive, Joseph comes to realize that this is "not the ideal long-term solution. [54] It may be that Joseph numbed himself by living his life in what Waskow terms "a spiral of ambition" as overseer or boss. Four times he was appointed to rule over those with whom he might have felt some solidarity but did not: with his own family (Gen. 37:5-11); with his fellow slaves in Potiphar's household (Gen. 39:1-6); with his fellow inmates in prison (Gen. 39:19-23); and with all of Egypt as supreme overseer, second only to Pharaoh (Gen. 41:37-49).[55] Zornberg suggests that "Joseph's conscious memory of himself fails, as he works to survive in pit, prison, and palace."[56] When his brothers appear in Egypt, Joseph involves them in his "involuntary" reconstruction of the past. He jails Simeon (Gen. 42:24) just as he had been jailed, and he orders Benjamin to be "brought down" to Egypt just as he had been.

The layers of confrontation between Joseph and his brothers focus on the three instances of Joseph's weeping.[57] The first time, he weeps in response to his overhearing their regrets: "Alas, we are paying the penalty for what we did to our brother; we saw his anguish when he pleaded with us, but we would not listen. That is why this anguish has come

---

54. Samuel Mann, "Joseph and His Brothers: A Biblical Paradigm for the Optimal Handling of Traumatic Stress," *Journal of Religion and Health* 40, no. 3 (Fall 2001): 340. Mann suggests that "Joseph was unable to forgive until he finally experienced the depth of his emotional pain." Mann cautions therapists to look for ongoing unconscious defenses in apparently "successful" trauma survivors and the late impact of psychological trauma.

55. Arthur I. Waskow, "In the Dark: Joseph and His Brothers," *God Wrestling* (New York: Schocken Books, 1978), pp. 34-35.

56. Zornberg, *The Beginning of Desire*, p. 274.

57. Their confrontation unfolds within a larger family dynamic. Jacob has already split the brothers in his naming of them. Clearly, Rachel's sons, Benjamin and Joseph, are beloved. The naming expresses the split in the parents' own psyches that fuels intergenerational conflict. We have seen how Jacob and Esau also reflected their parents' favoritism (see Chapter Two). See David W. Augsburger, *Helping People Forgive* (Louisville: Westminster John Knox Press, 1996), pp. 52-53.

upon us" (Gen. 42:21). The brothers don't recognize Joseph, and they don't know that he can hear and understand them. They speak to him through interpreters. Joseph leaves the room to cry and then returns to order the jailing of Simeon. The second time, he hurries away to weep after Benjamin is brought to him. He has to wash his face before he comes back into the room and then gives orders to serve the meal (Gen. 43:30-31). "Each time he weeps," Zornberg points out, "something opens up in him, an unplanned response, which is at first a mere parenthesis, as he turns away and then turns back to his tyrannical role. . . . As they [he and his brothers] speak of what is not in the past, a new relationship is suggested, woven of regret, empathy, loss. Listening to them, Joseph begins to be."[58] His weeping releases repressed memories.

The third time, Joseph can "no longer control himself." He sends all the attendants away, instead of leaving the room himself, and declares, "I am Joseph. Is my father still alive?" (Gen. 45:1-3). This time, "his weeping is an eruption of the pain of his loss, intensified to a point that compels him to give up the masquerade."[59] He has found pieces of his lost self. His brothers are so "terrified" (in Hebrew, *bahal*) that they cannot answer him. The Talmud suggests that they are too ashamed to answer. Joseph fills the silence and claims a connection with them: "I am your *brother*, Joseph." (45:4; our emphasis). He rehearses their painful history and points to God as the one who brought them back together: "for God sent me before you to preserve life" (Gen. 45:5). Not hiding what his brothers did to him, Joseph gives what Zornberg calls a "therapeutic narrative, full of expressions of relationship . . . allowing God to take up the slack of that distance [between them]."[60] Forgiveness is not simply human work. It requires God to "take up the slack" of the distance separating us from others. In this sense, forgiveness is a gift from God.

Taking Up the Slack

God may well take up the slack, but we still have our own work to do. Giving completely to God what is essentially ours to do reflects sloppy responsibility. What do we learn from Joseph's story about our own

58. Zornberg, *The Beginning of Desire*, p. 307.
59. Zornberg, *The Beginning of Desire*, p. 309.
60. Zornberg, *The Beginning of Desire*, p. 311.

stories? We observe the repetition of a cycle: "You hurt me, so I'm going to hurt you back." We think we can see the situation clearly, and we say to ourselves, "All Joseph needs to do is X, Y, and Z." Our suggestions tumble out. Ah, but it's not so easy. We too are caught in the endless cycles of repeating the same thing over and over again until we are able to come home to ourselves. Then we own up to the hurt that others have inflicted on us and that we have inflicted upon them and future generations.

Looking directly at how Joseph handles the triggering emotion in his situation offers us another way to take up the slack. Joseph's story begins with anger: his brothers' anger at his favored status as Jacob's son and Joseph's anger at his brothers' betrayal. Thrown into a pit, his cries ignored by his brothers, Joseph becomes angry. As Andrew Lester explains, "The capacity to experience anger . . . is only activated when we perceive that we are in danger or threatened."[61] Joseph pours this anger into a questioning story when his brothers, many years later, come down to Egypt for food: "Where do you come from? . . . You are spies. . . . Here is how you shall be tested" (Gen. 42:7, 9, 15). Joseph transforms his threatened narrative in steps that correspond to those outlined by Lester for beneficially harnessing anger's transformative power:[62]

1. Recognize anger when it occurs. The omniscient narrator suggests that Joseph recognizes his anger by describing Joseph's encounter with his brothers in this way: "When Joseph saw his brothers, he recognized them, but he treated them like strangers and spoke harshly to them" (Gen. 42:7). The word play with two words from the same root *(nakar)*, "recognize" and "treat like strangers," drives this point home.

   Instead of denying or avoiding this anger — something we often do, either out of fear or guilt over anger as sinful — Joseph expresses it. Suppressing our anger can be dangerous; unidentified anger can interfere with our ability to deal with anger responsibly. We need to learn to identify our unique physical, mental, and behavioral signs of anger.

2. Acknowledge anger by naming and claiming anger as ours. Joseph

---

61. Andrew Lester, *The Angry Christian: A Theology for Care and Counseling* (Louisville: Westminster John Knox Press, 2003), p. 90.

62. For these steps, see Lester, *The Angry Christian*, pp. 226-46.

acknowledges his anger in Genesis 42:8. The narrator tells us a second time that "Although Joseph had recognized his brothers, they did not recognize him." This painful lack of recognition on the brothers' part prompts Joseph to remember in verse 9 his earlier dreams about ruling over them. Joseph accepts what he feels by allowing himself to remember. Instead of suppressing it, Joseph unleashes his anger in accusation. He insists that his brothers are spies when he knows they are not. When we acknowledge anger as Joseph did, we often struggle to overcome our fear, guilt, or shame about being angry.

3. Demobilize our bodies by controlling them without suppressing anger. Joseph turns away from his brothers in 42:24 to weep after overhearing them admit to ignoring his anguish after they threw him into the pit. Trying to control his body in front of his brothers, he turns away to weep. We might exercise, meditate, listen to or play music, or pray in order to demobilize our bodies.

4. Identify the narrative threatened. The narrator uses the brothers to tell the story that has simmered in Joseph all these years. Hearing his brothers tell the story of how they did not listen to his pleas for help when he was in the pit (42:21) helps Joseph to identify why he was angry. He acknowledges this memory by choosing to jail his brother Simeon while the rest return to Jacob to get Benjamin (42:24). Simeon's name comes from the root *shema'*, "to listen." Like Joseph, we can use anger as a "diagnostic tool" to uncover what feels threatening.

5. Evaluate the validity of the threat. Joseph decides that his angry stories are no longer necessary or appropriate when he reveals himself to his brothers when they return to Egypt: "I am your brother, Joseph, whom you sold into Egypt" (45:4). He no longer hides who he is from them. Instead, he reclaims the family relationship by using the phrase "your brother." Like Joseph, we are called upon to evaluate what's going on in terms of our faith and values.

6. Transform the story that made us vulnerable to threats. Joseph changes the frame of his story so that anger no longer drives it: "Now do not be distressed, or angry with yourselves, because you sold me here; for God sent me before you to preserve life" (45:5). Joseph now allows God to co-author his story. Likewise, we begin to revise our threatened stories so that they come more into line with our faith narratives.

7. Change patterns of dealing with anger. Joseph modifies his actions toward his brothers. He no longer lords it over them, treats them like strangers, or hides his tears. Instead, "he kissed all his brothers and wept upon them; and after that his brothers talked with him" (45:14-15). We might need to change patterns of silence, nagging, violence, passive-aggressiveness, or hostile humor.

8. Express anger creatively. Joseph releases his anger and rechannels it by going beyond Pharaoh's instructions to give his brothers wagons and provisions for their journey back home and adding some humor: "Then he sent his brothers on their way, and as they were leaving, he said to them, 'Do not quarrel along the way'" (45:22-24). We might not be as witty as Joseph and might therefore journal or express anger to a trusted other instead.

When we forgive, we oscillate between groveling, which leaves our knees bloody, and hubris, which leaves our noses bloody. Some of us know one extreme better than the other, but both are damaging to the soul. We have experienced our selfhood being torn to shreds by humiliating forces outside of our control, so we stay small and low to avoid being hurt more. And still we get hurt. We have experienced our selfhood being torn to shreds by humiliating forces outside our control, so we puff up and beat our chests to avoid being hurt again. And still we get hurt. What breaks this mind-numbing, repetitive cycle?

Joseph weeps. "And he wept so loudly that the Egyptians heard it, and the household of Pharaoh heard it" (Gen. 45:2). Joseph weeps so profoundly that he both loses himself and finds himself in the experience. His is no ordinary weeping. It's not even about the tears, but rather about the soul-altering transformation that occurs. What breaks this cycle is his recognition that repeating the cycle doesn't work — it only harms everyone. To break the cycle, we sink into or soften the tender heart of sadness, and we allow tears to wash away all that interferes with our humanity as beloved creatures of God.

This spiritual experience acknowledges real pain and does not seek an outlet in self-flagellation or blaming others. Our softening moves us very personally inward as we continue to confront what we see and not turn away from it. We may like or dislike some of what we see. What matters is that we love ourselves through it all with a commitment to live toward shalom. As we do, we allow ourselves to come face to face with the many, many others who long to return home to themselves.

<small>QUESTIONS FOR REFLECTION</small>

- How do you know when you're angry? What are the unique physical, mental, and behavioral signs of your anger?
- What do you usually do to demobilize your anger?
- What emotions does Joseph's treatment of his brothers in Egypt evoke in you?
- In what ways have you used "unconscious defenses" to repress pain?
- Identify your moments of awareness and reckoning in a process of forgiveness that you have experienced. If this has not yet occurred, why not?

Inviting and Practicing Forgiveness

Dylan's Story

I (Michael) went to the playground with my two-year-old nephew, Dylan, and learned something about ease-filled self-forgiveness. Step by step, Dylan hoisted himself up the small rock-climbing wall as I stood close by. When he was almost to the top, his foot slipped on one of the plastic rocks, and he went sliding down the wall (thankfully, only about three feet high). I expected to hear him scream in tears. As I helped him stand, dry-eyed, he said, "Didn't make it." Then he walked to a new site of play. That was it.

•   •

Dylan didn't return to the climbing wall that day, but he has in the months since the incident. These words of a toddler — "Didn't make it" — recommend themselves as a self-forgiveness mantra for adults. Such a mantra can help us to overcome the many "experiential vectors" that contribute to conflicted forgiveness, including personality habits, psycho-biological composition, family patterns, cultural dynamics, power differentials, social injustice, and inter-generational memories. Many of these vectors direct us toward negative self-assessments in the face of challenges: "I'll never get there," or "Who do I think I am, trying this?" or "This is too difficult for me, so I should quit." We can, instead, choose a gentler form of self-talk: "Didn't make it today." We might practice this mantra until it becomes familiar. Practice can free us up from paralysis and prompt us to try again. Pastoral leaders can model this mantra practice and help people to identify the experiential vectors that resist it.

Forgiveness as a practice of the heart involves more than seeking an abstract knowledge of forgiveness and its definitions. The practice of forgiveness requires an internal recognition of wrongdoing accompanied by an external change in behavior.[63] Our understanding needs to seep into the actual experience and actions of our lives. Another practical dimension of this "seeping" is our relative ability or inability to genuinely say "I'm sorry; I did wrong." This invitation to forgiveness may or may not prompt forgiveness from the one wronged. Pastoral leaders support the practice of forgiveness by modeling the ability to say "I'm sorry; I did wrong" and by encouraging others to do so in their mending of relationships. In this way, congregations can take one more step toward becoming communities that embody forgiveness. The practice of speaking in this way builds up our capacity for forgiveness, much like exercise every day builds up our muscles and lung capacity.

Simply saying "I'm sorry" may not be enough if we use the phrase as a blanket to cover over the absence of appropriate actions. Saying it when it isn't our fault in order to take responsibility for someone else's deed is dishonest. Saying it as a means to smooth over tension without constructively working through differences is cowardly. Saying it without the accompanying "I did wrong" simply expresses regret and may or may not imply a request for forgiveness. A "Pearls Before Swine" comic from Stephan Pastis showed Mouse announcing that he had decided "to start saying sorry" for his wrongdoings. When asked by Pig if it was because he'd realized all the pain he had caused, Mouse replied, "Because I've realized sorry is just a word and you can say it without meaning it."

---

63. For other definitions of forgiveness, see Michael McCullough, Kenneth Pargament, and Carl Thoresen, *Forgiveness: Theory, Research, and Practice* (New York: The Guilford Press, 2000). They define forgiveness as "intraindividual pro-social change toward a perceived transgressor that is situated within a specific interpersonal context" (p. 9). See also F. LeRon Shults and Steven J. Sandage, *The Faces of Forgiveness: Searching for Wholeness and Salvation* (Grand Rapids: Baker Academic, 2003). They speak of forensic, therapeutic, and redemptive forgiveness: "a process of (a) reducing one's motivation for avoidance and revenge and (b) increasing one's motivation for good will toward a specific offender" (p. 20).

Some argue that Western culture has made forgiveness into a therapeutic notion in need of theological integrity.[64] Self-deception can all too easily occur with forgiveness. We can let ourselves "off the hook" without facing the moral music. In this vein, Susan Bauer has studied twentieth-century public apologies in the United States — for example, those of Bill Clinton, Jimmy Swaggart, and Bernard Cardinal Law. She has observed that they have become exercises in self-defense that "often serve as red herrings, drawing the eye and ear away from the missing confession."[65] "I did wrong" offers a confession, or an admission of fault. Such admission means that the individual takes responsibility for what happened. This is the second and perhaps more difficult step in the invitation-to-forgiveness process. Denise and I urge communities and individuals to be on guard against the tendency toward self-deceptive forgiveness and moralizing through forced forgiveness. In the name of forgiveness, communities can coerce people to "Get over it," "Forget about it," "See God's purpose in it," or "Move on" before they're ready. This, too, can be a problematic form of deception. Genuine forgiveness comes as God's gift and is known by God's freeing power.

Questions for Reflection
- When have you offered "I'm sorry" as words that didn't mean anything? What prompted you to do so?
- When have you practiced self-deceptive forgiveness? Why?
- Try to identify your "experiential vectors" that support self-deceptive forgiveness.

Forgiveness in the Hebrew Bible

In the Hebrew Bible, covenant frames forgiveness. Consequently, forgiveness often, but not always, hinges upon repentance. The Hebrew word translated "repent" comes from the verb *shub*, meaning "to turn,

---

64. L. Gregory Jones, *Embodying Forgiveness: A Theological Analysis* (Grand Rapids: Wm. B. Eerdmans, 1995). Jones discusses how forgiveness has been co-opted by "a therapeutic grammar of modern Western life" (p. 47). Contra Jones, see David Augsburger's *Helping People Forgive*; he brings resources from Scripture, theology, and the social sciences together to explore the complicated nature of forgiveness.

65. Susan W. Bauer, *The Art of the Public Grovel: Sexual Sin and Public Confession in America* (Princeton: Princeton University Press, 2008), p. 2.

to turn around onto the right path, to turn away from wrong, to return." It is both an attitude and an action that concretizes confession of wrongdoing. Repentance is central to Deuteronomistic theology and its message to the exiles: "If you . . . return to the LORD your God . . . then the LORD your God will restore your fortunes and have compassion on you, gathering you again from all the peoples among whom the LORD your God has scattered you" (Deut. 30:1-3). Repentance is embedded in covenant relationship, according to Walter Brueggemann, and it "became a decisive theme in response to the exile,"[66] when Israel questioned whether or not its covenant relationship with God had ended.

The final form of the book of Jeremiah, for example, addresses the exiles. Jeremiah repeatedly calls for Israel's repentance or "turning" *(shub)*, as well as reiterates God's willingness to forgive. "Return, faithless Israel, says the LORD. I will not look on you in anger, for I am merciful. . . . Only acknowledge your guilt, that you have rebelled against the LORD your God" (Jer. 3:12-13; also 3:14). Again in 3:22 God declares, "Return, O faithless children, I will heal your faithlessness" (cf. 4:1-2). The people respond to God's command/invitation with confession in 3:25: "Let us lie down in our shame, and let our dishonor cover us; for we have sinned against the LORD our God." Even Jeremiah himself is invited by God to turn back *(shub)* after he has uttered one of his gut-wrenching laments full of reproach of God. God responds, "If you *turn back,* I will *take you back,* and you shall stand before me. . . . It is they who *will turn* to you, not you who *will turn* to them" (Jer. 15:19, our emphasis). God's words call Jeremiah to refocus his prophetic role and continue what he has been doing: speaking God's word. For Jeremiah, these are "words of reassurance and reaffirmation"[67] rather than words of rebuke.

Ezekiel 18 is saturated with *shub* language in response to questions from the exiles about the fairness of what God has done. Many of them blame parents and grandparents for their current situation in exile: "What do you mean by repeating this proverb concerning the land of Israel, 'The parents have eaten sour grapes, and the children's teeth are set on edge'?" (Ezek. 18:2). The prophet stresses that each generation

---

66. Walter Brueggemann, *Reverberations of Faith: A Theological Handbook of Old Testament Themes* (Louisville: Westminster John Knox Press, 2002), p. 172.
67. Terence E. Fretheim, *Jeremiah* (Macon, Ga.: Smyth & Helwys, 2002), p. 242.

must accept responsibility for its own sin. Turning toward God means life; turning away from God brings death. The final word from God is this: "For I have no pleasure in the death of anyone, says the Lord GOD. Turn [*shub*], then, and live."

God's Conflicted Forgiveness

The pre-exilic (eighth century B.C.E.) prophet Hosea offers us a poignant glimpse into the conflicted heart of God in 11:1-9. Here, God struggles to forgive. The metaphor of God as parent creates a "love sandwich": God's love (vv. 1-4 and vv. 8-9) in both the past and the future brackets God's anger and disappointment over Israel's present sin (vv. 5-7). God remembers tenderly the nurturing of Ephraim (another name for Israel) in the wilderness. Nostalgia trumps the reality of Israel's complaining in the wilderness. Yet Ephraim has "refused to return [*shub*] to me," God complains. "My people are bent on turning away [*shub*] from me" (vv. 5, 7). The consequence will be severe: "They shall return [*shub*] to the land of Egypt, and Assyria shall be their king" (v. 5). Israel will experience a reversal of the Exodus from Egypt and return to enslavement, this time under Assyria. God's compassion overcomes God's anger, however. "How can I give you up, Ephraim? How can I hand you over, O Israel? . . . My heart recoils within me; my compassion [probably *rechamim*, "womb-love"] grows warm and tender. I will not execute my fierce anger" (Hos. 11:8-9a).

We also find a conflicted God in the story of the Flood in Genesis 6:6: "The LORD was sorry that he had made humankind on the earth, and it grieved him to his heart." The Hebrew for "was sorry" is not from the root *shub* but from *nchm* — literally, "to change one's mind." In the story of the Flood, this divine change of mind has negative consequences for humankind. It is associated with God's refusal to forgive.

In Jeremiah 18:8, God's change of mind is positive and offers hope for forgiveness. After God points out to Jeremiah at the potter's house that God can rework clay spoiled in the potter's hands, God declares, "If that nation, concerning which I have spoken, turns from its evil, I will change my mind [*nchm*] about the disaster that I intended to bring on it. . . . Turn now [*shub*] . . . and amend your ways and your doings" (vv. 9, 11). The tension that God feels about forgiveness in Jeremiah emerges in God's command to Jeremiah not to pray or intercede for the people, "for I will not hear you" (7:16-17; cf. 11:4; 15:1). God expresses this tension by weeping over the people's inability and unwillingness to follow God (Jer. 8:18–9:2, 17-19).

Forgiveness as Advocacy

In Genesis 18:16-33, Abraham argues with God over the fate of the city of Sodom, forcing God to reconsider obliterating the entire city for the sin of some: "Far be it from you to do such a thing, to slay the righteous with the wicked. . . . Far be that from you! Shall not the Judge of all the earth do what is just?" (Gen. 18:25). Samuel Balentine explains, "Here, God speaks, Abraham prays, and *then* God's word is executed."[68] God does not offer forgiveness or punishment automatically. What Abraham says affects God's action. Abraham reminds God of God's character, calls God to God's self and to covenant responsibility. Abraham confronts God and pushes God closer and closer to justice. "He is blunt, persistent, and nontraditional," says Terence Fretheim.[69] Abraham shows us that "intercession counts for something; Abraham's intercessory advocacy makes a difference."[70] What does this mean for our attitudes about forgiveness? Can confrontation block forgiveness? Promote it? Do we sometimes need to push on behalf of others for forgiveness?

As Abraham's encounter with God makes clear, forgiveness means meeting God head on. Rather than slithering away in meek resignation, we can learn to stand up to God, trusting that our protests on behalf of others will be received by God. Our advocacy makes an impression upon God, who modifies divine action accordingly. We need to reframe advocacy and confrontation as positive rather than negative faith practices. We must avoid equating confrontation with being "pushy." Forgiveness as advocacy takes active, prayerful, intentional work in a back-and-forth exchange. Forgiveness does not occur in one fell swoop. Forgiveness as advocacy does not rest upon individuals alone but belongs to the entire community.

68. Samuel E. Balentine, *Prayer in the Hebrew Bible: The Drama of Divine-Human Dialogue* (Minneapolis: Fortress Press, 1993), p. 145.

69. Terence Fretheim, "Genesis," in *New Interpreter's Bible,* vol. 1 (Nashville: Abingdon Press, 1994), p. 468.

70. Fretheim, "Genesis," p. 479.

A QUESTION FOR REFLECTION

- When has someone intervened and urged you to consider forgiveness? How did they help you to change your mind?

Jonah's Conflicted Forgiveness

If God can be conflicted about forgiveness, how much more so can God's creatures? The prophet Jonah, for example, runs in the opposite direction when God calls him to prophesy against the Assyrian city of Nineveh. Jonah makes it clear in 4:1-4 that he ran away because he knew God would be a pushover and forgive the Ninevites: "That is why I fled to Tarshish at the beginning; for I knew that you are a gracious God and merciful, slow to anger, and abounding in steadfast love [*chesed*], and ready to relent from punishing" (4:2). Jonah wanted no part of a too-merciful God, except when he found himself in the belly of the fish. He wanted to die rather than give the wicked a chance to repent. God's forgiveness would upset the proper order of things: the wicked are punished, and the righteous are rewarded. Jonah's anger in 4:1 blocks his ability to forgive, but in 4:4, God asks, "Is it right for you to be angry?" By asking this question, God challenges Jonah's anger. As Phyllis Trible points out, "The divine questioning offers the opportunity to work it through and to work through it."[71] The book ends, however, with God's rhetorical question: "Should I not be concerned about Nineveh . . . ?" This suggests that Jonah is still working through the idea of forgiveness.

Jonah's demand for Nineveh's punishment seems to contradict the thanksgiving he offered up to God in the belly of the fish in chapter two. As Trible notes, the focus of Jonah's prayer is not really on God but on Jonah himself. He egotistically uses the first-person singular twenty-six times in eight verses.[72] How ironic that Jonah raises himself above idol worshipers in 2:8-9: "Those who worship vain idols forsake their true loyalty. But I with the voice of thanksgiving will sacrifice to you." The words "true loyalty" translate the Hebrew word *chesed*, which means "covenant loyalty." Mentioning idol worshipers connects Jonah

---

71. Phyllis Trible, "Jonah," in *New Interpreter's Bible,* vol. 7 (Nashville: Abingdon Press, 1994), p. 524.

72. Trible, "Jonah," p. 508.

back to the sailors in chapter one and forward to the Ninevites in chapter three. Both groups stand outside the covenant, yet they pray and do what honors God. Jonah's piety appears false and hypocritical in contrast. When Jonah declares in 2:9 that "deliverance belongs to the LORD!", "it has a nauseating effect." No wonder the fish "vomited Jonah" (2:10). God delivers the fish "from an indigestible burden."[73]

Jonah does not exhibit what Steve Sandage terms the interpersonal characteristics of "ego-humility"[74] that enhance the process of forgiveness. These characteristics include (1) little need to control defensively interpersonal encounters, (2) an intersubjective capacity to empathize and take the perspective of others, (3) a willingness to acknowledge and take responsibility for one's own actions and wrongdoing and seek repair when appropriate, (4) a stronger sense of gratitude than entitlement, and (5) a proclivity to view others as one's equal. Jonah sets himself above idol worshipers (the sailors and the Ninevites). His sense of entitlement trumps his sense of gratitude. He doesn't take responsibility for his actions. He's defensive. He doesn't empathize with the Ninevites and doesn't consider them his equals.

Lest we think we can manipulate God to forgive, Jonah 3 reminds us that forgiveness comes as God's gift. The king of Nineveh takes Jonah's announcement of judgment on the city (3:4) seriously and proclaims a fast and the wearing of sackcloth for everyone, including the animals:

> "All shall turn [*shub*] from their evil ways and from the violence that is in their hands. Who knows? God may relent and change his mind [*nchm*]; he may turn [*shub*] from his fierce anger, so that we do not perish." When God saw what they did, how they turned [*shub*] from their evil ways, God changed his mind [*nchm*] . . . and he did not do it. (3:8-10)

The question "Who knows?" is filled "with possibility and uncertainty."[75] It echoes the ship captain's use of "Perhaps" in 1:6. God's forgiveness is not automatic and cannot be coerced by human action.

---

73. Trible, "Jonah," p. 507.
74. Shults and Sandage, *The Faces of Forgiveness*, p. 93.
75. Trible, "Jonah," p. 514.

QUESTIONS FOR REFLECTION
- Which characteristics of "ego-humility" do you exhibit? Which are most challenging for you?
- Is it reassuring or challenging for you to acknowledge that God's forgiveness cannot be coerced? Why?

Penitential Laments

Six of the laments of the Psalms model a process of confession. Psalm 51, which often finds its way into our liturgies, provides "the basic themes and vocabulary of confession."[76] In verses 1-2, the psalmist asks God to show grace, covenant loyalty, and mercy by gracing, blotting out, washing, and cleansing. The wrong the psalmist has done is pervasive, as expressed by the repetition of terms for sin — transgressions, iniquity, sin, evil, guilt — in the first five verses. The psalmist offers no excuses but simply states "I know" (51:3; cf. penitential Psalm 32:5), in the sense of "I acknowledge," "I admit." God is in the right (v. 4). The psalmist does not whine, coerce God, or use language of obligation. In verse 7, the psalmist refers to a public ceremony of ritual cleansing as outlined in Leviticus 14:2-9, 48-53 and Numbers 19:6, 18. Sometimes we need witnesses to the act of confession and forgiveness. The community witnesses forgiveness within the covenantal frame. In verse 13, the psalmist as "wounded healer" vows that after cleansing is complete, "I will teach transgressors your ways." The psalmist "pays forward" God's forgiveness by teaching others.

Christian communities pray the Lord's Prayer in unison. We pray, "Forgive us our sins, as we forgive those who sin against us." By praying together, we unite individual, communal, and intercultural intention. A friend joined almost two million people on the Mall in Washington, D.C., to witness the inauguration of President Barack Obama. Rev. Rick Warren of the Saddleback Church in southern California concluded the opening prayer with the words of the Lord's Prayer. Though she questioned the use of a sectarian prayer in an intercultural and interreligious context, our friend acknowledged "the awesome sense" that came with thousands of people praying

---

76. Walter Brueggemann, *The Message of the Psalms* (Minneapolis: Augsburg Press, 1984), p. 98.

these words in unison. She realized that forgiveness roots itself in individual and collective prayer. The church practices and embodies forgiveness as a community and thereby enfolds each member of the body into the embrace of this radical idea. When individual members are unable to forgive, the community does the work the person is not yet able to do. Sometimes we can make a "forgiveness decision,"[77] intentionally deciding to forgive even though we don't feel it in our bones. So we wait for our attitude and actions to catch up to our decision. Sometimes, the most a person or congregation can do is sense the need for forgiveness. Unable to do the work ourselves, we "pray it forward" so that future generations are released from the bondage of being unforgiven.

Not Forgiving

At times, forgiveness may not be possible or imaginable because the hurt is too traumatic. Individuals, families, and congregations affected by the patterns of alcoholism, for example, may struggle with forgiving someone for continuing to do harm to self and others by drinking. Theirs is a conflicted forgiveness that may never come into full expression. Children of alcoholics need to focus on learning strategies to cope with living in a family with an alcoholic parent. Since alcoholism affects one in four Americans, this is an issue that the church cannot avoid. A powerful video that grew out of a camp for children of alcoholics (entitled "Lost Childhood: Growing Up in an Alcoholic Family"[78]) describes the dynamics present in an alcoholic household: chaos, unpredictability, and broken promises. Children in an alcoholic household internalize these messages: Don't talk; Don't feel; Hide the pain; Don't trust anyone else. One child shares that "they blamed it [the alcoholism] on me. I thought it was my fault." Such experiences leave deep scars that erode a healthy sense of selfhood.

The video picks up sixteen years later, focusing on two of the chil-

77. Kenneth Briggs, *The Power of Forgiveness,* based on a film by Martin Doblmeier (Minneapolis: Fortress Press, 2008).

78. See www.lostchildhood.org. Jerry Moe started a camp for children of alcoholics, and in this video he interviews some of the children years later.

dren interviewed at the camp who have grown into adulthood. They have learned valuable lessons: Alcoholism is "not my fault"; "I'm not alone"; "You can't control another person's drinking"; "Don't protect the behavior of the alcoholic"; and "Take care of yourself." We can all benefit from the practices urged in the video: excavate buried emotions, identify psychological defense mechanisms; make sense of nonsensical family and institutional dynamics; and build a solid sense of self in community.

SMALL-GROUP EXERCISE

As a group, watch the film *The Power of Forgiveness*.[79] What stories and images strike you the most? Take care to listen fully to each person's response.
- How do you define forgiveness?
- How do you know that you have been forgiven? How do you know that you are in the process of forgiving?
- Can you imagine creating a "forgiveness garden" or some other ritual space to help you and other people heal? How might this be more problematic than helpful?
- What would you like to have forgiven in your life?
- What are some things that others want you to forgive?
- Think of ways to "pay forgiveness forward."

TAKE-AWAY POINTS

1. Start small; forgive what is possible.
2. Give yourself credit/grace for wherever you find yourself on the forgiveness continuum.
3. Surrender the idea that the ability to forgive is a measure of faith.
4. Avoid language of obligation when dealing with forgiveness.
5. Invite forgiveness.
6. Practice forgiveness.
7. Cultivate "ego-humility."
8. Identify unconscious psychological defenses against forgiving.
9. Avoid self-deceptive forgiveness.
10. Say "I'm sorry" and "I did wrong."

79. See thepowerofforgiveness.com to order this documentary.

CARE PRAYER
God of All People,

You meet us in the gaps. Standing in these strange places, we often bristle, stiffen, turn away, typecast, and judge with closed hearts and minds. We trade genuine experience for trite beliefs about nations, cultures, and one another. We domesticate the wild in service of the tamed. Stir us with compassion to pry open the hallowed doors of closed consciousness to experience your goodness living through all. When we meet walls of resistance, help us to know conflict's source: fear of retribution, bruises inflicted by others, or harm done to ourselves. Embrace us with your fierce tenderness as first invitation to forgive and to release, however possible, leaning toward a future of reconciliation. Amen.

Chapter 7

Covenant Care Community

At a recent retirement party for Julie Arenstein, beloved Director of Facilities at Wesley Seminary, the reflection below was read. She had written it years earlier.

The Forest That Was

I watched from my kitchen window as the sun came up over the mountains to spread its warm glow over the forest below. I began to feel that first excitement of spring as my eyes turned to a young sapling — the one planted so many years ago. I thought he had grown so straight and tall. I felt quite pleased with myself, as I had nurtured him through drought and avalanches of snow.

I was told there was a plague that was killing our forest. Not my young tree, I said to myself. I've taken such care that no plague would dare infest him. Yet I watched the forest grow thin. No, they must find a cure so the forest will be thick and lush again. I turned back to my tree and, to my horror, I saw no new leaves.

I ran into the forest, and everywhere I turned I saw trees without new leaves. I ran to my tree and gathered his leaves about me as if I could put them back one by one. As his leaves drifted back to the ground, his bare branches gently brushed against me as if to say, "Stop — you can do no more. There is no cure. The plague is spreading everywhere."

This plague is AIDS, the young tree is my son, and the forest is my fellow human beings.

Imaging Covenant Community

To mark Julie's retirement, the Seminary collected funds to plant a tree in honor of her service and to memorialize her son, Douglas. Enough money was raised to plant several trees, so many that we joked about "Julie's grove." That day, this grove of trees became for us an image of covenant care community. Through this metaphor, we felt connected to one another, to Julie's son, and to the past, present, and future of our Seminary. We honored Julie's tears over the loss of her son with our own tears and expressed mutual gratitude for working together. We recognized that we are all planted, with our roots intertwined, in God's garden.

Psalm 1 evokes this image of rooted covenant care community. As the Psalter's "hermeneutical entry point,"[1] Psalm 1 frames our interpretation of the psalms that follow. Contrasting the fate of the righteous and the wicked, the psalmist expresses the theme of the Two Ways in wisdom thinking (see "path" in vv. 1 and 6[2]). This theme, also called act/consequence, posits that the righteous are rewarded and the wicked are punished; we get what we deserve. The righteous are "like trees planted by streams of water, which yield their fruit in its season, and their leaves do not wither" (1:3), while the wicked are "not so, but are like chaff that the wind drives away" (1:4). The righteous tree is nourished by the waters of *torah* — "instruction" (v. 2). It is no coincidence that the Psalter is divided into five books to echo the five books of the Torah in Jewish tradition: the Pentateuch (Genesis, Exodus, Leviticus, Numbers, and Deuteronomy). Psalm 1 connects righteousness with the steady growth of well-rooted and well-watered trees and offers hope that we will grow like these trees if we tread the right path through life. It also democratizes tree imagery that was traditionally

---

1. William A. Brown, *Seeing the Psalms: A Theology of Metaphor* (Louisville: Westminster John Knox Press, 2004), p. 55.

2. Brown, *Seeing the Psalms,* p. 56. Brown notes the chiastic (from the Greek *chiasm,* meaning "X") structure of Psalm 1, which strengthens the contrast of the Two Ways:

    A description and fate of the righteous: the metaphor for "path" (vv. 1-2)
        B metaphor for the righteous: "tree" (v. 3a-b)
            C conclusion: success (v. 4a)
            C′ introduction: lack of success (v. 4a)
        B′ metaphor for the wicked: "chaff" (v. 4b).
    A′ description and fate of the wicked: the metaphor for "path" (vv. 5-6)

descriptive of the righteous rule of the king (Isa. 11:1; Jer. 23:5-6; Zech. 3:8; 6:12; Ps. 72:2-3). Psalm 1 applies this imagery to every righteous person watered by *torah*.

Related to this image of the righteous trees is the image of God as divine gardener[3] who plants Israel in Sinai or Zion (Jerusalem; see Isa. 37:18-20, 31-32; Exod. 15:17). The gardener tends a greenhouse, as Psalm 52:8 suggests: "But I am like a green olive tree in the house of God" (cf. Ps. 92:12-14). The Temple is portrayed as refuge and "metaphorically a 'hothouse' for growth in righteousness."[4] Reflecting on Psalm 1 in light of Julie's retirement party, Michael and I can identify the unspoken but palpable feeling that our Seminary community is a "hothouse" for covenant care, a place of mutual support, teaching, and cooperative accountability for our journey together on God's path.

QUESTIONS FOR REFLECTION

- In what ways are you "planted" in God's garden? What kind of plant are you?
- Have you experienced times when you felt like chaff blown away by the wind? Why?
- How would you describe the path you are on in life?
- What would your faith community look and act like if it were a "hothouse" for growth in righteousness?

From the "Group Think" of Babel to Community

As Babel and its "group think"[5] community indicate, not all communities are hothouses for growth. A comforting community can lull us into a false sense of security, suffocating newness. Irritations that shake things up can be a spur to healthy change. Community often em-

---

3. Brown, *Seeing the Psalms,* pp. 70, 77. See also Vigen Guroian, "The Christian Gardener: An Orthodox Meditation," *The Christian Century,* 28 February 1996. Guroian calls Christians "sacramental gardeners" rather than co-creators with God because we garden to symbolize our "acceptance of our responsibility and our role in rectifying the harm done to the creation by sin" (p. 230).

4. Brown, *Seeing the Psalms,* p. 76. Psalm 1 co-opts the symbol of trees and sacred poles (*'asherah*) as representing illicit worship of other gods (e.g., Deut. 16:21).

5. Irving L. Janis, *Group Think: Psychological Studies of Policy Decisions and Fiascoes,* 2d ed. (Boston: Houghton Mifflin, 1982).

bodies the tension between comfort and disturbance. Which is which will depend upon where we stand in the community. If we read the Bible *from* the center toward those on the margins to teach them what to do to occupy privileged space, we promote comfort for those in power. If we read the Bible *to* the center from the margins, we challenge that comfort and the sense that it is normal.[6] For example, the commandment in Exodus 20:8-10 about not working on the Sabbath makes no sense to the poor who can't get work for even a single day.[7] Only the dominant, employed culture can focus on taking Sabbath rest. This contrast echoes what W. E. B. DuBois has described as the "double-consciousness" of blacks in this country — that is, "this sense of always looking at one's self through the eyes of others."[8] This "two-ness" is built on marginalizing stereotypes imposed by those in power.

Reading from the center to the margins can co-opt covenant and genuine relationships and contribute to the creation of shadow community. Distinguishing characteristics of shadow community or pseudo-community[9] include fear of being one's genuine self and feeling "shut down" from expressing differing thoughts, feelings, and opinions. Shadow communities exert pressure on individuals to conform to certain beliefs and practices, shun people who question authority figures, betray the trust of vulnerable members,[10] and draw boundaries to exclude rather than include questioning people. Shadow communities value insularity and typically exalt their way of life above all others. Genuine communities, by contrast, are marked by their intentional effort toward love, justice, inclusivity, safety, and open communication.

Echoes of shadow community can be heard in the story of Babel in Genesis 11:1-9. This story begins by declaring, "Now the whole earth had one language and the same words." This statement seems to contradict Genesis 10:1-32, which lists the descendants of Noah and their

---

6. Miguel De La Torre, *Reading the Bible from the Margins* (Maryknoll, N.Y.: Orbis Books, 2002), p. 31. Unfortunately, De La Torre often lapses into the "centered" stereotypes of Jews in the Gospel stories.

7. De La Torre, *Reading the Bible from the Margins*, p. 4.

8. W. E. B. DuBois, *The Soul of Black Folks* (New York: Bantam Books, 1989), p. 3.

9. Margaret Kornfeld, *Cultivating Wholeness: A Guide to Care and Counseling in Faith Communities* (New York: Continuum Publishing, 1998, 2008), pp. 18-19. Kornfeld distinguishes between "pseudo" and "real" community.

10. See James N. Poling, *The Abuse of Power: A Theological Problem* (Nashville: Abingdon Press, 1991), pp. 122-23.

different languages. Genesis 10 does not comment negatively on these differences. It simply ends with "nations spread abroad on the earth after the flood" (v. 32). Clearly, the blessing and the commission ("Be fruitful and multiply and fill the earth") given to Noah and his sons in Genesis 9:1 (a re-affirmation of God's initial commission in Genesis 1:28) are being worked out in Genesis 10. Yet traditional (from the center) interpretations of the Babel story view the scattering of the inhabitants of Babel as divine punishment for building "a tower with its top in the heavens" (v. 4). The building is viewed as an act of human pride. God's "punishment" sets the stage for the new divine initiative in God's call of Abraham in Genesis 12.

These traditional interpretations are skewed[11] by the focus on the tower of Babel and its association with Mesopotamian temple-towers or ziggurats, the most famous of which was in Babylon. Verse 4, however, speaks of "a city and a tower," combining two words to express one compound idea, as in "night and day" and "heaven and earth." This literary technique, called hendiadys, suggests that Babel is a citadel or fortified city rather than simply a tower. To say that "its top [was] in the heavens" was to use typical urban terminology for big-city fortifications (Deut. 1:28; 9:1; Jer. 51:53; Judg. 9:46-47). Thus, rather than building a tower to become like God, the people of Babel fortify their city in an attempt to gain security apart from God. The anti-urban judgment is chilling. Cain, the first murderer, was also the first city-builder in Genesis 4:17. Babel represents an imperial center of power and exclusion that challenges God. One can't help but think here of the Twin Towers destroyed on 9/11 and the attack on the Pentagon. The buildings symbolized the financial and military power of the United States.

Babel is nothing more than an ancient gated community. Terence Fretheim rightly focuses on the motivation for building rather than on what is built.[12] The people of Babel want to "make a name" for themselves (v. 4). They fear the future: "otherwise we shall be scattered abroad upon the face of the whole earth." By choosing isolation, self-preservation, and homogeneity, they resist the divine command to fill the earth in Genesis 1:28. This puts the creation at risk. Theirs is a forti-

---

11. For much of what follows, see Frank Frick, *A Journey through the Hebrew Scriptures,* 2d ed. (Belmont, Calif.: Wadsworth, 2003), pp. 137-39.

12. Terence Fretheim, "Genesis," *New Interpreter's Bible,* vol. 1 (Nashville: Abingdon Press, 1994), p. 412.

fied city of "group think" rather than a community. God's scattering "promotes diversity at the expense of any form of unity that seeks to preserve itself in isolation from the rest of the creation."[13] Laurel Dykstra reminds us of our kinship with the Egyptian pharaoh who presides over an empire of oppression: "[Our] refusal to know the strangers in [our] midst is often the beginning of violence against them," as in Exodus 1:8, 10: "Now a new king arose over Egypt, who did not know Joseph."[14] How appropriately ironic that the word for "bricks" *(lebenah)* occurs only twice in the Hebrew Bible: in Genesis 11:3 ("Come, let us makes bricks") and in Exodus 1:14 (the Egyptians "made [the Hebrew slaves'] lives bitter with hard service in mortar and brick").[15] Empire builds on oppression and exclusion.

Troubling/Disturbing the Community Narrative

Liberation theologian José Míguez Bonino views the scattering at the end of the Babel story positively by reading from the margins to the center. Shaped by the history of the European conquest of Latin America, Bonino argues that God wants to disturb the attempt to unify all humanity around one city, one name, and one language. God intends a diverse humanity that finds its unity in the blessing for all the families of the earth. "God re-creates the diversity that some want to homogenize," he says.[16] A popular bumper sticker affirms such diversity: "Co-Exist." It incorporates the faith symbols of cross, star of David, and crescent. In the same way, the popular bumper sticker "God Bless America" is challenged by its protest versions: "God Bless All Nations" and "God Bless Everyone (No Exceptions)." Another example of the tension between unity and diversity can be seen in Nogales, Mexico. In downtown Nogales, a steel wall separates the city from U.S. territory. Blue spray paint on the wall declares, "Las paredes giradas de lado son puentes," which means "Walls turned sideways are bridges." Superim-

13. Fretheim, "Genesis," p. 413.

14. Laurel Dykstra, *Set Them Free: The Other Side of Exodus* (Maryknoll, N.Y.: Orbis Books, 2002), p. 109.

15. Dykstra, *Set Them Free*, p. 109.

16. José Míguez Bonino, "Genesis 11:1-9: A Latin-American Perspective," in *Return to Babel: Global Perspectives on the Bible*, ed. Jon Levison and Priscilla Pope-Levison (Louisville: Westminster John Knox Press, 1999), p. 16.

posed on these words are white crosses with the names of those who have died trying to cross the U.S.–Mexico border.[17]

"Group think," which infests faith communities and governments, can foster dangerous optimism, lack of vigilance, and slogan thinking about the weakness and immorality of out-groups.[18] Such thinking contributes to an atmosphere of "We're right and they're wrong." This reinforces divisions among us. Leaders need consistently to work against patterns within self and communities that encourage smug satisfaction or self-righteousness. Optimistic assessments of one's community as wonderful and welcoming, for example, need to be explored. What shadow side might be overlooked? Is there room for improvement? Was the journey to becoming welcoming a rocky one that is now forgotten or suppressed?

QUESTIONS FOR REFLECTION
- In what ways do you read the Bible from the center? From the margins? What is it like to read in the opposite direction to which you are accustomed?
- What do you look for in community?
- What do you fear about community?
- In what ways do you live in a fortified city? What would scattering look like in your life?

A Lesson: *Lars and the Real Girl*

In the movie *Lars and the Real Girl*,[19] actor Ryan Gosling plays a man fearful of intimacy. Lars expresses his affection for a life-size doll named Bianca (ordered online), much to the horror of his brother and sister-in-law, who live next door. The innocent drama plays out as Lars meets a real woman with whom he develops a genuine relationship. When the doll "dies" because Lars no longer needs her as a substitute

17. Mark S. Miles and Emily K. Snyder, "Strangers No Longer: Faithful Voices for Solidarity," *The Spire*, Vanderbilt University, 27, no. 1 (Fall 2008): 27. The authors argue that "the walls that we have constructed in our own minds are much more dangerous than these."

18. Janis, *Group Think*, p. 12.

19. *Lars and the Real Girl* is an MGM film released in October 2007 and directed by Craig Gillespie.

for the real thing, the small Lutheran church that his family attends recognizes the doll's death as real. They perform the same functions they would in any other circumstance of loss and gather around Lars. As one character in the movie says, "When someone dies, we come and sit. That's what we do." The camera scans a room of older women sitting in Lars's living room, busy with their knitting needles.

A take-away lesson from this film[20] is simple: covenant community holds us through the tense and intense moments. The community in the movie does not dismiss Lars's loss, but rather takes it seriously and does what congregations do during times of grief. The movie poignantly illumines a reality of genuine covenant care community — namely, that we are held in open arms, in prayer, with sustenance, because we exist. Covenant community embraces our totality even when selfhood seems fragmentary, foreign, unknown. Theologically stated, we are God's beloved, whether or not we can personally recognize this. If we can't, then the community does. To say that covenant community embraces us is another way of saying that the community loves us into the fullness of our being.

GROUP ACTIVITY

Watch *Lars and the Real Girl* together. Look for other examples in the movie of covenant community care.

Are these examples of what you consider to be traditional marks of covenant relationship? What surprised you about your list?

Covenant as Relationship

In the Hebrew Bible, covenant provides the foundation for community. Covenant exhibits both a vertical and a horizontal dimension. It defines Israel's relationship both to God and to its fellow human beings. The Sinai covenant is a "bilateral commitment";[21] in other words, it is a mutual agreement between people and God to take one another seriously in relationship. This God is not isolated and transcendent, but related and involved. The pronouncement "You shall be my people, and

20. For other uses of film in congregations, see Edward McNulty, *Praying the Movies: Daily Meditations from Classic Films* (Louisville: Geneva Press, 2001).

21. Walter Brueggemann, "Covenant," in *Reverberations of Faith: A Theological Handbook of Old Testament Themes* (Louisville: Westminster John Knox Press, 2002), p. 37.

I will be your God" functions as a prophetic covenant formula reaffirming this idea of bilateral commitment (Jer. 11:4; 24:7; 30:22; 31:33; 32:38; Ezek. 11:20; 14:11; 16:59-63; cf. Deut. 4:20). The idea of covenant saturates the book of Deuteronomy. In Moses' last sermon before the wandering Israelites cross over the Jordan into the Promised Land of Canaan, covenant is affirmed anew as the framework for Israel's life in the land. Jesus is steeped in covenant tradition. He quotes from Deuteronomy more than seventy-five times in the Gospels.

Deuteronomy makes primary the necessity of choice, every day, to commit to God or not: "See, I have set before you today life and prosperity, death and adversity. . . . Choose life . . ." (30:15, 19). Choosing life — that is, to keep covenant — will result in land, many descendants, and long life. Choosing death — that is, to violate covenant — results in none of these. Sanctions remind Israel that obedience is necessary for life. For Deuteronomy, the measure of covenant is the commandments: "If you obey the commandments of the LORD your God that I am commanding you today, by loving the LORD your God, walking in his ways, and observing his commandments, decrees, and ordinances, then you shall live and become numerous, and the LORD your God will bless you in the land you are entering to possess" (30:16). Jesus made a similar statement in the parable of the rich young man in Matthew 19:17: "If you wish to enter into life, keep the commandments." Jesus and his followers were called "ministers of a new covenant" (2 Cor. 3:6).

Covenant as living relationship-in-community entails a commitment to *listening* for God's call and *responding* to God in action. These two activities together put us on the path to understanding more fully what Dietrich Bonhoeffer meant by costly grace, as opposed to cheap grace. "Cheap grace means grace as a doctrine, a principle, a system," whereas costly grace is "the call of Jesus Christ at which the disciple leaves [the] nets and follows."[22] Bonhoeffer argues that a life lived in devotion and commitment to God through Jesus Christ requires obedience to the Living Word rather than assent to an ideology. Denominations in the Reformed church tradition make a similar assertion through the claim that Christ alone is head of the church and Lord of the conscience.[23] For Christians, listening to Jesus means choosing to

---

22. Dietrich Bonhoeffer, *The Cost of Discipleship* (New York: Touchstone, 1959), p. 43.

23. See, for example, "The Historic Principles of Church Government," G-1.0300 in *The Book of Order,* PCUSA. See www.pcusa.org/oga/publications/b0007-09.pdf.

keep covenant with God by living relationship in community and following wherever the path of life may lead.

Pastoral leaders help shape the covenant-keeping of community by using their authority in ways that respect cultural variances and psychological complexities. Pastors need to be mindful of people's differing needs and abilities for exercising agency and for recognizing personal and communal responsibilities. Several different dimensions inform the development of our worldview: locus of control (Is a person controlled by inner motivation or external requirement?) and locus of responsibility (Does a person take personal responsibility or assign blame to a system?). These two dimensions can be placed on a horizontal/vertical axis to produce four quadrants:[24]

Internal locus of control (IC) and internal locus of responsibility (IR): This person has a sense of personal control and personal responsibility.

External locus of control (EC) and internal locus of responsibility (IR): This person internalizes social expectations for responsibility and feels powerless against the system.

External locus of control (EC) and external locus of responsibility (ER): This person has little sense of personal control and feels powerless against the system.

Internal locus of control (IC) and external locus of responsibility (ER): This person has a sense of personal control while recognizing social barriers.

The Decalogue

The Decalogue, or the Ten Commandments (Deut. 5:6-21; Exod. 20:1-17), summarizes the essence of covenant. In Jewish tradition, the First Commandment is what Christians call the Prologue to the Decalogue: "I am the LORD your God, who brought you out of the land of Egypt, out of the house of slavery" (Exod. 20:2; Deut. 5:6).[25] This verse

24. Derald Wing Sue and David Sue, *Counseling the Culturally Diverse: Theory and Practice,* 5th ed. (Hoboken, N.J.: John Wiley & Sons, 2008), pp. 287-305.

25. In synagogues one can often see embroidered on the curtain of the ark that holds the Torah scrolls or above the ark itself an image of two tablets, rectangles with

asserts that the commandments given at Sinai originated in God's prior act of grace in the Exodus. Grace precedes law. Yet the Revised Common Lectionary reverses this order, treating Sinai texts before Exodus texts. This reinforces an old, inaccurate stereotype: the Hebrew Bible is a book of law and judgment, and the New Testament is a book of grace and love. Actually, the Decalogue can be seen as an act of divine grace. God guides Israel's response to God. These pointers create and safeguard a space in which Israel can experience a life of shalom, of wholeness and harmony in relationship with God and one another.[26]

This "introductory" commandment contextualizes the following commandments. God identifies God's self as a transformer of situations who brings freedom out of slavery. Paradoxically, this freedom allows us to enter into service to God. The Reverend Joseph Lowery, a veteran of the civil rights movement, echoes this understanding in his critique of the black community in the United States: Some "still have a slave mentality . . . you're not free because you do what you want to do. You're free when you do what you ought to do."[27] The "Prologue" tells us who we are called to be in entering into a covenant relationship with such a God. We must ask ourselves: Do our actions and social structures reflect this God of reversals?

Memory of the Exodus event functions as a constant source of reorientation for the people of God. "I am the LORD your God" reminds us that the authority of the Commandments, and thus of covenant, rests not in specific rules. Instead, it rests in the way that covenant "orients" persons and communities "around general values, principles, or

---

rounded or pointed tops (like old Jewish tombstones or monumental steles and boundary markers in the Ancient Near East), each with five lines consisting of the first two words of each of the commandments, five commandments on one tablet and five on the other. The First Commandment begins with *'anoki Adonai* ("I am the Lord") and refers to this verse.

26. See William Johnson Everett, "Recovering the Covenant," *The Christian Century* 10 November 1999, pp. 1094-97. Everett reviews *The Covenant Tradition in Politics* by Daniel Elazar (Transaction Publishers, 1999). Elazar suggests that we reintroduce the Bible as a source book for political theory and practice because it holds together the dynamics of power and justice. Freedom that serves our human need for trustworthy relationship is "federal liberty." Federalism comes from the Latin word for covenant, *foedus.*

27. Krissah Thompson, "Barack's Rock: A Veteran of the Civil Rights Battles Preaches about the Symbolism of the Nation's 44th President," *The Washington Post*, 14 January 2009, sec. C, p. 1.

virtues that reflect God's self-disclosure."[28] We can compare the Ten Commandments to the U.S. Bill of Rights and the United Nations Universal Declaration of Human Rights rather than to the U.S. Law Code. They are policy statements from which we develop legal guides for life and the character of covenant community.[29] In this way, the Bible moves us beyond reason to "imagination and emotions" and committed action.[30] It is not enough to memorize the Commandments, as some advocate.[31] Nor does simply posting them in a public place necessarily ensure that they are followed, even if we agree on which version and in what order.[32] What matters is what we *do* with them.

What we do with them is often spelled out in church mission statements. Religious and secular organizations take considerable time to craft such statements, which perform both an internal and an external function. They can provide a sense of cohesion, identity, and purpose for those within the community. They can also serve to introduce the community to those outside of it. In this sense, the Decalogue functioned as a mission statement for ancient Israel in covenant with God. Before he dies, Joshua leads the leaders of the people in a covenant renewal ceremony at Shechem (Josh. 24). He requests of them a renewed loyalty to the God of the Sinai covenant in word and deed ("with a true faithfulness," v. 14).[33] Israel is to "fear" the Lord (v. 14). Switching to "re-

28. Lisa Sowle Cahill, "Christian Character, Biblical Community, and Human Values," in *Character and Scripture: Moral Formation, Community, and Biblical Interpretation,* ed. William Brown (Grand Rapids: Wm. B. Eerdmans, 2002), p. 10.

29. Walter Harrelson, *The Ten Commandments for Today* (Louisville: Westminster John Knox Press, 2002), p. 17.

30. Cahill, "Christian Character, Biblical Community, and Human Values," p. 17.

31. See Bobby Ross Jr., "Nashville Ministry Tempts Children to Try Morality," *The Washington Post,* 28 December 2002, sec. B, p. 6. A retired flower-shop owner, George Kelley, started a ministry in his home. He would give ten dollars to any child under sixteen who could recite the Commandments to a pastor, rabbi, priest, teacher, or other authorized adult witness.

32. See Bill Broadway, "There Are 10, But Their Order Isn't Carved in Stone," *The Washington Post,* 21 February 1998, sec. D, p. 8. Broadway discusses the Jewish, Catholic-Lutheran, and Protestant versions of the Decalogue. Many of us may not be aware that a carving of Moses holding the two tablets with the Commandments forms part of a frieze of historic lawmakers on the south wall of the Supreme Court courtroom.

33. Robert Coote, "The Book of Joshua," *New Interpreter's Bible,* vol. 2 (Nashville: Abingdon Press, 1998), p. 715. This is possibly an example of hendiadys (two words expressing a single idea). Here, "the congruence of professed and actual obedience" is suggested.

vere" in the NRSV "reflects the contemporary change in many liberal churches from patriarchal piety to the piety of familiarity and friendship with God."[34] In the United States, this kind of loyalty is due the state whose laws we determine, which creates a disconnect with the notion of biblical covenant.

GROUP EXERCISE

How does your faith community reflect the God who brought Israel up out of Egypt?

How could your faith community do a better job of reflecting such a God?

Review the mission statement of your faith community. Does it articulate your understanding of covenant? Why or why not?

Design a service of covenant renewal for the first Sunday in the new year that includes your church's mission statement.

Mutual Watchfulness

In their negative form, the Ten Commandments cry out for community interpretation and debate. The first three commandments (in the Protestant order) express God's exclusive claims for allegiance: no other gods, no images, and no wrongful use of God's name to harm another. Commandments four and five treat God's basic institutions, the Sabbath and the family, as bridges that strengthen the relationship between community and God. The final five address basic human and social obligations and prohibit what damages life in community: murder, adultery, stealing,[35] bearing false witness, and coveting. These simple

---

34. Coote, "The Book of Joshua," p. 715. An example of the "piety of familiarity" is found in an article by Jacqueline Lapsley entitled "Friends with God? Moses and the Possibility of Covenantal Friendship," *Interpretation* 58, no. 2 (April 2004): 117-30. Lapsley argues that the intimate relationship between God and Moses offers a model of covenant faithfulness for the whole people of God. The God/Moses friendship is long-term and marked by reciprocity, self-assertion, and a full range of emotion. It is the "lack of genuine friendship" that led Israel to abandon God (p. 129).

35. See Robert Gnuse, *You Shall Not Steal: Community and Property in the Biblical Tradition* (Maryknoll, N.Y.: Orbis Books, 1985). Gnuse argues against the Western view that this prohibition undergirds the right to private property. Rather, it was meant to protect individuals and families by assuring them of the right of access to goods and possibilities necessary to productive existence within the community.

prohibitions leave us with questions. What constitutes Sabbath rest? What is adultery? What kinds of acts would show dishonor to parents? However, they do not leave the door open to "anything goes," as a cartoon from a few years ago suggests. It showed two blank stone tablets with a mallet and chisel next to them. The caption read, "The Ten Commandments Do-It-Yourself Kit." The negative form of the Commandments guides our debate. They "tell us what not to do. . . . These short prohibitions rule out certain forms of conduct."[36]

Knowing limits and watching boundaries are faithful practices of ministry. Boundaries and limits, while they can seem like walls, actually protect "the sanctity of the self in relationship."[37] Pastors who remain mindful of their level of competence as well as maintain a reasonable sense of their own limits are more likely to keep a balanced perspective on care. Without such knowledge, pastoral ministers may become emotionally fused or enmeshed (i.e., spend all of their pastoral care time with one person to the exclusion of others because they have made this person's problems their own); emotionally disengaged (i.e., unwilling or unable to visit people in the hospital in more than a perfunctory way); and/ or unaware of power dynamics related to differences of gender, class, and sexual orientation (i.e., either controlling others or being emotionally manipulated by others because they feel inadequate).[38] Pastoral ministers bear a primary responsibility for "monitoring the interaction of relational boundaries"[39] and "power dynamics" in care situations. Members of faith communities also participate in sacred boundary-keeping as they monitor dynamics in their own lives, families, and workplaces. Ministers and communities practice healthy relational boundary-keeping by honoring one another's right to say "yes" and to say "no." As covenant communities, congregations take care of boundaries and the ethical exercise of power as a faithful way of being in relationship.

Violating the Commandments shows us where we stand and frees us up for more positive behaviors. Further, the Decalogue gives us "ground for cries of protest and outrage, even when we may not know

36. Harrelson, *The Ten Commandments for Today*, p. 21.

37. "A Sacred Trust: Boundary Issues for Clergy and Spiritual Teachers," DVD Series, Part 1: "Boundaries, Power, and Vulnerability." Produced by the FaithTrust Institute. See www.faithtrustinstitute.org.

38. Carrie Doehring, *Taking Care: Monitoring Power Dynamics and Relational Boundaries in Pastoral Care and Counseling* (Nashville: Abingdon Press, 1995), pp. 74-103.

39. Doehring, *Taking Care*, p. 154.

exactly what we ought positively to recommend."[40] These categorical prohibitions ("You shall not . . .") need case law ("If you do X, then Y") to flesh out violations and specify penalties. These more specific case laws are not meant to promote legalism. Rather, they encourage *mutual watchfulness,* not to hound one another but as a means to hold one another in relationship. Such an approach to covenant community highlights "the *constructive* ways Scripture forms moral character and faith" and recognizes that "Scripture forms community as much as community forms the reading of Scripture."[41] The holding in relationship that characterizes mutual watchfulness is described as "watch care" in the black church tradition.[42] The black community in Washington, D.C., has reached out to the Obama family in "watch care" mode by extending numerous invitations to them to attend church, play golf, and even get their hair done. The aim is not to gain prestige but to watch out for the family and help them settle into their new city.

Questions for Group Reflection
- List ways in which your faith community expresses "watch care." What other ways might your faith community add to the list?
- Do you think the Ten Commandments are important for life today? Why or why not?
- How would you incorporate the Ten Commandments into a worship service?

Memory and Community

"Neighbor" is the defining moral category in the Ten Commandments, and it suggests a spatial neighborhood in which the Commandments operate.[43] The Commandments serve as the boundaries or fenceposts

---

40. Harrelson, *The Ten Commandments for Today,* p. 22. Harrelson sees the same dynamic at work in the parable of the persistent widow and the unjust judge in Luke 18:1-8.

41. See Brown, *Character and Scripture,* p. xi. Character ethics seeks "the *formative* as well as normative impact" that Scripture makes upon reading communities. It is the interpretation of Scripture that entails the appropriation of it (p. xii).

42. Avis Thomas-Lester, "Overtures to the Obamas," *The Washington Post,* 9 February 2009, sec. B, pp. 1, 5.

43. Patrick Miller, "The Good Neighborhood: Identity and Community through the Commandments," in *Character and Scripture,* p. 55.

for this neighborhood, which includes the *ger* or sojourner/newcomer/ alien who does not belong to the clan or family (Exod. 12:49; Lev. 20:2; 22:18; Deut. 29:11). Israel's compassion for the weak and disconnected is drawn from its own experience of deliverance in the Exodus: "You shall not oppress a resident alien [*ger*]; you know the heart of an alien [*ger*], for you were aliens [plural, *gerim*] in the land of Egypt" (Exod. 23:9; cf. 22:21-27). This "slave formula" reminds Israel of an identity,[44] which always involves a third party (the neighbor) and requires the one addressed to think about social issues. This view of covenant community challenges an exclusive focus on covenant as personal relationship with God. The Decalogue begins with "I am the LORD your God" and closes with "your neighbor." "Within those borders," Patrick Miller points out, "identity is given or made known and a community is formed."[45] Each party is defined in relation to the other, within the framework of memory and shared experience.

Covenant community strengthens the bonds between people and reaches beyond itself to include the transformative well-being of the whole creation. Of course, this is a tall order; such transformation could never be completely accomplished in one lifetime or by one community. This is exactly as it should be, since covenant community is historically mindful, present-focused, and future-oriented. Covenant community does not attempt to work toward a completely visionary utopia. Rather, it works with the nitty-gritty of daily life and responsibilities in order to forge a workable and sustainable harmony. Covenant community remembers even as it reshapes its past to live fully in the present. It opens itself to the possibilities and claims of future generations.

Not all memories are positive, however. Israel embraces many memories of the people's sinfulness, as we see in Jeremiah 2:1-8; Ezekiel 6:1-34; Psalm 106; and Exodus 32. But this is as it should be, according to Patrick Miller: "Both positive and negative memories are crucial to authentic self-understanding and identity, as well as to the shaping and reshaping of community."[46] Israel especially remembers

---

44. Bruce Birch, *Let Justice Roll Down: The Old Testament, Ethics, and Christian Life* (Louisville: Westminster John Knox Press, 1991), pp. 165-67. Birch cites Henry Nasuti on the slave formula in Deuteronomy 5:15 as the motive clause for law.

45. Miller, "The Good Neighborhood," p. 57.

46. Miller, "The Good Neighborhood," p. 72, n. 34. Miller refers to Jacqueline Lapsley here.

its wilderness wanderings after the Exodus from Egypt as a time of murmuring and complaint. Some of its complaints were legitimate: no water (Exod. 17:1-7; Num. 20:2-13), no food (Exod. 16). Others were simply illegitimate whining. In Numbers 11, for example, the people are sick of manna and crave what they had in Egypt based on a distorted memory. Israel does not hide these negative memories. They remain in the tradition to remind Israel that wilderness is transformed by God's presence into a place of no lack, of surprise, transformation, choice, and dependence upon God.[47]

Many factors influence the complex process of human memory. *What* we know about ourselves and other people is inseparably connected to past and present events. *How* the past is remembered — embodied, internalized, symbolized, and codified — will affect and shape each individual's present subjective reality.[48] The nature of memory is complex.[49] Memory is influenced by context; the brain stores memories in different ways; the brain may encode events in separate domains, making it difficult to construct a later story of the experience; and some memories are formed from fragments of experience. Memory is intricately related to meaning-making.

Pastoral leaders help people remember and interpret. We can draw insight from contemporary brain science to understand the complex interaction of imagination, memory, and story in the ritual practices of faith.[50] David Hogue notes that "the brain actually reconstructs our memories each time we recall them."[51] It follows that remembrance of a life event serves a cohesive function as it draws back together bits of ex-

---

47. Walter Brueggemann, *The Land: Place as Gift, Promise, and Challenge in Biblical Faith*, 2d ed. (Minneapolis: Augsburg Fortress Press, 2002).

48. Pamela Cooper-White, *Shared Wisdom* (Minneapolis: Fortress Press, 2004), p. 50; emphasis added.

49. Cooper-White, *Shared Wisdom*, pp. 52-54.

50. David A. Hogue, *Remembering the Future, Imaging the Past: Story, Ritual, and the Human Brain* (Cleveland: Pilgrim Press, 2003), p. 9. Two obvious types of memory rely on different brain structures: *working memory* (information needed for current living) and *long-term memory* (stored information needed beyond the present moment). Memories move from working memory to long-term memory when we learn. This is technically known as encoding neural pathways through the formation of engrams. Other dimensions of memory include *semantic memory* (knowledge of concepts and facts learned through experience); *procedural memory* (development of skills and habits); and *autobiographical* or *episodic memory* (recall of explicit information that influences our lives).

51. Hogue, *Remembering the Future, Imaging the Past*, p. 65.

perience that have been stored in what Hogue calls "distant vaults"[52] in the brain. In the final analysis, Hogue says, "the act of remembering is an act of self-reconstruction."[53] Congregational storytelling and caring can be restorative and healing for people, especially when memory fails or troubles us through lost, partial, painful, or distorted memories.[54]

Together, we tell stories around the biblical text as a way to remember what God has done, and to hear again what God is doing in our midst. We remember and tell these stories to each other, within communities and across generations, to remind ourselves of what we may have forgotten and to stir us to new possibilities for the future.

Effective pastoral leaders take note of the valuable meaning-making function of memories. In pastoral care, we help people and communities with meaning-making to allow for the surfacing of differing and sometimes contradictory memories and interpretations. We serve as trustworthy stewards of an ongoing process.

QUESTIONS FOR GROUP REFLECTION

- Who, concretely, is your neighbor? How might your covenant community expand its circle to include more neighbors?
- Reflect upon both the positive and the negative memories in your faith community's life. Which experiences were the most transforming and energizing?
- How has your faith community dealt with its negative memories? How could it deal more positively with these memories?

Covenant Care

Covenant is not a quid pro quo: "If you do this for me, I will do it for you" — or, in the words of one hapless minister, "Covenant is when you scratch my back and I scratch yours." Rather, God's covenant represents a radical pledge of mutual relatedness to creation so that love, justice, and righteousness may flower. Theological affirmations about covenant ring hollow if individuals and communities do not seek, moment by moment and day by day in each new situation, to live with

---

52. Hogue, *Remembering the Future, Imaging the Past*, p. 74.
53. Hogue, *Remembering the Future, Imaging the Past*, p. 75.
54. Hogue, *Remembering the Future, Imaging the Past*, pp. 68-74.

care-filled compassion. We practice by embodying love for one another in acts of service. Such love is not romantic love but covenantal love, which Walter Brueggemann describes as "a mutual commitment of trust, regard, and obedience between two partners."[55] The word *love* (*'ahav* in Hebrew) is found in public political treaties. Moses commands Israel to listen, love, and recite in Deuteronomy 6:5-7: "You shall love the Lord your God with all your heart, and with all your soul [being], and with all your might. . . . Keep these words. . . . Recite them." As Brueggemann explains, "The language of 'love' is used to speak of a solemn, public covenantal commitment that contains formal, concrete requirements that move beyond emotion and intentionality to enforceable obligation."[56]

The command to love God in verses 5-7 is introduced in Deuteronomy 6:4: "Hear, O Israel: The LORD is our God, the LORD alone." This verse is called the Shema in Jewish tradition, from the first word in verse 4 — "hear." The recitation of the Shema has become the centerpiece of Jewish daily worship. Jews are to recite the Shema twice a day. In Torah scrolls and in many prayer books, the letter *'ayin* at the end of *shema'* and the letter *dalet* at the end of *one* (in Hebrew, *'echad*) are written larger than the other letters, spelling the Hebrew word *'ed*, which means "witness." To recite the Shema is to testify or witness to the unity and uniqueness of this God with whom the Israelites are in relation. It is to witness not just with words but with actions, with the whole self (the word *nephesh* in verse 4 is better translated "being" or "self" than "soul").

To live in covenant and witness with "confidence" literally means *with trust*. The verb from which the noun is derived comes from the Latin *confidere*, "to trust." The word *faith* comes from the same root. It is no accident that the Center for Domestic Violence, founded by Dr. Marie Fortune, renamed itself The FaithTrust Institute. This renaming signals the close link between faith and trust at the center of this ministry, which addresses religious and spiritual issues of sexual and domestic violence. An international and multifaith organization, it trains

55. Brueggemann, "Love," in *Reverberations of Faith*, p. 126. In *Personal Commitments: Beginning, Keeping, Changing* (San Francisco: Harper & Row, 1986), Margaret Farley outlines several features of covenant, including the idea that God's commitment makes possible the breaking of otherwise insurmountable barriers within and between persons so that they can commit themselves to one another in some form of faithful love (p. 113).

56. Brueggemann, "Love," in *Reverberations of Faith*, p. 126.

and educates communities about the psycho-spiritual and physical damage done to persons by those who violate personal and professional boundaries.[57]

Covenant confidence emerges over time for persons and communities, and it takes many forms in each subsequent generation. We exercise covenant confidence when we acknowledge our own history of trust and distrust. We also exercise covenant confidence when we refrain from imposing requirements and obligations on others before they are ready or able to take steps of trust for themselves. In Erik Erikson's schema, trust forms the psychological foundation for all further development.[58] Trust influences the ability to form authentic relationships with God, within self, and among community. The close linkage between faith and trust spawns an essential pastoral theological tension. We know theologically that relationship forms the basis of covenant. Yet from a psycho-pastoral position, we know just how difficult relationship can be because it involves spoken and unspoken matters of the heart.

By "heart" we (Michael and I) don't mean something sentimental, purely intuitive or only feeling-based. Rather, "heart" references the quality of presence that receives, gathers, creates, and forms selfhood in community. We experience trust before we speak a word of language, since the bonds of positive emotional attunement develop between an infant and care giver in life's earliest months.[59] Trust is a matter of the heart, a quality *experienced* "as numinous — filled with light, security, and joy"[60] — *before it is named*. When pastors talk about trust without helping to embody it in community, their words may ring hollow to those who mostly know trust by its absence because of early abandonment and trauma. Pastoral leaders strengthen the heart of the community by building bonds of trust and nurturing covenant confidence. Pastors do this by exercising leadership that is "a *function of community,*

57. Dr. Marie Fortune founded FaithTrust in 1977. It is based in Seattle, Washington.

58. See Erik Erikson, *Identity and the Life Cycle* (New York: W. W. Norton, 1980); *The Life Cycle Completed: A Review* (New York: W. W. Norton, 1982); *The Life Cycle Completed: Extended Version on the Ninth Stage of Development by Joan Erikson* (New York: W. W. Norton, 1997).

59. See Roy Herndon SteinhoffSmith, "Infancy: Faith before Language," in *Human Development and Faith: Life-Cycle Stages of Body, Mind, and Soul,* ed. Felicity B. Kelcourse (St. Louis: Chalice Press, 2004), p. 129.

60. SteinhoffSmith, "Infancy," in *Human Development and Faith,* p. 129.

not of individuals."[61] Leaders help a community to realize its vocation by reminding it why it exists, giving it organizational direction, and enabling the translation of vocation into concrete tasks. In this way, pastors generate covenant confidence and trust.

From Broken Contracts to Covenant Care Community

How are we to trust in covenant or exercise faith when relational bonds have been severed or strained? Covenant-keeping looks different depending on where we stand. This became clear as the natural disaster called Hurricane Katrina painfully exposed shameful layers of our national story. We watched in horror as the stranded residents of New Orleans gathered at the city's Convention Center once the levees broke. Day turned to night and to day again as federal, state, and local officials scrambled to effect a rescue, especially of the poor and black residents who lacked the ability and/or the resources to evacuate. Clearly, America's social contract had been broken. The financial meltdown sparked by the sub-prime mortgage surge has also exposed broken contracts. In its wake, pensions have dried up, companies have closed, and people have lost their homes and their health insurance. Pastoral leaders need to bear in mind the multiple experiences with covenant-keeping and covenant-breaking that people in their congregations have experienced. How do we foster covenant when faith has been betrayed? How do we foster covenant-making with different age groups? For people of faith, ongoing covenant practice requires recalling the covenant promise, knowing the claim it makes upon us and the freedom it brings, and carrying out its demands.

Following governmental failure in New Orleans, more than one million volunteers journeyed there to serve its hurting community. According to Robert Green, who became known as "Ambassador of the 9th Ward," the area of the city that sustained the heaviest losses, "They offset what the government didn't do." Mr. Green's mother and granddaughter were killed in the devastation. Sister Mary Pat White, RSCJ, directs Duchesne House in New Orleans, which provides a home for a week for volunteer groups across the country. She muses that the im-

---

61. Daniel O. Aleshire, *Earthen Vessels: Hopeful Reflections on the Work and Future of Theological Schools* (Grand Rapids: Wm. B. Eerdmans, 2008).

age of "bright-eyed, bushy-tailed students with paint on their faces putting their hearts totally into their work" runs counter to the stereotype of "students on spring break partying all night." These volunteers keep covenant with God's people through the long haul and hard work of rebuilding in a city "so full of broken hearts and broken contracts." They are keeping covenant even when the social contract between the government and its people has been broken.

Small churches offer another arena of covenant-keeping in the midst of broken social contracts. Whether in cities, towns, or rural settings, people are visiting small churches in increasing numbers. Thirty-five percent of small-membership churches are growing each year.[62] Lewis Parks observes that five types of persons visit small churches: persons seeking surrogate family (because they are separated from their families by work, school, or the military); persons seeking an alternative to the anonymity of the workplace and the public square; persons weary of self-absorption and in search of a bigger corporate story to which they can contribute; persons who have a score to settle with God in a safe environment that sympathetically receives their anger and tears; and persons who are looking for a place to give back for the blessings they have received.[63]

We must be careful, however, not to assume that covenant community is the sole domain of the church. Meditation groups, yoga classes, and spiritual knitting circles[64] can all promote covenant community. Also, multiple covenant communities can exist within one congregation. What does this suggest for care? Covenant care strengthens bonds between people in the congregation, links groups within the church, and also develops relationships with people beyond the congregation. To image community in this way — with many layers and multiple, often overlapping connections — is to recognize the inherent complexity of covenant-keeping and caring in our time.

---

62. Lewis A. Parks, "Who Is Visiting Small Churches These Days?" in *Leading Ideas: A Resource for Church Leaders,* The Lewis Center, 24 September 2008.

63. Parks, "Who Is Visiting Small Churches These Days?" in *Leading Ideas.*

64. See, for example, Susan Izard and Susan Jorgensen, *Knitting into the Mystery: A Guide to the Shawl-Knitting Ministry* (Harrisburg, Pa.: Morehouse Publishing, 2003), and Susan Lydon, *Knitting Heaven and Earth: Healing the Heart with Craft* (New York: Broadway Books, 2005).

A QUESTION FOR REFLECTION

- Name the covenant communities of which you are a part. How could these communities strengthen their covenant bonds? How could they connect with one another?

Covenant Holiness and Guilting

One student of mine shared her frustration during a recent meeting of the colloquy I (Michael) co-led with a local pastor in our field education program. She was trying to build a solid adult Sunday school program in the rural parish in which she was interning. Attendance at Sunday-morning sessions was spotty at best, with as few as one or as many as three people. Rarely would there be a carryover from the previous week. Adding to her frustration was the common practice of parents dropping their children off for Sunday school and then returning for worship later. Our group agreed that this situation was not unique to this congregation. We live in a time of challenges to commitment-making and covenant-keeping, challenges which feed unrealistic expectations. Pastoral leaders sometimes assume that it is their job to cajole, entice, prod, or "guilt" people into discipleship. Does this approach build covenant community?

The Sinai traditions in Exodus 19–24 suggest that guilting does not build community. Exodus 19 opens with a theological declaration connecting the Exodus from Egypt with Sinai: "You have seen what I did to the Egyptians, and how I bore you on eagles' wings and brought you to myself. Now therefore, if you obey my voice and keep my covenant, you shall be my treasured possession out of all the peoples. Indeed, the whole earth is mine, but you shall be for me a priestly kingdom and a holy nation" (vv. 4-6). Once the people agree to do as the Lord says (v. 8), Exodus 19 continues with a call to consecration for the covenant-making ceremony, which is actually carried out in Exodus 24. God does not invoke the memory of the Exodus to guilt Israel into entering into covenant with God. The metaphor of God as eagle (see Deut. 28:49; 32:11-14) suggests God's nurturing protection and awesome power, rather than divine cajoling and manipulation. Further, the covenant is a conditional one — "*if* you obey." God does not manipulate by sugar-coating covenant. God requires. Much is expected of Israel as God's people. God's mighty theophany (appearance) on Sinai is described as a combination of violent thunderstorm and volcanic activity: "theophany is by definition disruptive," Walter Brueggemann points out.[65] The violence is not coercive, since Israel has already agreed to covenant with God before the theophany takes place.

God calls Israel to be "a priestly kingdom and a holy nation" (Exod. 19:6). Priests are a special class of leaders in Israelite society. Now all Israelites are to be holy (in Hebrew, *qadosh*). To be holy is to consecrate oneself, set oneself apart, or separate oneself for service to God. Israel bears special responsibility as God's people. Israelites must function among the nations as priests function in Israelite society to mediate the divine will and blessing. God's holiness is fundamental to God's character and identity. Holiness becomes the standard by which Israel judges itself: "You shall be holy, for I the LORD your God am holy" (Leviticus 19:1, part of the Holiness Code in Leviticus 17–26). Such holiness is not limited to the arena of worship and ritual purity but is expressed also in everyday living and acts of justice. So, for example, Leviticus 19:18 declares, "You shall not take vengeance or bear a grudge against any of your people, but you shall love your neighbor as yourself: I am the LORD." This theme of holiness as justice is also expressed in the Song of Hannah in 1 Samuel 2:2a, 4, 8: "There is no Holy One like the LORD. . . . The bows of the mighty are broken. . . . He raises up the poor from the dust. . . ." This theme is echoed by Mary's Magnificat in Luke 1.

The structure of Exodus 19–24 reveals what holiness means concretely for Israel. God calls Israel to holiness in Exodus 19, and enters into covenant with Israel in Exodus 24. Between the two chapters come the Decalogue and the Covenant Code (Exod. 20:22–23:33), which offer guidelines for holiness. Presented as if given to Moses by God, the Covenant Code, or Book of the Covenant (Exod. 24:7), actually developed over time to meet the changing needs of the Israelite community. It contains both categorical law ("You shall not steal"; Exod. 20:15) and case law ("If . . . , then"; Exod. 21:1–22:17).

A QUESTION FOR REFLECTION
- How do you define holiness?

---

65. Walter Brueggemann, "The Book of Exodus," *New Interpreter's Bible*, vol. 1 (Nashville: Abingdon Press, 1994), p. 838.

Getting the Guilt Out

Over a table conversation in seminary, I (Michael) sighed reluctantly as I realized how many of our religious practices can be motivated by the self-imposed guilt of parishioners and the demanding guilt of pastoral leaders. In exasperation I asked, "Why can't we do away with making people feel guilty?" A classmate immediately responded, "Well, how else do you think we can get people to do what we want?!" We may feel as if laying a guilt trip on people works. It may produce short-term results. For example, we may attend a Bible study because someone else wants us to, or to please others and make them feel valued. We may strongly urge people to make commitments to the church because we fear that without measurable growth in attendance, others may judge us harshly. Yet demanding, conniving, strong-arming, or guilting others or ourselves (however "nicely manipulative" it might be) has a boomerang effect. It comes back to hit us if we don't watch out. We also need to be gentle with ourselves and know the root of what motivates or prompts this behavior toward guilt. Without this knowledge, the cycle of dissatisfaction continues as the joy of life in community remains perpetually out of reach. Sustainable pastoral practices grow out of a different kind of soil. They sprout from a soil of trust, abiding presence, and sufficiency, not a soil of guilt, shame, coercion, and manipulation. Guilt screams, "This has to be different than it is." Trust says gently, "It will unfold as it will in God's time."

QUESTIONS FOR REFLECTION
- When have you "guilted" someone into doing something they did not want to do?
- When have you been "guilted" into doing something you did not want to do? How did that make you feel?

Practicing Covenant

Covenant practices can foster well-being and trust-filled relationship among all people and the entire created order.[66] Covenant practice is

---

66. For more on the qualities and practices of religious and nonreligious people working toward the common good, see Laurent Parks Daloz et al., *Common Fire: Leading Lives of Commitment in a Complex World* (Boston: Beacon Press, 1997).

not about doing something just when we feel like it, but most especially when we don't. Covenant practice as faithful commitment to God, creation, others, and self builds on the oneness of God and seeks our one-ness in the midst of our many-ness. Yet we must take care not to enshrine oneness so that it masks a normative sameness.[67] The United States has fostered such oneness by describing itself as a "melting pot," which obscures the individual "ingredients" of its composition. The "politics of difference," however, challenges those who would deny the uniqueness of particular social identities. We suggest "salad" as an apt metaphor. Ingredients can be identified in the whole yet together create something quite tasty that individual ingredients could not. Covenant practices honor these differences.

Covenant community is God's ingathering of people with sufficient room for all to belong and to bring with them all of their "unbelonging." This notion of "unbelonging" comes from Sathianathan Clarke, a systematic theologian at Wesley Seminary, who describes the creative tension in his own identity and life. "Belonging in my case is a reconciliation of multiple unbelongings," he says.[68] Sathi's is a continual effort to use "not fitting" as a source for healing the fragmentation in God's church and world.

The book of Esther also speaks to the issue of belonging and unbelonging, of the many and the one.[69] Read during the minor Jewish festival of Purim in the spring each year, Esther commemorates the deliverance from genocide of exiled Jews in the Persian Empire. During Purim, a festive meal is eaten, often accompanied by a Purimshpiel. Purimshpiels are farcical plays which parody the accepted authority of teachers, texts, and public readings of the scroll. People often dress up as the major characters in the book, wear masks, and even cross-dress.

67. *Ethnicity and the Bible,* ed. Mark G. Brett (New York: E. J. Brill, 1996), p. 4. Brett argues that ethnocentrism manifests this homogenizing oneness and "is ethically appropriate only when the cultural identity is that of a minority, embattled or, at any rate, non-hegemonic" (p. 19). Otherwise, it becomes racism for the dominant group. Ethics cannot be universalized.

68. Excerpted from an unpublished paper by Sathianathan Clarke, "Biblical Interpretation: Modes and Themes from an Indian Christian," delivered to the House of Bishops, Episcopal Church USA, on 20 March 2006.

69. For what follows, see Denise Dombkowski Hopkins, "Unmasking: Esther, Exile, and Creativity," in *Strangers in a Strange Land: A Festschrift in Honor of Bruce C. Birch,* ed. Lucy Hogan and D. William Faupel (Lexington: Emeth Press, 2009).

Participants boo and hiss whenever Haman's name is read or mentioned. (The Talmud *Megilla 7b* urges the drinking of so much wine on
Purim that people can no longer tell the difference between "Blessed be
Mordecai" and "Cursed be Haman.") Timothy Beal suggests that the
book of Esther is a farce and that "Purim invites us to recognize, and
even to celebrate, the otherness within us that we so often try to repress
or hide. Purim is, in this sense, a coming-out party. Purim crosses
boundaries, and invites others to do the same."[70]

The name "Esther" comes from the Hebrew root *satar,* meaning "to
hide" *(hiphil).* The book is preoccupied with hiding, masking, and mis-
representing otherness. Beal argues that Vashti is erased, banished
from the king's presence. However, her exscription "serves to mark territory by naming that which belongs outside it; yet precisely in this
process of marking off for oblivion, Vashti and her refusal are also in-
delibly *written into* the story in a way that will be difficult to forget."[71]
Beal thinks of the book of Esther as a kind of palimpsest — that is, a
story written, erased, and then written over with a new story, leaving
behind traces of the old.[72] This applies not only to Esther but to Mordecai as well. Like Vashti, Mordecai refused the powers by not bowing
to Haman (3:2-15), who is also an outsider in the Persian court. For Beal,
the book of Esther is not about models of Diaspora living but about
the identity crisis brought about by the Exile and dispersion.

In our story-sharing in company with the biblical story, we practice
covenant by crossing boundaries and remaining open to others. Covenant manifests itself when we stay with the stories we don't like or
can't understand, and honor different interpretations of them. We
read, listen, wrestle, and interpret together because we trust that the
word spoken and heard communally offers resonances we may not
know alone. At the same time, our individual reading, listening, and
wrestling infuse this communal covenant practice. Covenant-keeping,
as religious and spiritual practice for all of us, continually reaches
within and beyond ourselves to speak words of trust-filled promise and
embody deeds of love.

Covenant shapes the purpose of storytelling, since God calls us to

---

70. Timothy K. Beal, *The Book of Hiding: Gender, Ethnicity, Annihilation, and Esther*
(New York: Routledge, 1997), p. 124.

71. Beal, *The Book of Hiding,* p. 25.

72. Beal, *The Book of Hiding,* p. 29.

move from narrow self-interest toward shalom community. Jacqueline Lewis, in a study of pastoral leadership, argues that pastors of multi-racial and multi-ethnic congregations can lead people to "story a compelling vision in which cultural diversity is an ethical and moral imperative in the present, not a heaven-bound hope for the future," and embody "a pocket of the promise" of God's realm of peace.[73] Lewis notes common characteristics of effective leaders of multi-ethnic congregations: they empathize with the other, welcome the other, hold together cultural diversity, manage conflict, mediate resistance to change that inevitably comes with encountering difference, and celebrate and embody the church's multicultural and multi-racial mission.[74] Lewis underscores the power of stories to reshape personal and congregational identity into the vision of God's beloved community.

Pastors lead communities toward multicultural and multi-racial reality by (1) storying the vision through prophetic preaching, purposeful teaching, leadership development, and planning; (2) acknowledging and intentionally working against the counter-story of racism that thwarts living into the vision; and (3) drawing practical resources from the story lines of exemplary leaders and communities.[75] Lewis images a multicultural and multi-ethnic congregation as a *spiral* of "ever-deepening relationship with the self and the other" rather than as a continuum.[76] The "Pentecost Paradigm"[77] charts the phases through which congregations move: from a *monocultural* phase (being aware of the desire to diversify), to a *culturally diverse* phase (choosing to come to the fellowship table together), to a *multivocal* phase (allowing the stories at the table to co-author a new group story), to an *anti-racist phase* (taking table talk and the new story into the world; inviting new people and having new people do the inviting, which signals a power shift).[78]

---

73. Jacqueline Lewis, *The Power of Stories: A Guide for Leading Multi-Racial and Multi-Cultural Congregations* (Nashville: Abingdon Press, 2008).

74. Lewis, *The Power of Stories,* p. 3.

75. Lewis, *The Power of Stories,* p. 4.

76. Lewis, *The Power of Stories,* p. 95.

77. Lewis, *The Power of Stories,* p. 96.

78. Lewis's work intersects with that of Amy G. Oden, *God's Welcome: Hospitality for a Gospel-Hungry World* (Cleveland: Pilgrim Press, 2008). Oden points to the story of Abraham and Sarah at the oaks of Mamre in Genesis 18 as exhibiting the characteristics of God's radical hospitality: readiness, risk, repentance, and recognition. "Readiness expects God's welcome to transform both host and guest" (p. 19); "the risks of hospitality . . . force us to stay openhanded, ready to receive whatever outcome results" (p. 22); re-

The spiral returns to the culturally diverse phase as congregations continue to stay open to people of cultural diversity with stories to tell.

QUESTIONS FOR REFLECTION
- What "unbelongings" do you experience in your life?
- What boundaries have you crossed in your life?
- What are you hiding that distances you from other people?

Covenant practices enlarge the "me-centered" tendencies of contemporary life: self-aggrandizement, self-absorption, and self-preoccupation. Important covenant practices include the following:

engaging in mutual watchfulness
calling to one another to keep working on our promises
trusting together
crossing boundaries willingly
learning about, remembering, and working toward love
keeping "the least of these" at the top of our list
taking the first step when the last is completely unknown
fostering a culture of mutual accountability
healing all people and the whole planet
accepting different kinds of knowledge and stories
honoring the many in the one and the one in the many
remembering whose we are
acknowledging the complexity of memory
avoiding guilting and manipulation

Covenant practice can be demanding work. We are called to both a narrow focus as we look within ourselves and know who we are, and a broad vision as we see our connection to communities beyond our own culture and tribe. Covenant practices can be tension-filled, ambiguous, perilous, promising, hope-filled, and loving. Sometimes covenanting can happen harmoniously with little effort. At other times, we really have to work at it. It is not enough, as a once-popular bumper sticker declared, to "practice random acts of kindness." What is necessary is regularized, sustainable covenant action, rather than simply a whimsi-

---

pentance means not being regretful but turning to a new frame of reference (pp. 22-24); and "recognition sees beyond what appears to be to what truly is" (p. 27).

cal, one-time gesture that makes us feel good only for the moment. Covenant practice needs to be habit-forming.

Israel takes covenant to heart by making the covenant a habit — that is, by obeying the Commandments. Moses commends this obedience to the Commandments in Deuteronomy 6:7: "Recite them to your children and talk about them when you are at home and when you are away, when you lie down and when you rise." All of life is infused thereby with a sense of God's intention and a sense of human vocation. All of your comings and goings, says Moses, all of the business of living, ought to be touched by what God wills for you. Jacob Neusner argues that the rabbis post-70 C.E. who taught Torah actually "became" Torah, embodying the habit of covenant. That is, they became Torah revelation themselves by modeling Torah in their words and actions.[79] Moses continues in Deuteronomy 6:9: "Write them on the doorposts of your house and on your gates."

All of family and community life, the private and the public, rests under God's care. All of life offers encounter with God. Listening, reciting, and doing is habit-forming and life-shaping, both on the individual and on the communal level.

QUESTIONS FOR REFLECTION
- What covenantal habits might you and/or your faith community cultivate?
- Can you identify any negative covenantal habits?

Systemic Care: Recognizing Interconnections

Many of us struggle to care for individuals, communities, and systems. In a world constantly tugging at us, we wonder how we can possibly care for ourselves, let alone the whole of creation. We can feel over-

79. Jacob Neusner, *Introduction to Rabbinic Literature* (New York: Doubleday, 1994), pp. 5-7. Neusner argues that the Torah made "ample room" for the Hebrew Bible (written words) and for the Oral Torah (memorized words handed down at Sinai) "but also for gestures, indeed, also for persons. Consequently the sage could be received as a Torah and treated as such" (p. 6). This idea is not merely metaphorical, for the sage was the "model" of the Torah and had "the standing of the human embodiment of the Torah." The sage actually participated in the process of revelation. What he did and said was reported and often became law.

whelmed by stories of need and powerless against seemingly entrenched social structures. We can falsely assume that not being able "to do it all" renders any action futile. Yet the call of covenant care community propels us forward. Commitment to covenant care community doesn't mean we will be able to do everything. It does mean, though, that we can and must do *something* to extend God's care to the whole of creation. Changing the way we think about care can be a helpful first step.

Covenant-keeping means that we commit ourselves to embody this care. Embracing this commitment reverberates across the entire continuum of life, from the personal to the global. Larry Kent Graham offers a systemic perspective that recognizes these interconnections. This perspective assumes the following: (1) all elements of the universe are interconnected, standing in an ongoing reciprocal relationship to one another (i.e., we influence and are influenced by others, whether or not we are conscious of it); (2) reality is an organized totality with interrelated elements (i.e., each of us is created as a "whole" person and we are also "parts" of families and communities); (3) homeostasis (balance within the system) is maintained by communication, negotiation, and boundary management (i.e., healthy balance between people and within communities requires two-way interactions); and (4) creativity occurs in context, meaning that systems can transcend themselves (i.e., a family changes its entire structure with the birth of a new child). Graham's approach offers a much-needed expansion of the nature, scope, and practices of care.[80] Many pastors and congregations rightly would not want to give up the practice of caring for individuals. This remains a valuable and necessary ministry. But a perspective like Graham's can enlarge the frame of care so that pastors take into consideration multiple factors in the practice of care.

Group Exercise

Use John Wesley's Rule as a starting place for enlarging your perspective of care. Consider the various "actions" identified in the admonition below and expand them to think about how "you" — not as an individual, but as the community — can reframe covenant care.

---

80. Larry Kent Graham, *Care of Persons, Care of Worlds: A Psychosystems Approach to Pastoral Care and Counseling* (Nashville: Abingdon Press, 1992), pp. 38-41.

Do all the good you can,
By all the means you can,
In all the ways you can,
In all the places you can,
At all the times you can,
To all the people you can,
As long as ever you can.

Organizational Covenants

How can pastoral leaders care for systems? Leaders offer significant care by diagnosing systemic problems and shaping positive relationships within an organizational structure. Larry Kent Graham suggests that the purpose of covenant is to bring shalom or well-being to all relationships. Distressed patterns of relationship within organizations tear what Graham calls the "covenantal frame," or the intention toward shalom and well-being for all persons and communities. Ministers can stitch together the tears in the covenantal frame by caring for *people* and *patterns* of relationship. Specific strategies for helping to change impaired structural patterns toward contextual integrity include (1) restructuring inadequate boundaries (i.e., helping people to know their own needs and limits, and respecting those of others); (2) differentiating accountabilities and responsibilities in order to clarify structural order (i.e., helping members of families and congregations to establish clear lines of structure and accountability); and (3) responding to runaway systems (i.e., helping people and congregations through crisis and anxiety by offering appropriate words of reassurance, staying faithfully present, and making necessary referrals). A mark of effective system care is discernible movement, over time, from dysfunction, unworkability, fragmentation, and breakdown toward workability and functionality evident to more than just one person.[81]

Pastoral leaders can begin by developing collegial, respectful, and responsive interactions within congregations. Such activity reflects commitment to the biblical theme of covenant. Consider these suggestions:

---

81. Graham, *Care of Persons, Care of Worlds,* pp. 202-23.

1. Develop policies for volunteer and professional staff that protect the vulnerable and safeguard the well-being of each person and the whole community.
2. Establish clear descriptions for jobs and community responsibilities.
3. Create procedures for resolution of conflicts and disagreement.
4. Use a feedback loop (anonymous surveys, questionnaires, etc.) to assess the effectiveness of communication and the clarity of roles.

Care leaders covenant to regulate life together in order to minimize any possible harm to relationships within community.

Covenant (Cosmos) Community

Covenant community extends beyond human communities to include the whole creation. The biblical prophets long ago recognized this interconnectedness. In nine prophetic texts, the personified earth mourns (in Hebrew, 'abal) in response to human distress or violation of covenant (see Jer. 4:23-28; 12:1-4, 7-13; 23:9-12; Amos 1:2; Isa. 24:1-20; 33:7-9; and Joel 1:5-20). In these texts, according to Katherine Hayes, "the envisioned collapse of the nation or community is tied to the wasting away of the earth itself."[82] This "decreation" metaphor, says Hayes, introduces the earth as "an alternative arena in which the human audience can view the disorder that either pervades it or is about to engulf it."[83] This allows the Israelites to take in the prophetic announcements of disaster without being completely overwhelmed by them. The mourning earth mirrors their own distress, witnesses against them, and universalizes God's power and the consequences of human behavior.

Perhaps most striking among these prophetic texts is Jeremiah 4:23-28, which was the Hebrew Bible Common Lectionary text for the Sunday immediately following 9/11. In retrospect, the appearance of this text on that day was providential, but very few pastors preached from it. The "decreation" described so chillingly in these verses results from the

---

82. See Katherine M. Hayes, *"The Earth Mourns": Prophetic Metaphor and Oral Aesthetic* (Atlanta: Society of Biblical Literature, 2002), p. 240.

83. Hayes, *The Earth Mourns,* p. 243. The interplay between humans, creation, and God in these prophetic texts mirrors the same interplay Michael and I see in Genesis 1–11.

military invasion (4:19-21) of the "evil from the north" (4:6; 6:2) commissioned by an angry God (4:8, 26c: "the fierce anger of the LORD") because of Israel's disobedience. Jeremiah 4:23-27 intentionally echoes in reverse the repetitions of Genesis 1. The repeated phrases "God said," "and it was so," "God called," and "there was evening and there was morning [on day one/two/three]" in Genesis 1 communicate God's ordering activity in creation. However, the repetition in Jeremiah 4 communicates the opposite: God's de-ordering. "I looked" (or "saw") is repeated four times in four verses, and directly challenges "and God saw that it was good" repeated in Genesis 1. What Jeremiah "sees" is de-creation.

Both Genesis 1 and Jeremiah 4:23-28 begin with chaos (*tohu vabohu*, "a formless void"). However, Genesis 1 ends with order and God's resting, while Jeremiah 4 ends with God's anger. The quaking mountains (Jer. 4:24) symbolize the end of God's relationship with Israel. They contrast with God's Sinai theophany in earthquake and storm, symbolizing the beginning of God's relationship with the people in covenant (Exod. 19). In verse 26, "the fruitful land was a desert" alludes to both the wilderness wanderings and Israel's settlement in the land. Jeremiah's vision negates this history. What Jeremiah sees is "no one at all" (v. 25a). The land is empty. The invasion by Babylon means the return of chaos on all levels. How terrifying! Our human behavior has cosmic consequences.

In this regard, Terence Fretheim speaks of "the *creational* effects of human wickedness,"[84] and proposes "*a relational model of creation*" in which God and creatures act in interrelated ways in the "creative enterprise."[85] God takes a risk by ceding power to creatures for the sake of relationship, as evidenced in the Psalms. Psalm 8, for example, "is all about risk."[86] Despite the tiny place humans occupy in the created order (vv. 3-4), royal language is used for humankind in verse 5: "Yet you have made them a little lower than God and crowned them with glory and honor." God cedes power to humans by giving them dominion (v. 6).

The late pastoral theologian Howard Clinebell draws connections between the planet's health and human survival and well-being. Human disease and distress result in part from what Clinebell calls

84. Terence Fretheim, *Jeremiah* (Macon, Ga.: Smyth & Helwys, 2002), p. 105.

85. Terence Fretheim, *God and World in the Old Testament: A Relational Model of Creation* (Nashville: Abingdon Press, 2005), pp. 269-70.

86. Denise Dombkowski Hopkins, *Journey through the Psalms* (St. Louis: Chalice Press, 2002), p. 147.

"ecoalienation" — that is, rejection of our inherent earth-rootedness. This leaves us fragmented within ourselves and disconnected from other people. Greater consideration needs to be given to what Clinebell calls "ecobonding" or "ecotherapy," healing practices that nurture and sustain people and the planet. Covenant care community builds on Clinebell's ecoeducation principles that expand our body-mind-spirit selves in three ways. They help us (1) to become nurtured by nature; (2) to become more aware of our place in nature and the universe (what Clinebell calls ecological spirituality); and (3) to become more involved in active earth-caring.[87]

The National Council of Churches, through its Eco-Justice Program, urges us to care for the earth by sustaining biodiversity. Rates of extinction in some areas are fifty to one thousand times the natural rate because of habitat destruction, pollution, over-harvesting, invasive species, and endangered species trade. The NCC outlines personal and congregational actions that can be taken to slow the rate of extinction.[88] We can also care for the earth by following Norman Habel's advice to restore earth to "its proper place of honour in Genesis 1," where its revelation is a "geophany."[89] Unfortunately, we have too narrowly focused upon the human story in Genesis 1:26-30 at the expense of the earth's story. This hierarchical, human-centered focus relegates earth to secondary status. This narrow focus reduces the "unified cosmos" to a thing that must be subjugated ("subdue," vv. 26-28), setting the two stories in conflict with one another. How would the earth tell this story?

Group Exercise

Retell the stories in Genesis 1-11 from the viewpoint of the earth. How might the earth respond to the human command to subdue it? How would the earth respond to the Flood?

---

87. Howard Clinebell, *Ecotherapy* (Minneapolis: Fortress Press, 1996), pp. 61-88.

88. See "Tending the Garden: Stewardship of Biodiversity and Endangered Species," Eco-Justice Program, National Council of Churches of Christ, Washington, D.C. Visit their Web site at www.nccecojustice.org. They offer Resources, Take Action suggestions, and Lenten and Earth Day suggestions.

89. Norman Habel, "Geophany: The Earth Story in Genesis 1," in *The Earth Story in Genesis,* ed. Norman C. Habel and Shirley Wurst (Cleveland: Pilgrim Press and Sheffield Academic Press, 2000), p. 48. Habel is part of The Earth Bible Project, which seeks to read biblical texts from the perspective of earth.

Self-Care

Clinebell's work on ecotherapy draws a wide and encompassing circle around the many interrelated aspects of human care and earth care. How we care for ourselves, both individually and communally, influences the way we care for the earth.[90] Self-care becomes a covenant practice as we vow, in the presence of others, to care for ourselves in ways necessary to sustain pastoral ministry. As a classroom exercise, I (Michael) regularly invite students to make practical suggestions for self-care, and we usually generate a long list. Then I ask students to enter into covenant with one another by pledging to adopt a self-care practice, and to establish a check-in date with another person to see how it's working. Good self-care makes good sense, grounding us in community to receive, embody, and radiate the Living Word in practices of care with all of God's creation.

GROUP EXERCISE

- Make a list of practical suggestions for self-care. Choose a partner and enter into covenant to monitor each other's self-care commitments.
- Imagine how these self-care practices might contribute to the well-being of your family, community, and creation.

CARE PRAYER

O God of Covenant,
    In a world fragmented by fear, hostility, and pain, you call us into covenant care community. Mindful of memories, grievances, and histories that all too easily separate us from one another, we commit ourselves to remember and author a new future story for the human family, grounded in the old story of your abiding promise and presence. Inspire us to live into true selfhood as partners with Your creation, healers in Your community, and stewards of Your radically inclusive love. Amen.

90. Clinebell, *Ecotherapy,* p. 76.

Bibliography

"Academic Dishonesty." *Lex Collegii: A Legal Newsletter for Independent Higher Education* 30, no. 4 (Spring 2007): 1-6.

Ackerman, Susan. "Isaiah." In *Women's Bible Commentary*, exp. ed. with Apocrypha, ed. Carol A. Newsom and Sharon H. Ringe, pp. 161-68. Louisville: Westminster John Knox Press, 1998.

Aleshire, Daniel O. *Earthen Vessels: Hopeful Reflections on the Work and Future of Theological Schools.* Grand Rapids: Wm. B. Eerdmans, 2008.

Alter, Robert. *The Art of Biblical Narrative.* New York: Basic Books, 1981.

"American Politics." *Interpretation* 60, no. 2 (April 2006): 182-93.

Anderson, Herbert, and Edward Foley. *Mighty Stories, Dangerous Rituals: Weaving Together the Human and the Divine.* San Francisco: Jossey-Bass, 1998.

Anderson, Megory. *Sacred Dying: Creating Rituals for Embracing the End of Life.* Rev. and exp. ed. New York: Marlowe & Co., 2003.

Armistead, M. Kathryn. *God-Images and the Healing Process.* Minneapolis: Fortress Press, 1995.

Ashby, Homer Jr. *Our Home Is over Jordan: A Black Pastoral Theology.* St. Louis: Chalice Press, 2007.

Augsburger, David W. *Helping People Forgive.* Louisville: Westminster John Knox Press, 1996.

———. *Pastoral Counseling across Cultures.* Philadelphia: Westminster Press, 1986.

Balentine, Samuel E. *Prayer in the Hebrew Bible: The Drama of Divine-Human Dialogue.* Minneapolis: Fortress Press, 1993.

Balthazar, Pierre. "How Anger toward Absentee Fathers May Make It Difficult to Call God 'Father.'" *Pastoral Psychology* 55 (2007): 543-49.

Bauer, Susan W. *The Art of the Public Grovel: Sexual Sin and Public Confession in America.* Princeton: Princeton University Press, 2008.

Beal, Timothy K. *The Book of Hiding: Gender, Ethnicity, Annihilation, and Esther.* New York: Routledge, 1997.

Bibliography

Berryman, Jerome. *Godly Play: A Way of Religious Education.* San Francisco: HarperSanFrancisco, 1991.

Birch, Bruce C. "The First and Second Books of Samuel." In *New Interpreter's Bible,* vol. 2, pp. 949-1383. Nashville: Abingdon Press, 1998.

————. *Let Justice Roll Down: The Old Testament, Ethics, and Christian Life.* Louisville: Westminister John Knox Press, 1991.

————. "Old Testament Narrative and Moral Address." In *Canon, Theology, and Old Testament Interpretation,* ed. G. Tucker, D. Peterson, and R. Wilson, pp. 84-85. Philadelphia: Fortress Press, 1988.

Birch, Bruce C., and Larry L. Rasmussen. *Bible and Ethics in the Christian Life.* Revised and expanded edition. Minneapolis: Augsburg Fortress Publishers, 1988.

Birch, Bruce C., Walter Brueggemann, Terence E. Fretheim, and David L. Petersen. *A Theological Introduction to the Old Testament.* 2d ed. Nashville: Abingdon Press, 2005.

Blumenthal, David. *Facing the Abusing God: A Theology of Protest.* Louisville: Westminster John Knox Press, 1993.

Bohler, Carolyn. *God the What?: What Our Metaphors for God Reveal about Our Beliefs in God.* Woodstock, Vt.: Skylight Paths Publishing, 2008.

Bonhoeffer, Dietrich. *The Cost of Discipleship.* New York: Touchstone, 1959.

Bons-Storm, Riet. *The Incredible Woman: Listening to Women's Silences in Pastoral Care and Counseling.* Nashville: Abingdon Press, 1996.

Book of Order: The Constitution of the Presbyterian Church (U.S.A.), Part II. Louisville: Westminster John Knox Press, 2007.

Boyarin, Daniel. *Intertextuality and the Reading of Midrash.* Indianapolis: Indiana University Press, 1990.

Boyd, Marsha Foster. "Womanist Care: Some Reflections on the Pastoral Care and the Transformation of African-American Women." In *Embracing the Spirit: Womanist Perspectives on Hope, Salvation, and Transformation,* ed. Emilie Townes, pp. 197-203. Maryknoll, N.Y.: Orbis Books, 1997.

Boyd, Marsha Foster, and Carolyn Stahl Bohler. "Womanist-Feminist Alliances: Meeting on the Bridge." In *Feminist and Womanist Pastoral Theology,* ed. Bonnie Miller-McLemore and Brita Gill-Austern, pp. 189-209. Nashville: Abingdon Press, 1999.

Brett, Mark G., ed. *Ethnicity and the Bible.* New York: E. J. Brill, 1996.

Briggs, Kenneth. *The Power of Forgiveness.* Based on a film by Martin Doblmeier. Minneapolis: Fortress Press, 2008.

Brock, Rita Nakashima. *Journeys by Heart: A Christology of Erotic Power.* New York: Crossroad, 1988.

Brown, William. *Seeing the Psalms: A Theology of Metaphor.* Louisville: Westminster John Knox Press, 2002.

Brueggemann, Walter. "The Book of Exodus." In *New Interpreter's Bible,* vol. 1. Nashville: Abingdon Press, 1994.

————. "Covenant." In *Reverberations of Faith: A Theological Handbook of Old Testament Themes,* pp. 37-40. Louisville: Westminster John Knox Press, 2002.

————. "Holiness." In *Reverberations of Faith: A Theological Handbook of Old Testament Themes,* pp. 98-100. Louisville: Westminster John Knox, 2002.

————. *The Land: Place as Gift, Promise, and Challenge in Biblical Faith.* 2d ed. Minneapolis: Augsburg Fortress Press, 2002.

————. *The Message of the Psalms.* Minneapolis: Augsburg Publishing House, 1984.

————. *Texts under Negotiation: The Bible and Postmodern Imagination.* Minneapolis: Fortress Press, 1993.

————. *Theology of the Old Testament.* Minneapolis: Fortress Press, 1997.

Bush, Trudy. "Good Old Days?" *Christian Century,* 19 September 2006, pp. 30-33.

Butler, Trent C. *Joshua.* In *Word Biblical Commentary,* vol. 7. Waco, Tex.: Word Books, 1983.

Cahill, Lisa Sowle. "Christian Character, Biblical Community, and Human Values." In *Character and Scripture: Moral Formation, Community, and Biblical Interpretation,* ed. William Brown, pp. 3-17. Grand Rapids: Wm. B. Eerdmans, 2002.

Callahan, David. *The Cheating Culture: Why Americans Are Doing Wrong to Get Ahead.* New York: Harcourt Books, 2004.

Camp, Claudia. "Wise and Strange: An Interpretation of the Female Imagery in Proverbs in the Light of Trickster Mythology." *Semeia* 42 (1988): 14-36.

Campbell, Alastair. "The Courageous Shepherd." In *Images of Pastoral Care: Classic Readings,* ed. Robert C. Dykstra, pp. 54-61. St. Louis: Chalice Press, 2005.

Capps, Donald. "Bible, Pastoral Use and Interpretation of." In *Dictionary of Pastoral Care,* ed. Rodney J. Hunter, pp. 82-85. Nashville: Abingdon Press, 1990.

————. *The Depleted Self: Sin in a Narcissistic Age.* Minneapolis: Fortress Press, 1993.

————. *Living Stories: Pastoral Counseling in Congregational Context.* Minneapolis: Fortress Press, 1998.

Chilcote, Paul. "Grace upon Grace: Charles Wesley as Spiritual Mentor." *The Circuit Rider,* Sept./Oct. 2006, p. 7.

Chittister, Joan. *The Story of Ruth: Twelve Moments in Every Woman's Life.* Art by John August Swanson. Grand Rapids: Wm. B. Eerdmans, 2000.

Chopp, Rebecca. "Writing Women's Lives." *Memphis Theological Seminary Journal* 29 (Spring 1991), 3-13.

Clark, Stephen. *From Athens to Jerusalem.* Oxford: Clarendon Press, 1984.

Clarke, Sathianathan. "Biblical Interpretation: Modes and Themes from an Indian Christian." Paper delivered to the House of Bishops, Episcopal Church USA, on 20 March 2006.

Clinebell, Howard. *Ecotherapy.* Minneapolis: Fortress Press, 1996.

Cohen, Norman J. *Hineini in Our Lives: Learning How to Respond to Others through Fourteen Biblical Texts and Personal Stories.* Woodstock, Vt.: Jewish Lights Publishing, 2003.

————. *Self, Struggle, and Change: Family Conflict Stories in Genesis and Their Healing Insights for Our Lives.* Woodstock, Vt.: Jewish Lights Publishing, 1995.

Cohen, Shaye. *From the Maccabees to the Mishnah.* 2d ed. Louisville: Westminster John Knox Press, 2006.

Bibliography

Cooper-White, Pamela. *Many Voices: Pastoral Psychotherapy in Relational and Theological Perspective*. Minneapolis: Fortress Press, 2007.

————. *Shared Wisdom: Use of the Self in Pastoral Care and Counseling*. Minneapolis: Fortress Press, 2004.

Coote, Robert. "The Book of Joshua." In *New Interpreter's Bible*, vol. 2, pp. 553-719. Nashville: Abingdon Press, 1998.

Corey, Marianne Schneider, and Gerald Corey. *Groups: Process and Practice*. 5th ed. Pacific Grove, Calif.: Brooks/Cole Publishers, 1997.

Couture, Pamela. *Seeing Children, Seeing God: A Practical Theology of Children and Poverty*. Nashville: Abingdon Press, 2000.

Crenshaw, James L. "Introduction: The Shift from Theodicy to Anthropodicy." In *Theodicy in the Old Testament*, ed. James L. Crenshaw, pp. 1-16. Philadelphia: Fortress Press, 1983.

————. *Old Testament Wisdom: An Introduction*. Louisville: Westminster John Knox Press, 1998.

————. "Youth and Old Age in Qoheleth." In *Urgent Advice and Probing Questions: Collected Writings on Old Testament Wisdom*, pp. 535-47. Macon, Ga.: Mercer University Press, 1995.

Cross, Gary. *The Cute and the Cool: Wondrous Innocence and Modern American Children's Culture*. Oxford: Oxford University Press, 2004.

Crossan, John Dominic. *The Dark Interval: Towards a Theology of Story*. Niles, Ill.: Argus Communications, 1975.

Daloz, Laurent Parks, Cheryl H. Keen, James P. Keen, and Sharon Daloz Parks. *Common Fire: Leading Lives of Commitment in a Complex World*. Boston: Beacon Press, 1997.

Daniel, Lillian. "Kid Stuff: Raising Children in a Consumer Culture." *Christian Century*, 11 January 2005, pp. 22-27.

Davis, Patricia. *Beyond Nice: The Spiritual Wisdom of Adolescent Girls*. Minneapolis: Fortress Press, 2001.

De La Torre, Miguel. *Reading the Bible from the Margins*. Maryknoll, N.Y.: Orbis Books, 2002.

Dean, Kenda Creasy. *Practicing Passion: Youth and the Quest for a Passionate Church*. Grand Rapids: Wm. B. Eerdmans, 2004.

Dever, William G. *Did God Have a Wife? Archaeology and Folk Religion in Ancient Israel*. Grand Rapids: Wm. B. Eerdmans, 2005.

Diagnostic and Statistical Manual of Mental Disorders. 4th ed. Washington, D.C.: American Psychiatric Association, 1994.

Dittes, James. *Re-Calling Ministry*. St. Louis: Chalice Press, 1999.

Doehring, Carrie. *Internal Desecration: Traumatization and Representations of God*. Lanham, Md.: University Press of America, 1993.

————. *The Practice of Pastoral Care: A Postmodern Approach*. Louisville: Westminster John Knox Press, 2006.

————. *Taking Care: Monitoring Power Dynamics and Relational Boundaries in Pastoral Care and Counseling*. Nashville: Abingdon Press, 1995.

Dube, Musa. *Postcolonial Feminist Interpretation of the Bible*. St. Louis: Chalice Press, 2000.

DuBois, W. E. B. *The Soul of Black Folks*. New York: Bantam Books, 1989.

Duff, Nancy. "Locating God in All the Wrong Places: The Second Commandment and American Politics." *Interpretation* 60, no. 2 (2006): 182-93.

Dykstra, Laurel A. *Set Them Free: The Other Side of Exodus*. Maryknoll, N.Y.: Orbis Books, 2002.

Dykstra, Robert C. *Counseling Troubled Youth*. Louisville: Westminster John Knox Press, 1997.

———, ed. *Images of Pastoral Care: Classic Readings*. St. Louis: Chalice Press, 2005.

Dykstra, Robert C., Allan Hugh Cole Jr., and Donald Capps. *Losers, Loners, and Rebels: The Spiritual Struggles of Boys*. Louisville: Westminster John Knox Press, 2007.

Edson, Margaret. *Wit: A Play*. New York: Faber & Faber, 1999.

Eiesland, Nancy. *The Disabled God: Toward a Liberatory Theology of Disability*. Nashville: Abingdon Press, 1994.

Ekblad, Bob. *Reading the Bible with the Damned*. Louisville: Westminster John Knox Press, 2005.

Erikson, Erik. *Identity and the Life Cycle*. New York: W. W. Norton, 1980.

———. *The Life Cycle Completed: A Review*. New York: W. W. Norton, 1982.

———. *The Life Cycle Completed: Extended Version on the Ninth Stage of Development by Joan Erikson*. New York: W. W. Norton, 1997.

Everett, William Johnson. "Recovering the Covenant." *Christian Century*, 10 November 1999, 1094-97.

Farley, Margaret A. *Personal Commitments: Beginning, Keeping, Changing*. San Francisco: Harper & Row, 1986.

Fewell, Dana. *The Children of Israel: Reading the Bible for the Sake of Our Children*. Nashville: Abingdon Press, 2003.

Fiorenza, Elisabeth Schüssler. *Jesus: Miriam's Child, Sophia's Prophet*. New York: Continuum Books, 1994.

Fog, Jennifer J., and Joseph V. Gilmore. "Therapeutic Community." In *Dictionary of Pastoral Care and Counseling*, ed. Rodney J. Hunter, pp. 1273-74. Nashville: Abingdon Press, 1990.

Fontaine, Carole. *Smooth Words: Women, Proverbs, and Performance in Biblical Wisdom*. JSOT Supplement Series 356. Sheffield: Sheffield Academic Press, 2002.

Foster, Charles R., Lisa E. Dahill, Lawrence A. Golemon, and Barbara Wang Tolentino. *Educating Clergy: Teaching Practices and Pastoral Imagination*. San Francisco: Jossey-Bass, 2006.

Fox, Michael V. *A Time to Tear Down and A Time to Build Up: A Rereading of Ecclesiastes*. Grand Rapids: Wm. B. Eerdmans, 1999.

Frank, Arthur W. *The Wounded Storyteller: Body, Illness, and Ethics*. Chicago: University of Chicago Press, 1995.

Frankel, Ellen, and Herb Levine. "The Broken Tablets and the Whole: An Exploration of Shavuot." *Kerem: Creative Explorations in Judaism* 7 (5761/2001): 82.

Fretheim, Terence E. "The Character of God in Jeremiah." In *Character and Scripture:*

Bibliography

Moral Formation, Community, and Biblical Interpretation, ed. William P. Brown, pp. 211-30. Grand Rapids: Wm. B. Eerdmans, 2002.

————. "Genesis." In *New Interpreter's Bible,* vol. 1. Nashville: Abingdon Press, 1994.

————. *God and World in the Old Testament: A Relational Model of Creation.* Nashville: Abingdon Press, 2005.

————. *Jeremiah.* Macon, Ga.: Smyth & Helwys, 2002.

————. *The Suffering of God: An Old Testament Perspective.* Philadelphia: Fortress Press, 1984.

Freud, Sigmund. *Future of an Illusion.* Translated by W. D. Robson-Scott. New York: Liveright, 1949.

Frey, William. "Update." The Lewis Center for Church Leadership, Wesley Theological Seminary (14 May 2008).

Frick, Frank. *A Journey through the Hebrew Scriptures.* 2d ed. Belmont, Calif.: Wadsworth, 2003.

Friedman, Edwin H. *Generation to Generation: Family Process in Church and Synagogue.* New York: Guilford Press, 1985.

Friedman, Rabbi Dayle. "Introduction." In *Jewish Pastoral Care: A Practical Handbook,* ed. Dayle Friedman, 2d ed. Woodstock, Vt.: Jewish Lights Publishing, 2005.

————. "Letting Their Faces Shine: Accompanying Aging People and Their Families." In *Jewish Pastoral Care: A Practical Handbook,* 2d ed., ed. Dayle Friedman, pp. 344-74. Woodstock, Vt.: Jewish Lights Publishing, 2005.

Frymer-Kensky, Tikva. *Studies in Bible and Feminist Criticism.* Philadelphia: Jewish Publication Society, 2006.

Gerkin, Charles. *An Introduction to Pastoral Care.* Nashville: Abingdon Press, 1997.

Gilbert, Roberta M. *Extraordinary Relationships: A New Way of Thinking about Human Interactions.* Hoboken, N.J.: Wiley Press, 1992.

Gill-Austern, Brita L. "The Midwife, Storyteller, and Reticent Outlaw." In *Images of Pastoral Care,* ed. Robert C. Dykstra, pp. 218-27. St. Louis: Chalice Press, 2005.

Glasse, James. *Profession: Minister.* Nashville: Abingdon Press, 1968.

Gnuse, Robert. *You Shall Not Steal: Community and Property in the Biblical Tradition.* Maryknoll, N.Y.: Orbis Books, 1985.

"God Image Handbook for Spiritual Counseling and Psychotherapy: Research, Theory, and Practice." *Journal of Spirituality in Mental Health* 9, no. 3/4 (2007).

Graham, Larry Kent. *Care of Persons, Care of Worlds: A Psychosystems Approach to Pastoral Care and Counseling.* Nashville: Abingdon Press, 1992.

————. *Discovering God Images: Narratives of Care among Lesbians and Gays.* Louisville: Westminster John Knox Press, 1997.

Grant, Jacquelyn. "The Sin of Servanthood and the Deliverance of Discipleship." In *A Troubling in My Soul: Womanist Perspectives on Evil and Suffering,* ed. Emilie Townes, pp. 199-218. Maryknoll, N.Y.: Orbis Books, 1993.

Greider, Kathleen J. "From Multiculturalism to Interculturality: Demilitarizing the Border." *Journal of Supervision and Training in Ministry* 22 (2002): 40-58.

Grimes, Christopher. "God Image Research: A Literature Review." *Journal of Spirituality in Mental Health* 9, no. 3/4 (2008): 11-32.

Gunn, David, and Dana Fewell. *Narrative in the Hebrew Bible.* New York: Oxford University Press, 1993.

Guroian, Vigen. "The Christian Gardener: An Orthodox Meditation." *Christian Century,* 28 February 1996, p. 230.

Gutiérrez, Gustavo. *On Job: God-Talk and the Suffering of the Innocent.* Maryknoll, N.Y.: Orbis Books, 1987.

Gutstein, Naphtali. "Proverbs 31:10-31: The Woman of Valor as Allegory." *The Jewish Bible Quarterly* 27, no. 1 (2005): 36-39.

Habel, Norman. "Geophany: The Earth Story in Genesis 1." In *The Earth Story in Genesis,* ed. Norman C. Habel and Shirley Wurst, pp. 34-48. Cleveland: Pilgrim Press and Sheffield Academic Press, 2000.

Hammett, Edward, with James Pierce. *Reaching People under Forty while Keeping People over Sixty: Being Church for All Generations.* St. Louis: Chalice Press, 2007.

"Hang Up and Drive." *Vanderbilt Magazine* (Spring 2007): 22-23.

Hanson, Karen R. "The Midwife." In *Images of Pastoral Care,* ed. Robert C. Dykstra, pp. 200-208. St. Louis: Chalice Press, 2005.

Harrelson, Walter J. *The Ten Commandments for Today.* Louisville: Westminster John Knox Press, 2006.

Harrington, Sarah, and Thomas Smith. "The Role of Chemotherapy at the End of Life." *Journal of the American Medical Association* 299, no. 22 (11 June 2008): 2667-78.

Haugk, Kenneth C. *Don't Sing Songs to a Heavy Heart: How to Relate to Those Who Are Suffering.* St. Louis: Stephen Ministries, 2004.

Hayes, Katherine M. *"The Earth Mourns": Prophetic Metaphor and Oral Aesthetic.* Atlanta: Society of Biblical Literature, 2002.

Herman, Judith. *Trauma and Recovery.* New York: Basic Books, 1992.

Hileman, Linda S. "Keeping Up Appearances." *Circuit Rider* (March/April 2007): 14-15.

Hiltner, Seward. *The Christian Shepherd: Some Aspects of Pastoral Care.* Nashville: Abingdon Press, 1959.

Hindson, Ed, and Howard Eyrich. *Totally Sufficient: The Bible and Christian Counseling.* Rosshire, Eng.: Christian Focus Publications, 2004.

Hoffman, Louis. "A Developmental Perspective on the God Image." In *Spirituality and Psychological Health,* ed. Richard H. Cox, Betty Ervin-Cox, and Louis Hoffman, pp. 129-50. Colorado Springs: Colorado School of Professional Psychology, 2005.

Hogg, Tracy. *The Baby Whisperer Solves All Your Problems.* New York: Atria Books, 2005.

Hogue, David A. *Remembering the Future, Imaging the Past: Story, Ritual, and the Human Brain.* Cleveland: Pilgrim Press, 2003.

Hopkins, Denise Dombkowski. "Biblical Anthropology, Discipline of." In *Dictionary of Pastoral Care and Counseling,* ed. Rodney J. Hunter, pp. 85-88. Nashville: Abingdon Press, 1990.

————. *Journey through the Psalms.* Rev. and exp. ed. St. Louis: Chalice Press, 2002.

————. "Judith." In *Women's Bible Commentary,* exp. ed. with Apocrypha, ed.

Carol A. Newsom and Sharon H. Ringe, pp. 279-85. Louisville: Westminster John Knox Press, 1998.

―――. "Unmasking: Esther, Exile, and Creativity." In *Strangers in a Strange Land: A Festschrift in Honor of Bruce C. Birch,* ed. Lucy Hogan and D. William Faupel. Lexington: Emeth Press, 2009.

"How the Bible Is Read, Interpreted, and Used." In *New Interpreter's Bible,* vol. 1, pp. 33-212. Nashville: Abingdon Press, 1994.

Howe, Leroy. *The Image of God: A Theology for Pastoral Care and Counseling.* Nashville: Abingdon Press, 1995.

Howe, Neil, and William Strauss. *Millennials Rising: The Next Great Generation.* New York: Vintage Books, 2000.

Hummel, Leonard M. *Clothed in Nothingness: Consolation for Suffering.* Minneapolis: Fortress Press, 2003.

Hunsinger, Deborah van Deusen. "Paying Attention: The Art of Listening." *Christian Century,* 22 August 2006, pp. 24-30.

―――. *Pray without Ceasing: Revitalizing Pastoral Care.* Grand Rapids: Wm. B. Eerdmans, 2006.

Irish, Donald P., Kathleen F. Lundquist, and Vivian Jenkins Nelson, eds. *Ethnic Variations in Dying, Death, and Grief: Diversity and Universality.* Philadelphia: Taylor & Francis Publishers, 1993.

Izard, Susan, and Susan Jorgensen. *Knitting into the Mystery: A Guide to the Shawl-Knitting Ministry.* Harrisburg, Pa.: Morehouse Publishing, 2003.

Janis, Irving L. *Group Think: Psychological Studies of Policy Decisions and Fiascoes.* 2d ed. Boston: Houghton Mifflin, 1982.

Joh, Wonhee Anne. *Heart of the Cross: A Postcolonial Christology.* Louisville: Westminster John Knox Press, 2006.

Johnson, Elizabeth A. *She Who Is.* New York: Crossroad, 1992.

Jones, Beth Felker. "Spanking Away Sin." *Christian Century,* 1 May 2007, pp. 8-9.

Jones, L. Gregory. *Embodying Forgiveness: A Theological Analysis.* Grand Rapids: Wm. B. Eerdmans, 1995.

―――. "Embodying Scripture in the Community of Faith." In *The Art of Reading Scripture,* ed. Ellen Davis and Richard Hays, pp. 145-46. Grand Rapids: Wm B. Eerdmans, 2003.

Jones, W. Paul. *Worlds within a Congregation: Dealing with Theological Diversity.* Nashville: Abingdon Press, 2000.

Jung, Carl. *On Active Imagination.* Princeton: Princeton University Press, 1997.

―――. *Psychology and Alchemy.* In *The Collected Works of C. G. Jung,* vol. 12, trans. G. Adler and R. F. C. Hull. Princeton: Princeton University Press, 1980.

Justes, Emma J. *Hearing Beyond the Words: How to Become a Listening Pastor.* Nashville: Abingdon Press, 2006.

Karaban, Roslyn A. *Complicated Losses, Difficult Deaths: A Practical Guide for Ministering to Grievers.* San Jose, Calif.: Resource Publications, Inc., 2000.

Kaufman, Gershen. *Shame: The Power of Caring.* Cambridge: Schenkman Publishing Co., 1980.

Kelcourse, Felicity B. *Human Development and Faith: Life-Cycle Stages of Body, Mind, and Soul.* St. Louis: Chalice Press, 2004.

Kern, Kathleen. "Victims as Pariahs." *Christian Century,* 24 January 2006, p. 9.

Kille, D. Andrew. "Jacob: A Study in Individuation." In *Psychology and the Bible: A New Way to Read the Scriptures,* ed. J. Harold Ellens and Wayne G. Rollins, pp. 66-82. Westport, Conn.: Praeger, 2004.

Kim, Simone Sunghae. "A Korean Feminist Perspective on God Representation." *Pastoral Psychology* 55, no. 1 (2006): 35-45.

King, Philip, and Lawrence Stager. *Life in Biblical Israel.* Louisville: Westminster John Knox Press, 2001.

Kluckholn, Clyde, and Henry A. Murray. *Personality in Nature, Society, and Culture.* New York: Alfred A. Knopf, 1948.

Kohut, Heinz. *The Analysis of Self.* Madison, Wis.: International Universities Press, 1971.

Koppel, Michael S. *Open-Hearted Ministry: Play as Key to Pastoral Leadership.* Minneapolis: Fortress Press, 2008.

————. "Playing Church: Toward Critically Creative Pastoral Practices." *Pastoral Psychology* 55, no. 4 (March 2007): 431-40.

————. "Self Psychology and End of Life Pastoral Care." *Pastoral Psychology* 53, no. 2 (November 2004): 139-51.

Kornfeld, Margaret. *Cultivating Wholeness: A Guide to Care and Counseling in Faith Communities.* New York: Continuum Publishing, 1998, 2008.

————. "The Gardener." In *Images of Pastoral Care: Classic Readings,* ed. Robert C. Dykstra, pp. 209-17. St. Louis: Chalice Press, 2005.

Kottler, Jeffrey. *The Language of Tears.* San Francisco: Jossey-Bass, 1996.

Kushner, Harold. *When Bad Things Happen to Good People.* New York: Schocken Books, 1981.

Kyung, Chung Hyun. *Struggle to Be the Sun Again.* Maryknoll, N.Y.: Orbis Books, 1990.

Lambert, Christina, and Sharon Kurpius. "Relationship of Gender-Role Identity and Attitudes with Images of God." *American Journal of Pastoral Counseling* 7, no. 2 (2004): 55-75.

LaMothe, Ryan. "Render unto Caesar: Pastoral Care and the American Empire." *Pastoral Psychology* 55 (2007): 339-51.

Lapsley, Jacqueline. "Friends with God? Moses and the Possibility of Covenantal Friendship." *Interpretation* 58, no. 2 (April 2004): 117-30.

Lartey, Emmanuel Y. *In Living Color: An Intercultural Approach to Pastoral Care and Counseling.* 2d ed. New York: Jessica Kingsley Publishers, 2003.

Leslie, Kristen J. *When Violence Is No Stranger: Pastoral Counseling with Survivors of Acquaintance Rape.* Minneapolis: Fortress Press, 2003.

Lester, Andrew D. *The Angry Christian: A Theology for Care and Counseling.* Louisville: Westminster John Knox Press, 2003.

Lieber, David, ed. *Etz Hayim: Torah and Commentary.* New York: Jewish Publication Society, 1999.

Bibliography

Linafelt, Tod. *Surviving Lamentations: Catastrophe, Lament, and Protest in the Afterlife of a Biblical Book*. Chicago: University of Chicago Press, 2000.

Linn, Susan E. *Consuming Kids: The Hostile Takeover of Childhood*. New York: New Press, 2004.

Lydon, Susan. *Knitting Heaven and Earth: Healing the Heart with Craft*. New York: Broadway Books, 2005.

Lytch, Carol E. *Choosing Church: What Makes a Difference for Teens*. Louisville: Westminster John Knox Press, 2004.

Mann, Samuel. "Joseph and His Brothers: A Biblical Paradigm for the Optimal Handling of Traumatic Stress." *Journal of Religion and Health* 40, no. 3 (Fall 2001): 335-42.

Marshall, Joretta L. "Toward the Development of a Pastoral Soul: Reflections on Identity and Theological Education." *Pastoral Psychology* 43, no. 1 (September 1994): 11-29.

Masenya, Madipoane. *How Worthy Is the Woman of Worth? Rereading Proverbs 31:10-31 in African-South Africa*. Bible and Theology in Africa, 4. New York: Lang, 2004.

Maynard, Jane F. *Transforming Loss: Julian of Norwich as a Guide for Survivors of Traumatic Grief*. Cleveland: Pilgrim Press, 2006.

McCormick, Blaine, and David Davenport. *Shepherd Leadership: Wisdom for Leaders from Psalm 23*. San Francisco: Jossey-Bass, 2003.

McCullough, Michael E., Kenneth I. Pargament, and Carl E. Thoresen. *Forgiveness: Theory, Research, and Practice*. New York: Guilford Press, 2000.

McNulty, Edward. *Praying the Movies: Daily Meditations from Classic Films*. Louisville: Geneva Press, 2001.

Meyers, Carol L. "Everyday Life: Women in the Period of the Hebrew Bible." In *Women's Bible Commentary*, exp. ed. with Apocrypha, ed. Carol A. Newsom and Sharon H. Ringe, pp. 251-59. Louisville: Westminster John Knox Press, 1998.

———, ed. *Women in Scripture: A Dictionary of Named and Unnamed Women in the Hebrew Bible, the Apocryphal/Deuterocanonical Books, and the New Testament*. Boston: Houghton Mifflin, 2000.

Meyers, William. "The Hermeneutical Dilemma of the African-American Biblical Student." In *Stony the Road We Trod: African-American Biblical Interpretation*, ed. Cain Hope Felder. Minneapolis: Fortress Press, 1991.

Míguez Bonino, José. "Genesis 11:1-9: A Latin-American Perspective." In *Return to Babel: Global Perspectives on the Bible*, ed. Jon Levison and Priscilla Pope-Levison, pp. 13-16. Louisville: Westminster John Knox Press, 1999.

Miles, Mark S., and Emily K. Snyder. "Strangers No Longer: Faithful Voices for Solidarity." *The Spire*, Vanderbilt University, 27, no. 1 (Fall 2008): 27.

Miller, Alice. *The Drama of the Gifted Child: The Search for the True Self*. New York: Basic Books, 1981.

Miller, Patrick. "The Good Neighborhood: Identity and Community through the Commandments." In *Character and Scripture: Moral Formation, Community, and Biblical Interpretation*, ed. William P. Brown, pp. 55-72. Grand Rapids: Wm. B. Eerdmans, 2002.

————. *The Ten Commandments.* Interpretation: Resources for the Use of Scripture in the Church. Louisville: Westminster John Knox Press, 2009.

Miller-McLemore, Bonnie. "The Living Human Web." In *Images of Pastoral Care: Classic Readings,* ed. Robert C. Dykstra, pp. 40-46. St. Louis: Chalice Press, 2005.

Miscall, Peter D. "Introduction to Narrative Literature." In *New Interpreter's Bible,* vol. 2, pp. 539-52. Nashville: Abingdon Press, 1998.

Mitchell, C. Ben, Robert D. Orr, and Susan A. Salladay, eds. *Aging, Death, and the Quest for Immortality.* The Horizons in Bioethics Series. Grand Rapids: Wm. B. Eerdmans, 2004.

Mitchell, Kenneth R., and Herbert Anderson. *All Our Losses, All Our Griefs: Resources for Pastoral Care.* Louisville: Westminster John Knox Press, 1983.

Montilla, R. Esteban, and Ferney Medina. *Pastoral Care and Counseling with Latino/as.* Minneapolis: Fortress Press, 2006.

Moore, Mary Elizabeth. *Teaching from the Heart: Theology and Educational Method.* Minneapolis: Fortress Press, 1991.

Morton, Nelle. *The Journey Is Home.* Boston: Beacon Press, 1985.

Moschella, Mary Clark. *Ethnography as a Pastoral Practice: An Introduction.* Cleveland: Pilgrim Press, 2008.

Nanko-Fernandez, Carmen. *Perspectivas: Hispanic Theological Initiative.* Occasional Paper Series 3, no. 10 (Fall 2006): 58.

Nelson, Judith Kay. *Seeing through Tears: Crying and Attachment.* New York: Routledge, 2005.

Neuger, Christie Cozad. *Counseling Women.* Minneapolis: Fortress Press, 2001.

Neusner, Jacob. *Introduction to Rabbinic Literature.* New York: Doubleday, 1994.

Niemeyer, Robert A. *Meaning, Reconstruction, and the Experience of Loss.* Washington, D.C.: American Psychological Association, 2001.

Oates, Wayne. *The Presence of God in Pastoral Counseling.* Waco, Tex.: Word Books, 1986.

O'Brien, Julia M. *Challenging Prophetic Metaphor: Theology and Ideology in the Prophets.* Louisville: Westminster John Knox Press, 2008.

O'Connor, Kathleen. "The Book of Jeremiah: Reconstructing Community after Disaster." In *Character Ethics and the Old Testament: Moral Dimensions of Scripture,* ed. Daniel Carroll and Jacqueline Lapsley, pp. 81-92. Louisville: Westminster John Knox Press, 2007.

————. *Lamentations and the Tears of the World.* Maryknoll, N.Y.: Orbis Books, 2002.

————. "The Tears of God and Divine Character in Jeremiah 2–9." In *Troubling Jeremiah,* JSOT Supplement Series 260, ed. A. R. Pete Diamond, Kathleen O'Connor, and Louis Stulman, pp. 387-401. Sheffield: Sheffield Academic Press, 1999.

Oglesby, William B. Jr. *Biblical Themes for Pastoral Care.* Nashville: Abingdon Press, 1980.

Park, Andrew Sung. *From Hurt to Healing: A Theology of the Wounded.* Nashville: Abingdon Press, 2004.

Parker, Kenneth R. "Story-embodying." *The Journal of Biblical Storytelling* 5 (1995): 85-88.

Bibliography

Parks, Lewis A., and Bruce C. Birch. *Ducking Spears, Dancing Madly: A Biblical Model of Church Leadership.* Nashville: Abingdon Press, 2004.

————. "Who Is Visiting Small Churches These Days?" *Leading Ideas: A Resource for Church Leaders,* The Lewis Center, 24 September 2008.

Parks, Sharon Daloz. *Big Questions, Worthy Dreams: Mentoring Young Adults in Their Search for Meaning, Purpose, and Faith.* San Francisco: Jossey-Bass, 2000.

Pearl, Michael, and Debi Pearl. *To Train Up a Child.* Orange, Calif.: Gospel Truth Ministries, 1994.

Pembroke, Neil. *The Art of Listening: Dialogue, Shame, and Pastoral Care.* Grand Rapids: Wm. B. Eerdmans, 2002.

Peterson, Greg. "God on the Brain: The Neurobiology of Faith." *Christian Century,* 27 January 1999, pp. 84-88.

Pitzele, Peter. *Scripture Windows: Toward a Practice of Bibliodrama.* Los Angeles: Alef Design Group, 1997.

Pixley, Jorge. *Jeremiah.* St. Louis: Chalice Press, 2004.

Poling, James N. *The Abuse of Power: A Theological Problem.* Nashville: Abingdon Press, 1991.

Pratt, Mary Louise. *Imperial Eyes: Travel Writing and Transculturation.* London: Routledge, 2007.

Procter-Smith, Marjorie. *In Her Own Rite: Constructing Feminist Liturgical Tradition.* Nashville: Abingdon Press, 1990.

Pruyser, Paul. *The Minister as Diagnostician.* Philadelphia: Westminster Press, 1976.

The Rabbinical Assembly. *Etz Hayim: Torah and Commentary.* New York: Jewish Publication Society, 2001.

Radosevic, Tracy. "MULLing the Biblical Text." *The Journal of Biblical Storytelling* 11 (2001): 67-77.

Ramsay, Nancy J. *Pastoral Care and Counseling: Redefining the Paradigms.* Nashville: Abingdon Press, 2004.

————. "Teaching Effectively in Racially and Culturally Diverse Classrooms." *Teaching Theology and Religion* 8, no. 1 (January 2005): 18-23.

Richard, Suzanne. "Linen." In *Harper's Dictionary of the Bible,* rev. and updated, ed. Paul J. Achtemeier, pp. 562-63. San Francisco: HarperCollins, 1996.

Richardson, Ronald W. *Creating a Healthier Church: Family Systems Theory, Leadership, and Congregational Life.* Minneapolis: Fortress Press, 1996.

Ringe, Sharon H. *Wisdom's Friends, Community and Christology in the Fourth Gospel.* Louisville: Westminster John Knox Press, 1999.

Rizzuto, Anna Maria. *The Birth of the Living God: A Psychoanalytic Study.* Chicago: University of Chicago Press, 1979.

Rumi, Jalal al-Din. *The Essential Rumi.* Trans. Coleman Barks. San Francisco: HarperOne, 1997.

Russell, Letty M. *Church in the Round: Feminist Interpretation of the Church.* Louisville: Westminster John Knox Press, 1993.

————. *The Future of Partnership.* Philadelphia: Westminster Press, 1979.

Saliers, Don E. "Liturgy and Moral Imagination: Encountering Images in a TV Culture." In *Musicians for the Churches: Reflections on Vocation and Formation*, pp. 47-50. Yale Studies in Sacred Music. New Haven, Conn.: Institute of Sacred Music at Yale University, 2001.

————. *Worship Comes to Its Senses*. Nashville: Abingdon Press, 1996.

Samuels, Andrew. *The Political Psyche*. London: Routledge Press, 1993.

Sanders, James A. *Torah and Canon*. Philadelphia: Fortress Press, 1972.

Sasso, Sandy Eisenberg. *Cain and Abel: Finding the Fruits of Peace*. Illustrated by Joani K. Rothenberg. Woodstock, Vt.: Jewish Lights Publishing, 2001.

Saussy, Carroll. *The Art of Growing Old: A Guide to Faithful Aging*. Minneapolis: Augsburg Press, 1998.

————. *God Images and Self-Esteem: Empowering Women in a Patriarchal Society*. Louisville: Westminster John Knox Press, 1991.

Savage, John. *Listening and Caring Skills in Ministry: A Guide for Groups and Leaders*. Nashville: Abingdon Press, 1996.

Scheff, Thomas. *Microsociology: Discourse, Emotion, and Social Structure*. Chicago: University of Chicago Press, 1990.

Scheib, Karen D. *Challenging Invisibility: Practices of Care with Older Women*. St. Louis: Chalice Press, 2004.

Schimmel, Solomon. *Wounds Not Healed by Time: The Power of Repentance and Forgiveness*. New York: Oxford University Press, 2002.

Segovia, Fernando, and Mary Ann Tolbert, eds. *Reading from This Place: Social Location and Biblical Interpretation in the United States*. Minneapolis: Fortress Press, 1995.

Seow, Choon-Leong. "The First and Second Books of Kings." In *New Interpreter's Bible*, vol. 3, pp. 1-295. Nashville: Abingdon Press, 1999.

Shults, F. LeRon, and Steven J. Sandage. *The Faces of Forgiveness: Searching for Wholeness and Salvation*. Grand Rapids: Baker Academic, 2003.

Simundson, Daniel. *Faith under Fire: Biblical Interpretations of Suffering*. Minneapolis: Augsburg Press, 1980.

Sligar, Sam. "A Funeral That Never Ends: Alzheimer's Disease in Pastoral Care." *Journal of Pastoral Care* 41, no. 4 (December 1987): 343-51.

Smith, Mark S. *The Laments of Jeremiah and Their Contexts: Jeremiah 11–20*. Atlanta: Scholars Press, 1990.

Smith-Christopher, Daniel. *Jonah, Jesus, and Other Good Coyotes: Speaking Peace to Power in the Bible*. Nashville: Abingdon Press, 2007.

Sorajjakool, Siroj. *Child Prostitution in Thailand: Listening to Rahab*. New York: Haworth Press, 2003.

St. Clair, Michael. *Object Relations and Self Psychology: An Introduction*. Monterey, Calif.: Brooks/Cole, 1986.

Stairs, Jean. *Listening for the Soul: Pastoral Care and Spiritual Direction*. Minneapolis: Fortress Press, 2000.

SteinhoffSmith, Roy Herndon. "Infancy: Faith before Language." In *Human Development and Faith: Life-Cycle Stages of Body, Mind, and Soul*, ed. Felicity B. Kelcourse, pp. 129-46. St. Louis: Chalice Press, 2004.

————. *The Mutuality of Care*. St. Louis: Chalice Press, 1999.

Bibliography

Sternheimer, Karen. *It's Not the Media: The Truth about Pop Culture's Influence on Children.* Boulder, Colo.: Westview Press, 2004.

Suchocki, Marjorie H. *Divinity and Diversity: A Christian Affirmation of Religious Pluralism.* Nashville: Abingdon Press, 2003.

Sue, Derald Wing, and David Sue. *Counseling the Culturally Diverse: Theory and Practice.* 5th ed. Hoboken, N.J.: John Wiley & Sons, 2008.

Sugirtharajah, R. S. *Postcolonial Criticism in Biblical Interpretation.* Oxford: Oxford University Press, 2002.

Sullivan, Harry Stack. *The Interpersonal Theory of Psychiatry,* ed. Helen Perry and Mary Gawel. New York: W. W. Norton, 1953.

Swenson, Kristin. *Living through Pain: Psalms and the Search for Wholeness.* Waco, Tex.: Baylor University Press, 2005.

Tangney, June Price, and Kurt W. Fischer, eds. *Self-Conscious Emotions: The Psychology of Shame, Guilt, Embarrassment, and Pride.* New York: Guilford Press, 1995.

Taylor, Barbara Brown. *Leaving Church: A Memoir of Faith.* New York: HarperCollins, 2006.

Taylor, Daniel. *The Healing Power of Stories: Creating Yourself through the Stories of Your Life.* New York: Doubleday, 1996.

Thomason, Sally Palmer. *The Living Spirit of the Crone: Turning Aging Inside Out.* Minneapolis: Augsburg Fortress Press, 2006.

Tiffany, Frederick C., and Sharon H. Ringe. *Biblical Interpretation: A Road Map.* Nashville: Abingdon Press, 1996.

Towner, Sibley. "The Book of Ecclesiastes." In *New Interpreter's Bible,* vol. 5, pp. 265-360. Nashville: Abingdon Press, 1997.

Trible, Phyllis. "Beholding Esau." In *Hineini in Our Lives: Learning How to Respond to Others through Fourteen Biblical Texts and Personal Stories* by Norman H. Cohen, pp. 169-74. Woodstock, Vt.: Jewish Lights Publishing, 2003.

————. *God and the Rhetoric of Sexuality.* Philadelphia: Fortress Press, 1978.

————. *Texts of Terror: Literary-Feminist Readings of Biblical Narratives.* Philadelphia: Fortress Press, 1984.

Twenge, Jean. *Generation Me: Why Today's Young Americans Are More Confident, Assertive, Entitled — And More Miserable Than Ever Before.* New York: Free Press, 2006.

Ulanov, Ann. *Picturing God.* Boston: Cowley, 1986.

Ulanov, Ann, and Barry Ulanov. *The Healing Imagination: The Meeting of Psyche and Soul.* Einsiedeln, Switzerland: Daimon, 1999.

Vaage, Leif. "Learning to Read the Bible with Desire: Teaching the Eros of Exegesis in the Theological Classroom." *Teaching Theology and Religion* 10, no. 2 (April 2007): 87-94.

Valliant, George. *Aging Well: Surprising Guideposts to a Happier Life from the Harvard Study of Adult Development.* London: Little, Brown, 2002.

Van Leeuwen, Raymond C. "Proverbs." In *New Interpreter's Bible,* vol. 5, pp. 17-264. Nashville: Abingdon Press, 1997.

Volf, Miroslav. *Exclusion and Embrace: A Theological Exploration of Identity, Otherness, and Reconciliation.* Nashville: Abingdon Press, 1996.

Wall, John. "Human Rights in Light of Children: A Christian Childist Perspective." *The Journal of Pastoral Theology* 17, no. 1 (Spring 2007): 54-67.

Warrior, Robert. "A Native-American Perspective: Canaanites, Cowboys, and Indians." In *Voices from the Margin: Interpreting the Bible in the Third World,* new ed., ed. R. S. Sugirtharajah, pp. 277-85. Maryknoll, N.Y.: Orbis Books, 1995.

Waskow, Arthur I. *Godwrestling.* New York: Schocken Books, 1978.

Waterhouse, Steven. *Life's Tough Questions: What the Bible Says about Suffering, Depression, Demon Possession, Abortion, Suicide, Pastoral Care and Death Issues, Mental Illness.* Amarillo, Tex.: Westcliff Press, 2005.

Watson, Jeffrey. *Biblical Counseling for Today.* Nashville: Thomas Nelson, 2000.

Weems, Lovett Jr. "Leaders Know Themselves." *Leading Ideas,* 12 April 2006.

Weems, Lovett Jr., and Ann Michel. "Clergy Age Trends in the United Methodist Church, 1985-2007." Lewis Center for Church Leadership Report (2008).

Weems, Renita. *Battered Love: Marriage, Sex, and Violence in the Hebrew Prophets.* Minneapolis: Fortress Press, 1995.

West, Gerald. *Reading Other-Wise: Socially Engaged Biblical Scholars Reading with Their Local Communities.* Atlanta: Society for Biblical Literature, 2007.

White, James. *Introduction to Christian Worship.* 3rd ed. Nashville: Abingdon Press, 2000.

White, Michael, and David Epston. *Narrative Means to Therapeutic Ends.* New York: W. W. Norton, 1990.

Williams, Michael, ed. *The Storyteller's Companion to the Bible.* Nashville: Abingdon Press, 1991.

Wimberly, Edward. *Recalling Our Own Stories: Spiritual Renewal for Religious Caregivers.* San Francisco: Jossey-Bass, 1997.

————. *Using Scripture in Pastoral Counseling.* Nashville: Abingdon Press, 1994.

Winfrey, David. "Biblical Therapy." *Christian Century,* 23 January 2007, pp. 24-27.

Wink, Walter. *Engaging the Powers: Discernment and Resistance in a World of Domination.* Minneapolis: Fortress Press, 1992.

————. "Wrestling with God: Psychological Insights in Bible Study." In *Psychology and the Bible: A New Way to Read the Scriptures,* ed. J. Harold Ellens and Wayne G. Rollins, pp. 9-21. Westport, Conn.: Praeger, 2004.

Winnicott, Donald Woods. *The Maturational Processes and the Facilitating Environment.* New York: International Universities Press, 1965.

————. *Playing and Reality.* New York: Basic Books, 1971.

Wolterstorff, Nicholas. *Lament for a Son.* Grand Rapids: Wm. B. Eerdmans, 1987.

Women's Bible Commentary, exp. ed. with Apocrypha, ed. Carol A. Newsom and Sharon H. Ringe. Louisville: Westminster John Knox Press, 1998.

Wren, Brian. *What Language Shall I Borrow? God-Talk in Worship: A Male Response to Feminist Theology.* New York: Crossroad Books, 1989.

Yee, Gale A. "Hosea." In *Women's Bible Commentary,* exp. ed. with Apocrypha, ed. Carol A. Newsom and Sharon H. Ringe, pp. 207-15. Louisville: Westminster John Knox Press, 1998.

————. *Poor Banished Children of Eve: Woman as Evil in the Hebrew Bible.* Minneapolis: Fortress Press, 2003.

Zornberg, Aviva Gottlieb. *The Beginning of Desire: Reflections on Genesis.* New York: Doubleday–Image Books, 1995.

Zurheide, Jeffrey R. *When Faith Is Tested: Pastoral Responses to Suffering and Tragic Death.* Minneapolis: Fortress Press, 1997.

Author Index

Subject Index

Scripture Index